Praise f

M000310811

Caprice Hollins brings years of experience and nuance to her work guiding a wide range of organizations towards greater racial equity. In this practical and engaging handbook, she shares her expertise, taking readers from preparation to follow-up, at the personal, group, and institutional levels. In so doing, Dr. Hollins provides organizations an invaluable resource.

— Dr. Robin DiAngelo, author, *White Fragility:*
Why It's So Hard For White People To Talk About Racism

A brilliant tool! Dr. Hollins' masterful instructional style gives us the necessary insight, wisdom, and compelling information to influence our understanding, shift organizational behavior, and inform our path to racial healing.

— Debra Robinson Baker, MA, organizational development
practitioner, equity and social justice instructor

This is an excellent resource for anyone engaged in trying to move an organization towards equity and justice. The practical advice, examples, suggestions, and guidelines provide a toolkit for organizational and community change. Do the exercises, learn from the examples and you'll have what you need to jump right into the work. As Hollins writes "this work…is about learning so we can take action to make change." This book is essential for your racial equity work.

— Paul Kivel, educator, activist, and author, *Uprooting Racism:*
How White People Can Work for Racial Justice

This book is filled with wisdom and a wealth of information born out of years of extensive, hard-earned experience. I couldn't think of a more qualified author than Dr. Caprice Hollins. A practical resource and foundational toolkit, *Inside Out* is for every person committed to the work of racial justice, equity, and inclusion. It is a must-read for anyone who is tired of organizations "pimping diversity" and is ready to do the real work of dismantling institutional racist practices so all people can thrive. I highly recommend it!

— Dr. Brenda Salter McNeil, author, *Becoming Brave:*
Finding the Courage to Pursue Racial Justice Now

Dr. Hollins has created an invaluable resource for those seeking knowledge and skills on how to actively engage in the field of social justice. The book is accessible, personal, engaging, and informative. Those committed to social change will leave the book invigorated and better prepared for the vital work Hollins calls us all to do.

— Eddie Moore Jr., PhD, Founder/President, The Privilege Institute

An accessible, practical, and generous guide, *Inside Out* takes the guesswork out of building an anti-racist organization.

— Michelle MiJung Kim, award-winning author, *The Wake Up:
Closing the Gap Between Good Intentions and Real Change*

This is a great guidebook for anyone engaging in anti-oppression work. Caprice shares how her personal experiences have led her to this work and uses past research to help readers understand the ways that structural inequities exist in the United States. *Inside Out* provides a plethora of strategies to navigate barriers and challenges that arise when engaging in DEIB work, and invites readers to develop a necessary framework to guide them in anti-oppression work.

— Janice Gassam Asare, PhD, anti-racism consultant, writer, educator

INSIDE OUT

INSIDE OUT

THE EQUITY LEADER'S GUIDE TO UNDOING INSTITUTIONAL RACISM

CAPRICE D. HOLLINS

new society
PUBLISHERS

Cover design by Diane McIntosh.
Cover images: © iStock.

Printed in Canada. First printing October 2022.

Inquiries regarding requests to reprint all or part of *Inside Out*
should be addressed to New Society Publishers at the address below.

To order directly from the publishers, order online at www.newsociety.com

Any other inquiries can be directed by mail to:
New Society Publishers
P.O. Box 189, Gabriola Island, BC V0R 1X0, Canada (250) 247-9737

LIBRARY AND ARCHIVES CANADA CATALOGUING IN PUBLICATION

Title: Inside out : the equity leader's guide to undoing
institutional racism / Caprice D. Hollins.

Names: Hollins, Caprice D., author.

Description: Includes bibliographical references and index.

Identifiers: Canadiana (print) 20220390339 |
Canadiana (ebook) 20220390347 | ISBN 9780865719811 (softcover) |
ISBN 9781550927740 (PDF) | ISBN 9781771423700 (EPUB)

Subjects: LCSH: Racism in the workplace. | LCSH: Diversity in the workplace. |
LCSH: Organizational change. | LCSH: Corporate culture.

Classification: LCC HF5549.5.R23 H65 2022 | DDC 658.30089—dc23

Funded by the Government of Canada | Financé par le gouvernement du Canada

New Society Publishers' mission is to publish books that contribute in fundamental ways to building an ecologically sustainable and just society, and to do so with the least possible impact on the environment, in a manner that models this vision.

To the parents, families, and friends of Tamir Rice, Aiyana Jones,
Eric Garner, Michael Brown, Freddie Gray, Philando Castile,
Alton Stirling, Trayvon Martin, Walter Scott, Atatiana Jefferson,
John Crawford, Renisha McBride, Sandra Bland,
#sayhername, Breonna Taylor, Ahmaud Arbery, George Floyd,
and so many more Black women, men, and children
whose lives were tragically taken from us.
#Black Lives Matter.

Yes, All Lives Do Matter

I knew it when
the doctor first placed you in my arms,
your life mattered
I knew it when
you spoke your first words cook, cook, eat, eat
I knew it when I sent you off to school
I knew it when the police threw you to the ground
as you attempted to enter the mall
I knew it when
security was called because someone
thought you were breaking into your own car
I knew it when they
shot and killed you while playing with a toy gun
in the park, and at the store, at a stop light,
while walking, and riding your bike
I knew it when they took your life
in your grandma's backyard
I knew it when they
mistook you for a burglar
I knew it when you went for a jog
I knew it when
they put you in a choke hold,
I knew it when you cried out,

"Please, I can't breathe."

Contents

Foreword

What gets us into this work? What keeps us "in it" when the tasks of liberation toward equity are so arduous? Reading this book made me like and appreciate Dr. Caprice D. Hollins even more. She has undertaken a personal, practical, and vital approach to working with race and justice. As a clinician, consultant, educator, and well-known expert in working with ethnically diverse populations, Dr. Hollins has managed to bring forth a leadership framework, strategies, and sustainability in this invitational book that favors the beginnings, rather than endings, of conversations. This is not a set of instructions toward simplified solutions, rather a path to authenticity—which is how people and organizations manifest solutions.

The idea that people and institutions are too intransigent to change in the direction of liberation tries to interrupt potent anti-racism and anti-oppression. While there is no denying that facing not-ready faces full of contempt due to underlying fear of loss of comfort is most tiring, Dr. Hollins is one of the new voices unwilling to be daunted and unwilling to wait until all conditions are perfectly met. She brings us hard-earned wisdom revealed in her own authentic discoveries of what structural racism and systemic inequality really are and offers her elegant answers to seemingly impossible questions. This book invited me into humility and reignited my commitment.

As a multiracial Black woman, for whom coding and code switching are not mysterious, Caprice is trustworthy in her urgency that we free ourselves through truth seeing and truth speaking. In this book, she leads us to grow our capacity for truth in seeing the lie of race and the profound impact of systemic White supremacy—while supporting us in accountably engaging. Her credibility is nourishing to the reader who chooses to examine privilege and marginalization in non-performative and courageous ways. Dr. Hollins knows and role models how to initiate and keep returning to a regulated, centered state in the face of micro- and macroaggressions. These are not easy practices, but readers will embrace them for the sake of deep, lasting equity. And for those called to lead (not all are), it is an invitation to start the work with courage and with the comfort that we are not alone.

Of even more value, Dr. Hollins' grounded voice is not just teaching about liberation. She is carrying it out in this book by producing freedom from myths like meritocracy and by making visible what we are embedded in. Her clarity about how the inner work mirrors the outer, how we (on both sides of privilege and oppression) contain the tensions we are working to illuminate, how we are the "them" we were taught to distrust, have one result: The group we call "us" grows ever wider as fewer and fewer people are experienced as "other." Instead, the pervasive forces of dehumanization are observed, addressed, and, at times, neutralized.

This book calls for maturity in the work of social justice. More than pseudo-antiracism, we begin facing dehumanizing legacies of enslavement, ongoing brutalizing marginalization, and soul loss due to benefitting from both. Through the practices in this book, we explore what we learned and can unlearn what is false and toxic. Dr Hollins credibly shows how each person carries anything ever learned, and all grow up with misinformation and misconception. However, a part of growing up is to shed distortion. The time is now for truth-telling, for refusing to sink into despair, and for accepting the encouragement to reengage.

Dr. Hollins daringly illuminates dimensions that tend to dishearten social justice educators such as how to manage signals of unreadiness that are quickly perceived by BIPoC—who instinctively adjust. Or the reality that an inevitable multiracial society will not necessarily and automatically bring needed social changes. She leads by fostering true, genuine curiosity about what it might be like to live experiences of marginalization. And what conditions are needed for that grade of curiosity to arise. She warns of the impulse to place at the center experiences that are not representative. Showing how, for members of advantaged groups, shame shuts down higher brain function and blame blocks creativity. And how shame is just under the surface, covering fear of change. However, she sees anger as fuel for BIPoC if harnessed.

Inside Out sheds clarity about the tyranny of demand for answers and solutions—which reduce centuries of complex collective dynamics to a problem to solve, rather than a set of conditions to be encountered and ongoingly transformed. Dr. Hollins teaches that the work belongs to everyone who is harmed by racism through brutalizing marginalization, dehumanizing soul loss, or both. She skillfully urges us to notice impatience of wanting actions to take right away in order to get relief and put the challenge behind. Instead, Dr. Hollins would have us engage the practice of shifting each moment through regulation, readiness, availability, and coalition.

Because racism, and oppression in general, is a constant condition, Dr. Hollins invites us to acknowledge impact even when there may be other possible interpretation. She invites all to listen and believe those most expert. To lean in with true interest about what it is like to live an experience, to seek to have another feel understood—not to just settle for imagined understanding. Her approach is practical, taking into account the long arc of time and the immediate step. Individuals reading this book will come to see that equity and freedom work is always a collective endeavor, one that expands in time and influence. Readers will be filled by an author with dignity, compassion, and the call to justice.

— Leticia Nieto, PsyD. LMFT, TEP
Psychotherapist, Anti-Oppression Trainer, Socionomist
Professor Master of Arts in Counseling (MAC)
College of Education and Counseling
St. Martin's University | 5000 Abbey Way S.E. | Lacey, WA 98503

Preface

As I sit here thinking about what words can adequately express why I'm writing this book and the hopes I have for you as you read through the following pages, I can't help but let out a heavy sigh. Tomorrow will be the two-year anniversary of the murder of George Floyd. My desire is to lessen some of the psychological, emotional, and physical toll this work will have on your mind, body, and spirit as you lead racial equity in your workplace. As I guide your leadership, I am aware that working to end racism will come at a significant cost to you, no matter what I say or do. With that said, my desire is that this book will guide you in a way that leaves you feeling like you've found some missing pieces to your puzzle.

I have worked across the country delivering keynotes, facilitating workshops, coaching, and consulting on race, racism, and race relations for more than twenty years. Many people I've met along the way, whether they are leading because they saw the need, were hired specifically for a diversity position, had it added to their workload, or is a CEO trying to make change, one thing everyone has in common is that they struggle with how best to approach diversity, equity, inclusion, and belonging (DEIB) in their workplaces.

These are daunting times. People have become more emboldened by racism. There is a tug-of-war going on in the United States as hate crimes continue to rise, families are politically divided, and businesses face having to decide where they stand. There are those that will argue with conviction and hold firm to deeply rooted beliefs that the US is based on meritocracy, and that anyone who works hard can make it. They will search for any grain of evidence that, e.g., Black people are getting in their own way of achieving the American Dream, rather than seek to understand the structures in place that continue to hold a knee on the necks of Black folks.

Then there are White people who are quick to quote Martin Luther King Jr. in his "I Have a Dream" speech by stating that we need to judge one another by the content of our character rather than the color of our skin. Not only is this an oversimplification of racism, but it also totally misses the point of King's speech and it enables White people who say it to remain complacent with the structures of racism that continue to benefit them.

Some companies will create "diversity" statements with little intention of investing in real change. Leaders of these companies will be uncomfortable with conversations about race. They may hire a DEIB person but place them low on the organizational chart, exclude them from participating in important decision-making processes, and not provide them with the necessary resources to effectively do their jobs. They are often the only ones in their "department" with no staff to make meaningful change.

When I became the first Director of Equity and Race Relations for Seattle Public Schools, I didn't have a book to assist me in navigating these and other complex situations. When the new superintendent and school board shut down the department four years later, I was devastated. I had poured my heart and soul into trying to make a difference for students, families, and Staff of Color. When I ventured on my own to become a DEIB consultant, I talked to other consultants and read books to try and figure out how best to approach this work. I received helpful bits and pieces but, again, could find nothing comprehensive to guide me. So, I decided to write this book for anyone who is committed and courageous enough to lead DEIB in their workplace.

My hope is that this book serves as a compass in your journey toward justice, pointing you in directions that lead your organization toward meaningful change. Because no two organizations are exactly the same, there are things you will have to learn as you go, making adjustments along the way. *Inside Out: The Equity Leader's Guide to Undoing Institutional Racism* is written as a guide to help you anticipate challenges you are likely to face, overcome obstacles that will arise, as well as provide you with effective ways to lead equity, and dismantle racism in your organization, all the while reminding you of the importance of doing your own personal work. It is not a cookbook. There is not, nor will there ever be, a recipe that fits all organizations when it comes to dismantling the institutional racism the United States was founded on.

Introduction

BREAKING DOWN STRUCTURES of inequity is not something you should venture into without support and guidance. Through stories, real-life examples, and suggestions for approaches to take, *Inside Out* will leave you feeling less alone, and more confident and effective as a DEIB leader. While this book speaks directly to racism and is geared towards DEIB leaders working within organizations, the ideas in it apply to all forms of isms, and will be useful to other DEIB consultants like myself, who work from the outside in.

Section I: Preparing to Lead

I encourage you do the necessary personal work it takes to become a truly effective DEIB leader. You may be tempted to skip this section. Recognize that in it holds an important part of the answers you seek. Do not make the common mistake some DEIB folks make, believing they can successfully lead without being a part of the process. This section will help you explore what type of leader you want to be by
- becoming grounded in your *why* for racial justice
- having you do the work with those you lead, rather than to them
- establishing beliefs that will guide you in the process
- deepening your understanding of why cross-cultural race dialogue is so challenging

Section II: Finding a Framework to Guide You

Imagine you wake up and find yourself in the middle of a dense forest. You have water and food but no map. The trees are so condensed you have no idea what direction to begin heading. This section discusses the importance of having a framework that will serve as a guide to help you and others see where you are going and what you need to do to get there. Whether you use the one I offer up, find a different one, or create your own, understand that without a framework to think about what you are doing, where you are going, and why, you will become lost in the process and take those you are leading along with you.

The Framework shared with you in this book covers, in detail, four pillars to becoming an antiracist organization.

- Awareness—the personal work requiring individuals within your organization to deconstruct how they've been socialized.
- Knowledge—the work your organization does to grow in its understanding of the people they work with and serve.
- Skill development to effectively engage across cultures.
- Action and Advocacy—the purpose of DEIB work: ways to dismantle institutional and systemic isms that can't be done alone (which is why the first three pillars of bringing staff on board are essential).

Section III: Practicing Strategies for Engaging in Race Conversations

One of my favorite definitions of culture, I heard years ago, is that "Culture is what everybody knows, that everybody knows." Whether members within your organization are aware of it or not, there is an established, often unspoken culture for how to engage. If you are not explicit about what is needed to have conversations about race, racism, and race relations, you will unconsciously default to White patriarchy, Christian, heterosexual, cultural norms. Most of these norms are not going to be effective in addressing institutional racism. This section offers ways to approach race conversations and how to effectively engage in difficult conversations. Not only does this section include what needs to be considered when having conversations about race, it also provides you with practical tools and strategies for you to practice and teach to your colleagues. It covers some of the more difficult challenges you will face as race conversations surface and what needs to happen when conflict arises. As a result, you will be able to model courageous conversations and staff will be able to practice new ways of being in the workplace.

Section IV: Gaining Commitment and Institutionalizing Change

I don't watch television very often, but when I do it's usually to watch old black-and-white movies. It takes me back to when I was a little girl of six or seven, lying next to my grandmother drinking tea, eating leftover cookies from her catering business, watching old movies together. It wasn't until later in life that I realized how racist and sexist these movies were, but I digress. The 1940s movie *Gaslight* highlights how someone can be made to feel as if they are not psychologically sound when, really, it's the other person playing tricks on your mind.

In the movie *Gaslight*, the character Gregory, played by George Cukor, is intentionally making Paula, played by Ingrid Bergman, feel she is going "insane." The term *gaslighting* has become language used to explain how PoC are often made to feel—even when it isn't intentional—that we are the ones being irrational or foolish in our thinking. When leading equity work, you will have many experiences where things don't go as you planned. There will be people who will feel free to give you feedback that is hurtful rather than growth promoting. These experiences will cause you to doubt your ability to lead.

It is important you surround yourself with people who can not only help you lead this work, but with whom you can process your experiences, so you are able to discern the differences between your issues and theirs. Leaders need people who can tell them what they did well, but also help them think about how to improve as they move forward. Working in isolation is not only an ineffective change strategy because no one person can bring down institutional barriers alone, it will also make *you* an easy target (seen as "the problem") rather than your institution's policies and practices. This section identifies ways to bring others on board and provides you with a model to identify where your organization is currently at so together you can take the necessary step toward becoming an organization that values and appreciates its diversity.

**Section V: Sustaining Yourself
While Maintaining Your Commitment**

Leading equity work can feel like living your life in dog years. It will age you quickly. To help mitigate this effect, you will need to build into your routine an ongoing practice of self-care. While I can't tell you exactly what that looks like for you, I do offer suggestions you may not have considered (and some reminders) to help lessen burnout and fatigue.

At the end of many of the chapters, you'll find exercises, suggested videos to watch, and recommended readings, to help you grow in your understanding of DEIB and strengthen your abilities as a leader. Consider downloading an audible app on your phone so you can do some of the suggested "reading" while driving in your car, riding transit, or walking.

While reading, you may find yourself wondering why I use the term People of Color (PoC), instead of the more recent term Black, Indigenous, and People of Color (BIPoC). Rather than leave you speculating, I will briefly explain.

Throughout history, pitting one group against another has been a strategic ploy to keep us fighting one another, rather than the systems that are holding us back. When I hear or see the term BIPoC, I hear us and them. It's as if we're saying, let's talk about what's happening to Black and Indigenous people, and then if we have time, or the inclination, we can talk about the other two racial groups experiences, whose experiences are not significant enough to even name. It is another form of *othering*. Throughout history, especially during the Civil Rights Movement, it was the unity of diverse groups that strengthened us and led to change—and our division that destabilized our efforts and contributed to the preservation of institutional and structural racism.

Not only does the term BIPoC weaken us by creating an "us versus them" mentality, but it also continues the tokenization of Indigenous people. Based on what I've observed in institutions, conversations I've held, and books I've read, the true focus has been on the Black experience. Even if this isn't always the case, I've seen it more often than not. Ultimately, the "I" for Indigenous has become an add-on to assuage our guilt but does little to address Indigenous people's experiences of racism. It's as if by saying BIPoC we are tricking ourselves into believing we are being inclusive, when really, we are just pretending.

People of Color in the United States share a common experience in that no matter what decade we are born in, no matter our class, gender, sexual orientation, age, ability, citizenship, or religion, our race will be held against us many times throughout our lives. We must talk about this in a way that shows we are united against all forms of racism. Sometimes this will require we talk about and address our common collective experiences as PoC, while other times it necessitates our allyship, by fighting alongside one another and naming injustices done to a specific group, e.g., Black Lives Matter, Missing and Murdered Indigenous Women, Anti-Asian Hate, and Latine[1] children held in cages.

My generation, those born at the tail end of the Civil Rights Movement, fell asleep. It's as if we collectively, though unconsciously, agreed that the changes those before us fought and died for leveled the playing field for PoC. In truth, like the generation before them, Civil Rights activists did the laborious work of paving the way. It wasn't meant to end with the murder of Martin Luther King Jr. Thanks to Donald Trump and his followers, a blinding light has been shined on how far our country still must go. Not only did White supremacists quickly come out of the woodwork, but those who unknowingly internalized the values of White supremacy culture prompt us daily with a need to pick up where the generation before us left off. This has revitalized the fight in those who never stopped the work, woke up generation X, and lit a fire under millennials who refuse to turn the other way.

Another term you may be wondering about is my continued use of "White people," rather than Caucasian. This change is based on what I learned from reading "Getting Rid of the Word 'Caucasian'" by Carol C. Mukhopadhyay in the anthology *Everyday Antiracism* edited by Mica Pollock and further research. To give you a brief overview, Johann Friedrich Blumenbach, a physician and physiologist coined the term "Caucasian" in the eighteenth century creating a racial classification system in White people's favor, determining those of European descent to be closer to God, and thus the superior race. He deemed all other groups as inferior. How much inferior depended on where your "race" came from and how phenotypically different you were from those living in the Caucasus Mountains.

Ignoring the fact that the idea of race was a completely made-up concept, the United States used Blumenbach's concept of a superior race to determine who would have, and who would not. And though we no longer refer to people as Mongoloid or Negroid, two of Blumenbach's other classifications, to this day we still use race as a determining factor in every aspect of our society. By saying Caucasian, we are literally saying that "White people are superior."

Lastly, there will be times when I say "we," and other times I will refer to "PoC" and "Black people" as if I'm separate. It was challenging for me to write this book without being a part of what I'm sharing. So please excuse my vacillating between the two. I'm excited for you as you uncover the chapters that follow and wish you all the best in your journey for justice.

PREPARING TO LEAD

To change is to be vulnerable.
And to be vulnerable is to be alive.

—Alexis De Veaux

1

What's Your Why?

IT'S IMPORTANT YOU KNOW why you are embarking on this difficult and demanding journey of leading for racial equity. It won't be easy, to say the least. It isn't sexy, and it certainly won't make you the most popular person among many of your friends, family members, or colleagues.

Far too often I come across organizations tokenizing diversity to make it appear as if they are committed to Diversity, Equity, Inclusion and Belonging (DEIB). They will tout all the right language in their mission and vision statement, even going so far as to hire a Manager or Director of Diversity; but these organizations won't do the real work that benefits the needs of the PoC they work with and are there to serve. This is evident when there is no budget to support the work, when there is no department to lead it, and leadership see it as separate from their own roles, so they take no active part in the work.

Leading this work is not something you should take lightly. It's not a project, a four-year plan, or a onetime thing. It's not a jacket you take on and off depending on how hot or cold the weather is. It's a cultural shift. A way of being. And it will require your steadfast commitment and determination to lead your organization in a direction they don't understand and that lacks familiarity.

You will encounter White people who believe everything in your organization is functioning just fine, so why change it? What they are really saying is, it's been working fine for me. There will be People of Color (PoC) who resist because they've learned to be grateful for what they have. They've learned to go along to get along, and you bringing up race will rock the steady boat they've been sitting in. Some administrators who don't have experience with DEIB work won't understand or think it's necessary. Others will not be willing to take the risk of being vulnerable or appearing incompetent.

Whatever the reason for resisting change, the point is that you will need to be grounded in your own *why* for this work. It will serve as an anchor when things become most difficult, or others feel you are dividing the organization. So, think about it. What's your *why* for racial justice? Why do you believe it's necessary to address diversity, equity, inclusion, and belonging in your workplace? Consider not only your professional reason but your personal reason as well. Knowing your *why* will help you stay committed when the going gets tough. Because it will get harder before it gets easier.

My Why for the Work

I often feel emotionally, physically, and psychologically drained after facilitating race conversations, particularly when it's a mandatory learning opportunity for participants. It's not uncommon for one or two White individuals, sometimes even an entire group, to sit in the back of the room (or even the front), with arms folded and a visible attitude that appears to publicly convey *you can make me go to this workshop, but you can't make me learn*. It's amazing how many people are averse to learning about racism and how deep they will dig their heels into the floor to keep from opening themselves up to the experiences of People of Color. Even in educational settings, I've witnessed educators approach learning about racism like superman reacts to kryptonite. From their behavior, you would think it would weaken or possibly even kill them to learn more about the Students of Color they serve. These people are averse to having their world view challenged, and there is little you can do to that won't result in a power struggle.

Once while facilitating a full-day workshop with about sixty people in the room, there was a White man sitting near the front whose body language appeared to indicate that he didn't want to be there. Whenever groups participated in table talk to process content, he didn't join them. Several times during large group discussion, he would raise his hand but only to convey why he disagreed with what I was saying or teaching. As our time together came to an end, he raised his hand again. Given that thus far he had been unwilling to be curious or even slightly open to the learning, rather than allow him to ask his question, I asked him one instead. *"Scott, I've noticed each time you've spoken, it's been to disprove something I've said. We've been together for about six hours now, and I'm wondering if there is anything, even a small thing, you've found helpful in what I've shared?"* He paused for a moment as if he was genuinely contemplating my question, turned to look right at me, and simply said replied *"no."* I let out a visible sigh and then moved on to call on others who had their hands up. Rather than engage him further like I previously had, I realized it was best to engage those who were interested in learning. Many people came up to me after the workshop thanking me for what they learned. Some even apologized for the behavior of Scott and other resistant colleagues.

As you engage in this work, remind yourself that you may not be impacting everyone, but there are people in the room who are learning and growing because of your work. This is one of those moments where your *why* is critical. Don't let the Scotts of the world become a deterrent from what you know needs changing.

My *why* for staying in this work are twofold. My personal *why* has to do with my children. By the time my son, Matae, was a freshman in high school he was already over six feet tall, weighing 247 pounds, wearing size 16 wide shoes, and growing a beard. It didn't take long for him to tower over his 5'4" mother and come almost head-to-head with his 6'5" father. Nor did it take long for his father and me to become even more worried than we had always been for his safety. Matae has experienced many of the privileges our upper-middle-class status has afforded our family. But his father and I have always known that as a Black man growing up in this country, there was one thing our income would not protect him from: racism.

We do our best to help him understand the stereotypes placed upon him simply because of the color of his skin and what can happen when White people act on their assumptions. But it is difficult for many young People of Color who are sheltered by class privilege to listen and believe these truths. We have always talked with him and his sister about what being Black in the United States means. We've tried our best to prepare both children for the racial realities that exist in our society and provide them both with tools in which to navigate their way through the many challenges that lie ahead for them both.

During the time people were protesting the killing of 18-year-old Michael Brown in Ferguson, Missouri, I had a "what if" fright occur that I will never forget. I say, "what if" because every woke Black and Brown parent who hears about another killing can't help but wonder, *What if that was one of my children?"*

Matae was a freshman at O'Dea, a private all-boys school in Seattle, Washington. He and his friend would frequently walk to his dad's job to carpool home. One day, shortly after they began driving home, Gary received a call from the building manager at his workplace. Someone reported his car was being broken into. Even though my son and his friend were dressed in the required school uniform (slacks and button-down shirts) and the fact that my husband, a director in his company, was wearing professional attire, as he was unlocking *his* car at *his* assigned parking spot, they were criminalized. It was inconceivable to the caller that Black people own nice things. That person saw three black men and thought dangerous or thief. When my husband called to tell me about the incident, we intellectualized the situation and agreed to talk with Matae, yet again, about our society's views of Black people, particularly Black men.

It wasn't until a few weeks later that *"what if"* really hit me. It was during a faculty meeting at the Seattle School of Theology and Psychology, where I had been teaching part-time for the past 17 years. Our Dean, Dr. Derek McNeil, decided to open our meeting in prayer for Michael Brown's family. On August 9, 2014, their beautiful, smart, loving eighteen-year-old son had just been fatally shot in Ferguson, Missouri, by a White police officer. As Dean McNeil led us in prayer, I began to weep from the deepest parts of my being. Not only for Michael Brown but for the families of Trayvon Martin, Eric Garner, and so many other men, women, and children who had experienced the worst of the worst of what it means to be Black in the United States.

And so, I wept for my son, Matae, too. I don't want others to find his name in Wikipedia describing the "incident" that took his life. I do not want any of my sons or daughters, nieces or nephews, grandchildren, friends, or family members, or anyone to be remembered across the country in this way. I say all of this to say, my personal reasons have to do with my children, my grandchildren, my unborn grandchildren, and your children. I cannot deny that Barack Obama was president, Oprah Winfrey is a billionaire, Michael Jordan has his own line of shoes, nor that I have a doctorate. However, we must also recognize individual successes of PoC are the exception to the rule. Their successes are achieved despite institutional and systemic racism Black, Latine, Indigenous, and Asian peoples face daily.

Professionally, my *why* for staying the course, when it becomes extremely difficult to do so, has to do with those who came before me. I think of the abuse, cruelties, and millions of lives lost as I acknowledge Indigenous peoples' land I'm on, the long fight for Civil Rights, the imprisonment of Japanese Americans, Chinese excluded from citizenship, and other historical mistreatment of PoC. Through remembrance I recognize the shoulders I stand upon and can't help but feel a responsibility to do my part in the continued struggle to end racism.

Despite what many White people are determined to believe, we are far from being a post-racial society. This country's legacy of systemic racism has left an unlevel playing field in its wake. To see this, we need only listen to the stories of PoC, view social media, and turn to the research. These and other sources make evident the disparities that still exist within health care, education, economic, housing, judicial, and other systems. We need only turn on our televisions, computers, or phones and bear witness to the political discourse to understand we are nowhere near where we could or should be as a nation. Until we become united as a nation concerned about the well-being of all her people, there will remain much work to do, many conversations to be had, policies to eliminate, and changes to be made. Dismantling racist systems—that were designed from the start to put White people at an unfair advantage and PoC at an unfair disadvantage—will not come without challenges and won't change by sitting on the sidelines.

As I prepare for work each morning, I remind myself that the worst thing that could happen is I become frustrated with a person I encounter who becomes defensive about their White fragility, invalidates my story with their White privilege, or who walks out the room with self-righteous indignation. It is in these moments that I hold fast and remember my *why* for racial justice. Even if the risks I take mean I might lose my job, I will never ever worry I will be spit on, clubbed, bitten by German Shepherds, hosed, jailed, or lynched for my attempts to bring about racial justice. I keep in mind those who came before me, and I do my best to remain in the conversation, knowing that change is still needed even when my children can attend schools historically reserved for Whites only.

Know Your Why:
Commitment to Change and Be Changed

- What's your *why* for racial justice? What will keep you in this work when it becomes challenging, demanding, and fatiguing?

2

See Yourself as
Part of the Work

WHETHER YOU ARE A PoC or White, you cannot lead this work if you are not willing to take a good hard look at yourself. Not once or twice but constantly. This means exploring your own implicit biases, messages you have unconsciously and consciously taken in about your own identity groups and others. It means first acknowledging your privileges based on identities you hold whether it be your race, gender, sexual orientation, class, age, religion, ability, or national origin. It requires examining how you've done harm and ways in which you've colluded with racism whether intentional or not. It is critical you lead with humility, understanding that while you may have experienced oppression based on one or more of your group identities, you've also likely experienced privilege based on another. Without critically reflecting, without doing the necessary personal work, you will not be able to lead the way.

I am a light skin, multiracial (African American and White) 57-year-old, able-bodied, heterosexual, Christian woman, of upper-middle-class status, born in the United States, who racially identifies as Black. In case you are curious, I identify racially as Black because my White identity has always been ignored by Whites. I want to pause for a moment to speak to White people reading this. You may be offended that as a multiracial person, I identify racially as Black. At least, this is what I commonly hear from White people when entering discourse about why Barack Obama, born of a White mother and African father, identifies as Black.

When I was young, choosing multiple boxes to include all your races was not an option. I was hurt, angered, and confused by this as a little girl of six or seven. I couldn't understand why I was forced to choose one race when I knew I was born of two races. Both were important to how I saw myself and represented the love between my parents, and the love we had for each other. So, in defiance, when filling out a form I would create my own box, write next to it MIXED, and check it. But no matter how much I wanted to be accepted as both, White people didn't see me that way. Hearing the "N" word directed at me as a child, later applying for jobs that posted Help Wanted signs in their window even after I had applied for the job, and many other situations in my life caused me to stop fighting to be seen as both. While I identify racially as Black, ethnically, i.e., culturally, I identify as both Black and White.

Identifying ethnically with both races means there are some things about me culturally that align with Black norms, values, beliefs, and ways of engaging, while there are other things about me that more closely align with White culture. It wasn't until Obama became president, or until I came into my current role, that White people started saying, *"Hey wait a minute, that's not right. You're saying you are Black, but you are White too."* In other words, it isn't until White people want to receive some of the credit that they become willing to see us as a part of their race.

Back to the personal work this chapter is about. Though I identify racially as Black, I nonetheless benefit from the privileges having lighter skin grants me. I am, in all honesty, a part of both the oppressed and oppressor simultaneously. As a result, White people are more likely to feel comfortable being around me and are more likely to give me the benefit of the doubt. We are all more likely to see images of fair-skinned Black women portrayed as beautiful in the media than we are Black women with darker skin. Another example of a privileged identity I hold is when I travel. While I may be concerned that because of my race I could be stopped and searched in the airport, as a Christian in this country, I never worry my religious beliefs will cause others to view me as a potential threat. On the other hand, our Sikh, Hindu, and Muslim brothers, sisters, and gender diverse[1] siblings frequently experience being detained for hours in the airport no matter how they are dressed, the purpose of their travel, or when all evidence points to them being American. Being multiracial and Christian are just two examples of privileged identities I hold.

Though there may be moments in your life where your privilege works against you, they tend to be the exception to the rule. Leticia

Nieto in her book, *Beyond Inclusion, Beyond Empowerment: A Developmental Strategy to Liberate Everyone*, describes these moments as a "status loss." These are moments when your privilege works against you and occur so seldom that, when it does happen, you are likely to be taken off guard, rather than something you anticipate happening.

Peggy McIntosh first introduced the idea of privilege in 1988 through a paper she titled "White Privilege and Male Privilege: A Personal Account of Coming to See Correspondences Through Work in Women's Studies." Before being exposed to her work, I had never heard of nor thought about privilege in this way. While there was no doubt in my mind White men and White women were at an advantage in this country, McIntosh's article provided the language I needed to articulate my daily experiences of racism. Her work has aided countless people's understanding of privilege and has aided us in engaging in race discourse. Peggy McIntosh describes privilege in the following way:

> Privilege exists when one group has something of value that is denied to others simply because of the groups they belong to, rather than because of anything they've done or failed to do. Access to privilege doesn't determine one's outcomes, but it is definitely an asset that makes it more likely that whatever talent, ability, and aspirations a person with privilege has will result in something positive for them.[2]

Two years after graduate school, I became pregnant with my first child, Matae. I was contracting as a therapist at a school primarily attended by African American students in Seattle Public Schools, taught by a mix of both Black and White teachers. Another support staff, a White woman, was also pregnant with her first child. I frequently found myself talking with her and other colleagues about names Gary and I were considering, and the aches, pains, and joys that come with a typical pregnancy. One day, it suddenly dawned on me that she rarely ever spoke about her own pregnancy with anyone, not even me. This led me to wonder if my colleague might be a lesbian.

This was the first time her sexual orientation ever crossed my mind. As a married heterosexual woman, I had never concerned myself with what others would think, say, or do to me, if the person I loved and was having a baby with was another woman. If it hadn't been for my understanding of privilege and our joint pregnancies,

I doubt it would have ever crossed my mind that not everyone has the privilege of vocalizing their feelings and experiences about the upcoming birth of their first child. I did end up asking her, and yes, she was a lesbian, and yes, she was afraid of others finding out. I understood her fears so protected her secret.

A couple of years ago, I had a client who I had been working with for several years. My contact person was leading me to the room the workshop would be held in. I hadn't seen him in a while, so I began making small talk as we walked. I recalled he had children and inquired about their ages. As soon as he told me their ages, I responded by saying, "What a great age for Christmas." His reply to me was, "Or Hanukkah." I felt instantly embarrassed. I was on my way to talk with faculty about DEIB, and yet here I was, the facilitator, being exclusive in my language and thoughts. In that moment, my automatic assumption, in the form of exclusive reference to Christmas, revealed my Christian privilege.

Talking with White people about how they benefit from being White is probably one of the biggest challenges in this work, and the most needed to dismantle institutional racism. If White people don't recognize they have unearned advantages simply because of the color of their skin, they will continue to operate under the myth of meritocracy—believing opportunity is solely tied to hard work. As many have said before, racism cannot be undone by pulling oneself up by one's bootstraps, particularly if people don't have the boots or the straps. Those with power and privilege must become allies who take part in dismantling the very systems their racial group has created.

Like a fish doesn't know it's wet, it's difficult to see our own privileged identities, and ways we've benefitted. So, anyone who finds themselves leading DEIB work must immerse themselves in personal work exploring how they themselves show up in race conversations, ways in which they are not just a member of an unfairly disadvantaged group, but also how they are a part of an unearned advantaged group. Without personal self-exploration, it becomes too easy to hold an enemy image of the other, making everyone else out there into "the problem." Such people, as Annie Dillard says, become "leaders who oppress rather than liberate others." [3]

White people who see themselves as allies—but who don't engage in continual self-examination—risk distancing themselves from other White people whom they judge as not "where they ought to be" in understanding racism. Those with unexamined issues are more likely to shame or lash out at other White people, rather than meet them where they are at. The motivator is often a desire that PoC view the ally favorably and different from "those other" Whites. Rather than approaching with humility, recognizing they once held a similar way of thinking, behaving, or acting.

Because PoC live racism every day, they will sometimes take the stance that change is only White people's work. While it is true, this type of thinking keeps participating PoC from the personal growth needed to heal. Not only do PoC unconsciously internalize messages of White superiority and PoC inferiority, but it is also impacts them mentally, physically, psychologically, and spiritually. There is a reason why skin-lightening cream is sold around the world, why Blacks spend more money on hair care products than any other racial group, and YouTube videos can be found for Asians seeking to temporarily widen their eyes. We each must uncover how racism is affecting us as well as to reveal ways in which it pervades every aspect of our society.

The shame and blame approach seldom moves race conversations forward. If you are brave enough to take on the role of a Racial Equity Leader, it doesn't mean just sharing your knowledge; it also involves having the courage to be a part of the process by showing up authentically. This includes modeling vulnerability, sharing your stories, and owning your mistakes. As a leader in this work, you will continually be learning while at the same time leading the way, as you support others in their DEIB journey.

Personal Work: Commitment to Change and Be Changed

- Read Peggy McIntosh's article, "White Privilege and Male Privilege: A Personal Account of Coming to See Correspondences Through Work in Women's Studies" or her shorter version "Unpacking the Invisible Knapsack." Both can be found online but be sure to pay for copyright permission before making multiple copies.
- Read the section titled *The ADRESSING Model* in Leticia Nieto's *Beyond Inclusion, Beyond Empowerment: A Developmental Strategy to Liberate Everyone.*

Privilege Pie

On a blank sheet of copy paper make a big circle. Draw horizontal, vertical, and diagonal lines so you end up with a circle with eight sections/slices of pie. On the inside of each individual slice, write with a pen or pencil each of the following privileged identities: cisgender male,[4] middle-/upper-class, no disability, 21–65, US born, Christian, White, heterosexual. Using a highlighter, shade in those slices where you have privilege. What insights do you have as you look at identities where you hold privilege and where you don't? Consider how intersections of identities might change a person's experiences? For example, someone who is middle- and upper-class with a disability will have a different experience from someone who is from a lower socioeconomic background with the same disability. What identities do you think about the most or least, and why might that be? Are all slices of the pie equal?

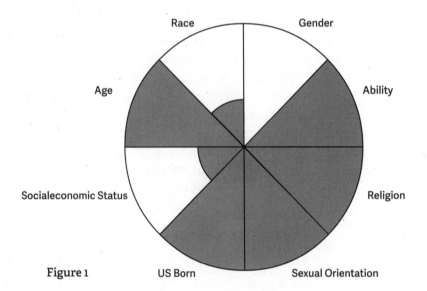

Figure 1

Watch the Race Forward video on YouTube with Sonny Singh discussing intersections of privilege: https://www.youtube.com/watch?v=VDozOrDEvAc. You can also go to RaceForward.org and watch other videos exploring intersections of identities when you have time.

3

Why We Don't Know How
to Talk About Race

WHEN YOU WERE GROWING UP, what were the messages you
received about race, racism, and race relations? You can think
about this question in a couple of different ways. Think about your
K-12 education experience. Was race, racism, and race relations a part
of the school's curriculum? A couple of years ago, I was in an elementary school library preparing to facilitate. As I was waiting for teachers and staff to arrive, I decided to pull a book off the shelf. The first
book I opened talked about how Native Americans *moved* to other
lands. I thought to myself, *well, isn't that sweet, they just "moved" to
other lands.* Native Americans didn't move to other lands, they were
forced. In the process men, women, and children were slaughtered,
coloring the earth red with their blood.

It wasn't until graduate school that I began seeking a different
understanding of race beyond the racist curriculum and narrative
taught by mostly White educators. I desired to know more about the
contributions of African Americans beyond Dr. Martin Luther King
Jr., peanut butter, sports, and music. Once I started teaching graduate
courses, I expanded my knowledge to experiences and contributions
of other ethnic groups. Through my work with my company Cultures
Connecting, I began rethinking the language I was using. As a result, I
no longer refer to Japanese as being interned but rather incarcerated,
I don't talk about Blacks as slaves but instead enslaved people, nor do
I say Whites and Non-Whites when speaking about race dynamics.
My language, initially, centered conversations around Whites. You are
either White or something other than White, not even valued enough
to be named. I share these few examples simply to make the point

that I did not begin to examine or challenge what I had been taught until I was a grown adult in my early thirties.

Another way to explore what you were taught growing up is to think about conversations with relatives. What did your parents or grandparents say about people who were different from you? What were conversations like when driving in the car with your family? Did they ever point out differences, and if so, what did they say? Did you ever comment out loud about people who looked different from you, and if so, how did the adults in your life respond? When thinking about the messages you received about differences, don't just consider what was said verbally. What isn't said to children is just as important as what is said. If race wasn't talked about, you were still making meaning of it. You formed thoughts, assumptions, and beliefs not only about people who were different from you but also about your own groups. You were just left to do it without guidance. What were the messages you received as a child?

Themes tend to come up when I ask people to share what they were taught. Whites tend to tell stories of color-blind thinking—being taught not to notice differences. They commonly share growing up in predominantly White homogenous communities where there were few, if any, PoC. It isn't until later in life when they leave their town, go off to college, or work for an organization where race is a part of the conversation that they even begin to explore what it means to be White. When White people do grow up in multicultural communities, even when they are the minority, there are usually no conversations about race. When they are raised by parents who are liberal or more open to diversity, once they reach dating age, they begin to hear contradictory messages and realize their parents didn't mean embrace diversity in *that* way.

Sometimes White people will describe having Friends of Color or growing up in the military. It's not uncommon to hear *"our differences weren't an issue,"* or *"it was about survival not race."* Whites should be asking *"Was racism not an issue for the PoC in my life, or did they just not talk about it with me? If so, why might that be?"* In many cases, PoC don't talk with their White friends and colleagues because it's not safe to do so. The subtle and not so subtle ways in which White people give clues as to their perspectives on race leaves many, if not most, feeling it's best not to waste their breath—or that it's in their best interest to keep the peace, and sometimes even their jobs.

PoC are having conversations about race and sharing experiences of racism with people who look like them, or with White allies whom they know they can trust. Talking with people who believe that racism is real is much less fatiguing for PoC than working to defend or prove their racial reality. Unfortunately, unbeknownst to many White people, their cross-cultural relationships operate at a superficial level, even when the relationship goes as far back as childhood. This causes them to assume race isn't important rather than understanding that race is relevant in every aspect of all our lives, White people's lives included.

On the other hand, when PoC are asked what they were taught about race growing up, I tend to hear altogether different responses. For example, more recent Immigrants of Color will say they didn't even know they were a Person of Color until they got here. (Note: I am intentional about saying "*recent*" since the United States is a nation of immigrants. Of course, Indigenous people are not immigrants, nor are African Americans whose ancestors were brought here in chains. And we should reconsider whether most Mexican Americans are immigrants, considering whose borders were crossed. But everyone else is an immigrant. It's just a matter of how many generations ago their families came to this country.) When Immigrants of Color come to the US with hopes of the American Dream, they quickly discover they must navigate the barriers associated with the racial stereotypes of the group they are most like.

When Asian Americans and Latine Americans share what they were taught growing up, two different yet common themes come up, both around assimilation. One is that parents fear their children are rejecting their heritage in place of White culture—which for many in this country has become synonymous with "American." The other theme is that parents encourage their children to assimilate into White-dominant culture. Assimilation has been a common approach to access and opportunity in this country, particularly during the turn of the twentieth century when millions of Italians, Irish, Germans, Polish, Greeks, and others of European descent left the familiarity of their homelands, some as refugees, all in anticipation of a better life in the United States.

Like our Latine and Asian American brothers, sisters, and gender diverse siblings, immigrants of the early twentieth century learned if they wanted to partake in the American Dream, they must make their ethnic differences invisible. This often meant changing their name, style of dress, foods, language, and other cultural markers. They only needed to read the signs *"Irish need not apply"* to understand the depths of prejudice and the barriers that ensued in "the land of the free."

This has not changed as much as we would like to believe, and most Asian and Latine Americans know this. They too want the same opportunities for their children and their children's children. So, they teach their children how to make White people feel comfortable around them, in many of the same ways European immigrants did, i.e., not teaching their children their home language, changing their names to sound more "American," and minimizing other cultural markers that denote them as "other." These parents know racism exists and that race matters, so they do what they can to help their children navigate barriers by adopting the values, beliefs, and attitudes of White culture.

Assimilation puts Asian and Latine in a double bind. Their experiences of racism are often marginalized, particularly for Asian Americans because they have been labeled the "model minority." Asians' proximity to Whiteness places them above other PoC in the minds of many White people, yet they still hold a status secondary to Whites. While they are never fully accepted into the constructs of White society, this partial acceptance is more favorable to what other PoC contend with. This results in yet another dynamic of "us against them"—pitting other Groups of Color against Asians. In these instances, Asians blame Black people for their own plight, *"Stop making waves,"* while Blacks minimize the racism Asian Americans face daily, *"You don't have it so bad."* This dynamic keeps us from working together in similar ways to what was done in the early twentieth century between Blacks and Irish shortly after they arrived on Ellis Island.

Initially, the Irish were kept at the lowest rungs of US society alongside Blacks. They too received the lowest pay and most dangerous jobs. Together, these two groups advocated for more advantageous labor laws. Eventually, through the gradual process of assimilation, Irish Americans began to gain favor among majority Whites, placing them above Blacks, producing a racial divide between the two groups. Rather than lift Blacks up, as Irish began to be included in the White race, they adapted the myth of meritocracy and other attitudes that viewed Blacks as inferior to the White race.[1]

The difference between White Americans and Black, Asian, Indigenous, and Latine Americans, in most cases, is their *phenotype*. Observable characteristics reveal who PoC are, making full assimilation impossible for the majority of minorities. Whereas, with White people, it is near impossible to discern who is Irish, Italian, Scottish, Polish, German, Greek, etc., or any combination of these identities, making their assimilation, and therefore access to opportunities, possible. I'm not suggesting that anyone should try to assimilate to thrive in the United States. Quite the opposite. I'm reminding you, the reader, that what existed long ago is still playing out today. In 2020 Donald Trump named COVID-19 the "Chinese virus," making this deadly coronavirus about the people rather than the disease. This type of thinking not only serves to increase the division, the hate, and the daily micro-aggressions that, in this case, Asians experience, it conveys a message that, in order to be American, Asian Americans must be less Asian. Our goal should not be exclusion but inclusion, without having to lose one's identity in the process.

When Blacks and Indigenous are asked what messages they received about race, I get an altogether different response. Indigenous people often convey a mistrust of White people. Receiving the worst of the worst land, forced into boarding schools, having to fight for basic human rights, e.g., advocating to bring a halt to the Dakota Access Pipeline often causes them to pause when Whites maintain they have their best interest at heart. Based on experiences, Black people also have a mistrust of Whites. As a result, many will teach their children they will have to work twice as hard to get half as far as their White counterparts. In addition to this, adolescents are taught how to navigate White space for their own safety. For many Black people, conversations about race were a central part of their growing up experience. Their parents, grandparents, aunties, and uncles talked about racism.

I liken this to teaching children about *stranger danger*. A parent isn't given a guidebook on how to talk with their children about strangers when they birth, adopt, or foster a child. Instead, they are left to figure it out on their own, each doing the best they can to inform their child of the dangers in the world in hopes of keeping them safe. They are not always sure of what to say or how often to say it or even what is developmentally appropriate to say. What they do know is there are strangers out there who will do their child harm.

Talking about stranger danger is a delicate balance. On the one hand, parents don't want their child running eagerly to the man standing in front of the van encouraging their child to come over and pet the puppy. At the same time, parents don't want to bring their child to work, introduce them to a coworker, and have their child start screaming "Stranger danger! Stranger danger!" In this way, talking with children about race is no different. Parents don't have all the answers, the correct ways of speaking about it, or a manual informing them of what to say and when. What they do know is that they must prepare them for the racial realities that exist. And because they want their child to come home alive to them, they talk about racism.

Gary and I have been talking with our children about racism since they were very young. The conversation changed depending on their age, gender, and which child we were talking to. When our son reached high school and was more independent, we needed him to understand that the moment he stepped out our front door, our middle-class status would not protect him from how he would be treated because of his race. For our daughters, the conversation has evolved more around *counternarratives*—messages that run contrary to the stereotypes held about Black women. This means frequently reminding them of their brilliance, beauty, and goodness. We don't want White cultures' definition of beauty, or what it means to be a girl, to take root in their heads.

White parents of White children, and White parents of Children of Color, tend not to talk with their children about race. They believe taking a color-blind approach will differentiate them and their children from *those* White people over there who are overtly racist. Rather than noticing differences and seeing them as negative in the way their own parents or family members did, the pendulum swings in the opposite direction to "*It only matters what's on the inside.*" The contrary is true for Parents of Color raising Children of Color. They don't have the luxury of pretending race doesn't matter and are more fearful of what could happen if their children weren't prepared.

With differences in experiences and approach, it becomes understandable why we don't know how to have healthy, productive conversations about race, racism, and race relations. When a PoC has known their whole life their race matters and engages a White person who is just now entering into these conversations, they are going to be in very different places. In these cases, a White person's interpretation of a PoC's experiences, i.e., the impact of systemic racism in politics, health care, judicial, housing, economic, and education systems, will lead to minimization, microaggressions, and failed attempts at understanding racism by divulging their own class, gender, and ability oppression.

PoC are confronted with significant challenges as they come across too few White people who are willing to become genuinely curious about and those who are naïve about racism. Exhausted from these encounters, rather than wondering *"Why he/she/they (Whites) see things the way they do? What were they taught? How did they come to understand it that way?"*—PoC often lash out or avoid race conversations altogether. Meeting White people where they are at isn't easy, in fact it's downright fatiguing, particularly when the White person they're engaging has just said or done something offensive.

Even though Parents of Color talked with their children about race, they weren't likely to teach them how to engage in conversations about racism with White people. I say this to remind you if you identify as a PoC, being so doesn't make you skilled at meeting White folks where they are at in a way that helps move conversations forward. You no doubt understand racism exists, have plenty of scars to prove it, but do you know how to invite White people into the conversation in a way that plants seeds of curiosity? Or do you push them off a cliff, so they never ever want to stand so close to the edge again, subsequently losing a potential ally rather than gaining one? Keep in mind that White people are exactly where our society has intentionally kept them: in the dark. Racism from the perspective of those most impacted has not been a part of our educational system. White parents didn't start talking with their children about racism until after the murder of George Floyd. And look at how far White people on the far right are willing to go to keep Critical Race Theory out of our schools. White people are manifesting what they have been taught and what they haven't been taught. Racism may be old news to you, but the idea of its insidiousness is likely new news to them.

More importantly, wherever you hold privilege and power, it is imperative that you are the one who leans into the experiences of those without. When it comes to racism, this means White people have the responsibility of becoming genuinely curious and wonder about the other, *"Why does this person see things the way they do? What have their experiences been that led them to look at the situation through a racial lens?"* Far too often PoC have encountered White people who have determined they are the experts of their racial reality even though many, if not most, haven't even begun to explore what it means to be White. White people determine when PoC are "playing the race card" (whether their story is valid, what research is valid, how things would be different if they just worked harder, or how a life wouldn't have tragically been taken if the PoC being discussed just didn't run, hadn't played with a toy gun, worn a hoodie, committed a crime, sat in a parked car, jogged down that street, or slept in their own bed).

Talking about race, racism, and race relations is foundational to undoing institutional and systemic racism. If we don't figure out how to talk about it, there will be no unpacking and dismantling centuries of power, privilege, and oppression. My colleague Kurt Hatch explained the importance of learning how to have the conversation by stating, *"The process is the first part of the product."* We must talk about racism to address racial inequities. And we must figure out how to do it better than we have done in the past. As an Equity Leader, your role in part will be to meet people where they are at and guide PoC and White people through the conversation.

Why We Don't Know How to Talk about Race: Commitment to Change and Be Changed

- Explore what you were taught about race growing up, spoken and unspoken message.
- When did you first realize your race mattered?
- Take 15 minutes to watch my TEDx Talk, "What White People Can Do to Move Race Conversations Forward," to further understand the concepts explored in this chapter: https://www.youtube.com/watch?v=7iknxhxEn1o&t=58s.

4

Establish Your
Foundational Beliefs

ONE REASON DEIB LEADERS, Equity Teams, and organizations are
ineffective in this work is they fail to identify, and agree upon,
Foundational Beliefs. Foundational Beliefs serve as a guide for how to
think about and approach race conversations. Think of Foundational
Beliefs like an internal compass used to influence the direction you go,
when having difficult conversations. Foundational Beliefs assist you
in seeing the person or people you are interacting with from a place
of curiosity—particularly when you are being triggered. They will
also help you to meet them where they are at while at the same time
holding them accountable for their words and actions. And when
you make mistakes or take an approach that runs contrary to your
beliefs, they will help you course correct. When DEIB leaders, Equity
Teams, and organizations are not grounded in their Foundational
Beliefs, there is more reacting rather than thoughtful responding.
This exacerbates any conflict you are trying to resolve, makes people
feel unsafe, and hinders DEIB progress. When everyone is clear about
their organization's Foundational Beliefs, they can hold one another
and themselves accountable while learning to engage in a way that
aligns with what is needed to move race conversations forward.

When determining Foundational Beliefs consider any of the following questions:

- What do you believe is necessary to hold front and center when
  having conversations about race?
- What values and beliefs will guide you and others throughout the
  conversations, particularly when the work becomes challenging?
- What do you hope will happen because of race conversations?
- Is my current approach furthering the division or bridging the
  racial divide?

In our book *Diversity, Equity, and Inclusion: Strategies for Facilitating Conversations on Race*, you can find a more complete list of Cultures Connecting's beliefs. The next section of this chapter describes six of our Foundational Beliefs, including strategies that align with those beliefs. You are welcome to use our beliefs, adapt them to fit your approach, or make a list of your own. What's important is that you have Foundational Beliefs, so you are mindful in how you model and lead DEIB work.

Hurting, Shaming, and Blaming Are Not Effective Tools for Opening Minds and Changing Attitudes and Assumptions

Some Equity Leaders approach the work from a place of self-righteousness. They have little tolerance for people and organizations who are in the earlier stages of their DEIB learning journey. They will often exhibit a predatory style of listening, ready to pounce the moment someone says something they disagree with. Some who use this methodology are at their wits' end with the slow pace and progress, and will demand immediate change, rather than work alongside their White colleagues.

It is not uncommon for this type of Equity Leader to point fingers, seeing this work as something everyone else needs to do, as if they themselves have "arrived." They are more prone to calling White people "out" rather than "in" when they unknowingly offend. While they may have done a great deal of external DEIB work, they've likely done little inside work. They will lack the skills and emotional capacity to meet people and the organization where they are at. You are more likely to hear, "*You're racist*" than you are "*Would you be open to hearing how what you said is racist?*" There is little humility for how they came to be where they are at in their understanding of institutional racism, nor recognition that they too have made mistakes and will continue to do so. They appear to have forgotten the ways in which they colluded with racism and focus their energy on individuals rather than systems.

Shaming and blaming can serve several functions for White people. It can assuage their fear of being perceived like *those* White people over there, i.e., the ones that are *really* racist. It can help them gain favor with Friends and Colleagues of Color, by conveying, "*See, I'm on your side.*" Shaming and blaming can relieve some of the guilt felt for their unearned White privileges and ease their shame for past roles they played in perpetuating racism. It's also possible that they believe calling White people out and shutting them down is allyship. While the latter is often necessary, i.e., at a rally when white supremacist groups show up, a self-righteous approach is rarely necessary or helpful in most workplace settings.

Whatever the reason, conscious or unconscious, when White people are overzealous in how they deal with racism, it rarely leads to change. It becomes about their own needs rather than serving the interests of PoC. When the "hit 'em hard" method is used, PoC are still left to worry about the psychological and physical safety of family. On the other hand, the "ally" pats themselves on the back for their *contribution* to "the cause," thinking *I sure told them.* While their intentions may be good, the impact keeps racism alive.

I can think of a few reasons why some PoC take a shaming and blaming approach when leading DEIB work. They may be in the earlier stages of their DEIB journey and are more prone to react to the spoken and unspoken pressures from other PoC. These leaders fear they will be viewed as not doing enough or seen as not truly invested in eradicating institutional racism. Comments from other PoC like *"You're being too soft,"* and *"That's just their White fragility,"* or *"I'm tired of taking care of White people!"* can imply their approach is part of the problem. Taking a tough stance when White people offend or make mistakes can show how determined they are to effect change and serve to gain acceptance and approval from other PoC who support this approach.

Another reason for a less thoughtful approach can be due to a fear of being seen as not Black, Asian, Native, or Latine enough? (You fill in the blank.) This can be particularly true for multiracial people who are lighter complexed, adopted into White families, have grown up in White communities and schools, or who have been raised in middle- or upper-class households. There can be a need to fit in with their Colleagues of Color, particularly those from their own group, to prove they belong.

But the main reason I encounter Leaders of Color who shame and blame people into understanding is because they are tired. The combination of historical racial trauma, current racism, and everyday microaggressions in their workplace leave them emotionally, psychologically, and physically drained. They experience workplaces that tout diversity, equity, and inclusion, commitment statements, and job announcements, but efforts and actions are little to nonexistent. Staff of Color are asked to lead DEIB initiatives in addition to their existing role, serve on Equity Committees with no compensation, and lead DEIB initiatives without support staff and any real power or ability to influence change. They witness nominal investment from executive leaders who don't devote time for personal work, and who see the change as something others do *to* their organization without their involvement. In other words, the climate and culture remain the same while their mission or vision suggests dedication. PoC are angry from hearing rhetoric like, "*These things take time,*" while PoC are getting paid less than their White counterparts and literally dying while waiting for that change. Suggesting they "*Meet White people where they're at*" or being told "*This time things will be different*" isn't enough. Some PoC, rightfully so, won't easily buy into what so far seems to be nothing more than empty promises. I have on many occasions provided DEIB workshops where Staff of Color have reached out to me privately and said something to the effect of, I appreciate your trainings but I just want you to know, leadership is not serious about making changes.

When Leaders of Color encounter White people who offend or behave in racist ways, it reinforces the feeling that nothing will ever change, so PoC shift to a more forcible approach which often includes shaming and blaming White people into understanding. Being thoughtful and intentional when engaging White people can just take too much energy that they don't have.

Whether you are a PoC leading this work or White, learning and practicing ways to effectively engage is a part of your role as an Equity Leader. It is important you develop your communication skills, and it will involve shifting your approach from calling people out to calling them in.

Strategies for Shifting from
Shaming and Blaming to Bridging the Divide

- Explore why you approach race conversations the way you do. What pain, fears, concerns, experiences underly your approach?
- Consider what you gain from shaming and blaming this person? Has it worked in the past? How are they likely to respond? What do you hope will happen as a result? Why are you being triggered?

- Ask yourself, "Am I lashing out at an individual when it is the system that is to blame?"
- Find someone who you can vent and process your experiences with before engaging the person who said or did that thing.
- Continuously question your motives, "*How does how I want to be seen by my Peers of Color contribute to how I approach DEIB conversations?*" If you are White, consider "*Are my actions driven by my desire for acceptance by PoC?*" If you are a PoC, consider "*How have I been practicing self-care so that I'm better able to meet White people where they are at?*"
- Name what you are experiencing in the moment, "*I'm finding myself being triggered by...*" Wait to respond until you've had time to think through what you want to say. I find it helpful when the conversation is through e-mail to write my initial thoughts and then go back and edit it later after I've had time to calm my nerves.
- Ask yourself, "*Will my approach align with my Foundational Beliefs about what is needed to move race conversations forward?*"
- Explore questions you could ask to meet the other person where they are at.
- If you are White, examine how your approach is aligned with allyship.

Hurt People Hurt People

When a White person does or says something racially offensive, it can trigger anger and harsh words from the Person of Color. This can easily initiate defensiveness from the person who offended. While anger is a normal reaction to racism, and defensiveness is a common way White fragility shows up, focusing on the anger or fragility results in a missed opportunity to surface the hurt and trauma caused by racism. Focusing on the fragility will also increase the likelihood you will center whiteness rather than the PoC and their pain. I know I have fallen into this trap and have regretted it each time.

In some institutions and situations, expressing anger is the only way a PoC feels they will be heard. Focusing on the hurt recognizes that underneath anger is the pain from a lifetime of racism. Unfortunately, many White people don't see it that way and are uncomfortable with anger, particularly when it is expressed by Black and Brown people. This is due to the stereotypes that we are dangerous and intend harm. In situations where hurt people hurt people, you need to check your stereotypes and discern between anger and true threat. Lastly, focusing on a PoC's anger when White fragility shows up lets White people off the hook in that it prevents them from examining their words or actions that initiated the PoC's anger in the first place.

The United States' long and painful history of racism, the daily impact it continues to have on the lives of PoC, and feelings of frustration and anger that change isn't transpiring fast enough are real. PoC are literally becoming sick from racism and are tired of waiting for White people to get on board. Patience is wearing thin as the years go by with seemingly little progress.

While it is OK to be angry, it isn't OK to use that anger to dehumanize or threaten to harm someone. I was facilitating a virtual workshop where a Black woman became angry with a White woman and said, "I felt like slapping her." While she wasn't threatening to harm her, this type of comment is hurtful and divisive and not what this work is about. In this situation, I did my best to explore with the Black woman similar experiences she's had with White women that were at the core of her anger. I didn't want the group to stereotype this Black woman or see her as the problem. My hope was to get to the root of her inappropriate statement where she could name her pain. The aim wasn't to get her to go too deep in front of a group of White people but rather help her to engage in a way that this White woman and others could hear and understand how she's been harmed yet again.

While you may not be a psychologist or have a degree in counseling, you likely have the capacity for empathy (if not, stop reading this book and please don't take on a leadership role in racial equity). If you do care, *regardless of your race*, talk with PoC in your organization and in your personal life. If you are a PoC, it's important to broaden your understanding beyond your own experiences. Conversations lead to understanding and can deepen your *why* for diversity, equity, inclusion, belonging and strengthen your commitment to becoming a change agent. It may also lead PoC to believe someone genuinely cares. Whether you are a PoC or White, your care and concern for the experiences of PoC in your organization increase the likelihood they will take an active role in the change.

Hurt people hurt people. Pain, fear, sadness, loss, hurt, and grief may be cloaked in anger and harder to recognize if anger and frustration are the only things paid attention to. Anger can serve as a protective measure for PoC to keep the more vulnerable emotions at bay. Underneath it all is a fear that their children, families, and their own emotional, social, psychological, economic, and physical well-being will never be made a priority in your organization or this country.

Strategies for Engaging PoC When They Express Anger

Invite

Find out if they are open to talking with you about what's going on for them. A simple statement like *"Would you like to talk about it?"* can get a conversation going. Or something more specific may work, such as *"I really care about you. It's clear this is really affecting you. Would you be willing to share with me what your experiences have been like that led to that comment?"* Move to a private area, if you are virtual, open a separate room for them and go in and talk with them or ask to talk with them after the meeting ends. This creates a safe place for them to be more open about their experiences. This same conversation could and should happen if you are supporting a group of people. Connect with them later if you don't have enough time in the moment.

Listen and Ask Questions

Show you genuinely care, are concerned, and are interested in hearing about their experiences of racism in the workplace and beyond. Seeking clarification, paraphrasing, and asking follow-up questions are good ways to demonstrate this.

Connect

If you are White engaging a PoC, name your Whiteness to get the conversation going. *"Being White has granted me a lot of privileges. I won't be able to truly understand your experiences around race, but I do care that everyone in this organization is treated fairly, has opportunities to advance, and that their race isn't a barrier to success. If you'd be willing to trust me with your experiences, I'm willing to listen. It will help me to better understand the work I need to do to improve our workplace."* Avoid comments like *"I understand exactly how you feel"* or using your own marginalized identities, e.g., class or gender, to connect. Just listen and try to empathize as best you can.

Connect

If you are a PoC engaging with another PoC, find ways to connect to their story. Show some level of vulnerability around your own experiences of racism without taking up too much time. This is a time for you to create space for their pain and just listen.

Avoid Offering Alternatives

"I'm sure they didn't mean it that way" or suggesting a "better" way for them to feel: *"Maybe if you didn't get so angry."* When anger surfaces for PoC, it is an accumulation of many situations over time that have happened to them, people they love, and people who look like them.

Thank Them

It takes a lot for a PoC to share their story, particularly when filled with pain. Convey appreciation that they trusted you with their stories and their willingness to be vulnerable. Name something they shared that will stay with you, helped you to understand, or touched your heart.

Tell Them

While you may not be able to do anything about what they shared in the moment, you can allow their story to touch your heart and keep you motivated and committed to equity work, especially on days you feel like giving up. Tell them their story has become a part of your why for this work. Do not overpromise and underdeliver. Share your own concerns such as how slow the organization is moving. Explain to them what you are doing, your approach, and why you believe it can lead to change.

Brainstorm

Talk with this person in the moment or later about how they can play an important role in moving the work forward if they have the emotional capacity and interest. For example, this person may be willing to serve on your Equity Team (see Chapter 17). Actively participating on the Equity Team will give them the opportunity to be a part of the solution and, if done right, help them feel empowered.

Regardless of your race, if you see their anger is creating a barrier to moving the work forward, the angry person should hear from you that it's not their anger that worries you. You may be angry too. After all, anger is an appropriate response to racism. It's important they understand your concern is how they use their anger and the impact it is having on DEIB work. You need their help in finding solutions and approaches that lead to changing people and therefore the organization.

Sometimes It's Normal For White Women to Cry

It's not uncommon for PoC to voice feeling annoyed when White women cry during conversations about race. It is problematic if we take a binary approach to their tears, i.e., it is either good or bad. It's much more complex than that, and there are many occasions when I feel relief that they are willing to be present in the conversation to the point it brings up emotions. But before we move to that, let's go beyond what we see on the surface.

The good, kind, loving, moral, ethical White person entering race discourse will likely feel disequilibrium as they begin to see themselves and the world in ways they've never seen before. Taking off the rose-colored glasses they've worn their entire lives and replacing them with an equity lens is an emotional process. When White women are experiencing a transformation, they are likely to experience emotions that bring about tears, just as PoC are expressing anger. Occasionally I will come across White men who cry in race conversations. However, it is much more common for White women to break down crying when exploring their racism and the harm done to PoC.

One reason White women cry is because they are having an awakening. If they stay in this work long enough, they will eventually shift from an intellectual understanding to an internalized one. These types of tears are a normal part of their development and should be welcomed. To connect to another person's pain is a sign they are present, engaged, and alive. White women's tears in this case tell me they care about what is happening to PoC and the impact racism is having on them.

Another cause for White women's tears is because they've been called in for their words or actions. In her thought-provoking book, *White Fragility: Why It's So Hard for White People to Talk about Racism*, Robin DiAngelo names this and other phenomena that occur in racial discourse. DiAngelo describes White fragility as the common ways Whites react in race conversations when their cultural narrative is being confronted. When challenged to explore what it means to be White, their power, and privilege, it typically creates an unnerving experience causing them to kick and scream their way down the path of denial. DiAngelo, a White woman herself, says this behavior serves *"to regain our racial position in society"* and dismisses PoC's experiences as real.

When White women cry out of a feeling of victimization, their tears invite their colleagues to feel sorry for them. Tears in this case don't come from new insight or understanding but are the result of the White woman feeling shame or guilt. Her tears turn the focus around whereby she becomes victim. Intentional or not, it has the impact of moving the conversation away from the PoC who originally experienced harm. These are the tears you don't want to encourage. Colleagues, both Whites and PoC, will often try to take care of the White person by affirming they are a "good" person. This is an attempt to jump in and "rescue" the White woman.

When colleagues step in to rescue White women from their discomfort, it is usually an automatic response done with little conscious thought. PoC may rescue because they've been conditioned over the years to make White people feel comfortable and know that White people's pain rarely results in a positive outcome for PoC. Assurance is one way PoC rescue White women. *"It's OK, I know you didn't mean it," "We've been friends for a long time, and I know you're not like that."* Reminding them of their goodness, hugging, and rubbing their back are different ways PoC release White people from having to do personal work.

White people become uncomfortable when they see their White colleagues being called in on something they said or did that was harmful. They can easily imagine what it would be like to have been in their White colleagues' shoes and may worry they could be next. White people respond to their White colleagues' tears by going to someone above you and suggesting that conversations and workshops about race are divisive. If you are a PoC, they may reframe the way you called their White colleague in as attacking. Believe me. This will baffle you. Just when the White person who was called in experiences discomfort, a necessary part of this work, the opportunity for growth, is snatched away. Rescuing keeps White people complacent and from having to do the deep person work necessary for change.

Strategies for Addressing White Women's Tears

- First discern why she is crying so you don't approach all crying in the same way.
- Pay attention to your internal reactions when White women cry so you don't come to their rescue. Allow White people to experience the disequilibrium when it is due to their gaining insight about racism.
- When their tears are because you or someone else called them in and they feel victimized, switch the attention back to the PoC they have harmed. Check in with the PoC to find out how they are doing, the impact the White person's words or actions had on them, and other similar experience.
- It is not uncommon for White women to leave the room in tears when they are being held accountable for their words or actions. That's OK. Let them go. Later you can check in with them to see if they have had some insight. Better yet, if you are a PoC, have a White ally check in with them. The goal is for them to look internally for insight, rather than externally for affirmation. What you don't want to do is make White people the center while ignoring PoC's experiences.
- When you are in a group situation and a White woman leaves the room, explain to the group why you are not following after her: *"Let's give her some space to be alone. Someone can check in with her later. Right now, I'm concerned about the impact this has had on Ashley."*
- When the tears are due to having an awakening, assist them in exploring what's going on for them. *"Why are you crying?"*, *"What are you feeling right now?"* and *"What triggered your emotional reaction?"* can help them process their emotions.
- Let White people do their own work. If you feel yourself working too hard, you are probably doing most of the work. Learning to ask thought-provoking questions is a tool to prevent this.

Although PoC May Bring a Personal Understanding of Racism, This Doesn't Mean They Understand Dynamics of Racism, Power, and Privilege

This belief comes from a quote by Jamie Washington, a Black man who said, "*Just because I am, doesn't mean I do know, and just because I'm not, doesn't mean I don't.*"[1] Don't assume that because someone is a PoC they have in-depth knowledge of how racism operates or the tools needed to dismantle it. Many PoC are living their lives day by day, trying to survive as they navigate the barriers perpetuated by racism. Far too often, PoC are expected not only to understand how racism functions but to assume the role of expert for their entire group's experiences. Conveying to a PoC in any manner that they should know more than they do can cause them to feel embarrassed because "they should know more."

During my daughter's sophomore year in high school, her teacher told the students to put away their books. They would be doing something different that day. Makena was initially excited for the change in routine, that is, until she learned they would be talking about race. She described having that sunken "*oh no*" feeling in the pit of her stomach, not sure of what "*talking about race*" would lead to. They were broken up into small groups to discuss vignettes that focused on Black people's experiences. She was one of two Black students in her class and the only one sitting amongst her White and Asian peers. As they were discussing the vignettes, just as she feared, her friends repeatedly asked for her opinion. Makena said to me, "*Mom, I was familiar with some of the situations, but not all of them, but it didn't matter. They all assumed I would know.*" Then with frustration she said, "*They don't ask me my thoughts and opinion on other subjects. Why only when it's about race?*"

While PoC are often automatically assumed to be the authority on race issues and particularly when it comes to their own racial group, White people on the other hand are often ignored for any insights or understanding they may bring to the work. This belief can be perpetuated by PoC: "*What can you teach me about something I experience every day?*" Malcolm X in his earlier years held this same belief. It wasn't until he went to Mecca that he realized that dismantling racism requires the joint effort of both those who experience oppression and the oppressor. Whites can also hold the belief they have nothing to offer: "*Who am I to talk about race?*" Though White people, according to many definitions of racism, can never experience racism, they can develop their understanding enough to play a critical role in dismantling racist systems. A better question is, "Who am I not, to talk about race?" Rather than leave the burden and responsibility on the shoulders of PoC, White people must be a part of the solution.

Strategies for Engaging Diverse Voices and Perspectives

- Don't tokenize PoC by asking them to lead just because they are a PoC. Invite them because of what they will bring to the conversation. If what they bring are their experiences as a PoC, be honest and let them know it's why you need them. Story can be a powerful tool for change. And if there are things about them that you value, their willingness to name racism when they see it, their ability to connect with different people, name those things as well.
- If you have few PoC in your organization and they have little knowledge or expertise in how institutional and racism functions, see if they are interested in learning and leading alongside you.
- If you don't have any PoC in your organization (besides yourself), work with what you do have. If there are any White people who are already doing the work to better understand institutional and systemic racism, invite them into the conversation. The lack of PoC can become part of your *why*.
- Be intentional about when to lead and when to step back. Don't always make your voice the one that needs to be heard. This has always been a challenge for me. I tend to get excited about DEIB conversations and want to share my stories, thinking, and feelings. I need to remember that other people want to, too.
- Embrace the idea of learning and growing together as a group. If you have been doing this work for a while, don't approach the work as if you are an expert. See yourself as someone who has some expertise in some areas but also who is developing it in others.

Everyone Deserves to Be Treated with Dignity and Respect

Well, maybe not everyone. But in most situations, this is the case, and even when it's not, seeing the humanity in another person can be a great tool to guide you in moving these conversations forward. This will be one of the more difficult Foundational Beliefs to live by, particularly if you tend to react or avoid rather than respond when your buttons get pushed. No matter what someone says or how much you are triggered by their words or actions, dehumanizing them with name calling, labeling, and hateful words puts you in the role of doing one of the very behaviors you are working so hard to change.

Whether you are a PoC or a White person leading racial equity work, you will frequently come across people who unintentionally trigger an emotional reaction in you. Your old brain is likely to kick into automatic pilot, ready to go into fight or flight mode. In these moments, slow down and call on your new brain, the one you've been exercising to develop muscle around. It's the one that theoretically knows that engaging by leaning in with questions and curiosity in triggering situations will get you further than attacking or avoiding. You may not feel this person deserves your time and efforts, but change won't occur without engagement. They are the work. You cannot change an organization without the aid of people within. Remember, many White people are doing exactly what they were taught to do. Their harmful, sometimes even painful comments reveal their socialization by White dominant culture.

Both White people and PoC who didn't begin to explore racism until later in life when they joined your organization are products of their environment. If you want them to think, behave, and act differently, you will need to be the one to show them the way. This, in part, is the role of a Racial Equity Leader: teaching people a new way of seeing and being in the world. If everyone were where you wanted them to be, there wouldn't be a need for you to take on this work. Model what you want to see in others.

You will encounter some people in your organization who will resist DEIB work every step of the way. I refer to this group as the 10% on the far left of the bell curve (see Figure 2 below). They are usually a small but mighty group of people, and you will want to avoid giving more power to them. No matter what strategies you try, how you present the information, your level of expertise, or what the data shows, they will insist DEIB work is the problem not the solution. The 10% on the far left will take every opportunity to deter the conversation sometimes publicly sometimes in private. They will find a hundred ways to push back against any and all DEIB efforts.

My advice to you is don't engage. When White people refuse to lean into a PoC's experiences or intentionally try to provoke you, don't

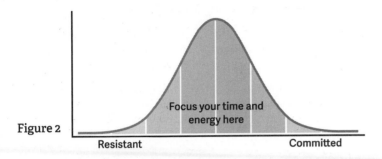

Figure 2

invest your time and energy in them. I once tried to engage a White family member in the 10% who was angry about the term White privilege. After lengthy conversation, I asked him if he would be willing to read some of the research on White privilege. His response was "*If it's valid.*" I immediately aborted the mission and only wished I paid attention to the clues sooner. I knew before this moment that he would find a way to refute that White privilege is a real thing no matter what evidence was put in front of him.

If you try to convince them, guide them, or prove to them their thinking is wrong, it will turn into a power struggle, and there will be no winners. Power struggles in organizations lead to "*us versus them*" and further divide staff. There will be those who may have gotten on board over time but who now align with the resistant person, who in their eyes, you attacked. And there will also be people who understand what you were trying to do, possibly even commend your approach, and who will support you along the way. What occurred between you and the resistant person will further their anger at the racism within your organization.

So, what can you do about the 10% on the far left? Sometimes you may need to call them out on their words or actions, particularly when it has a big impact on PoC, e.g., "*That's a racist thing to say. If it were true that our organization hires the most qualified person for the job, we would have more PoC in leadership positions.*" But in most situations, you will need to either ignore or set boundaries depending on what they are saying and doing because none of the other strategies I'm teaching you will work with this group. Hopefully your organization will become so invested in DEIB that the 10% eventually decide to change or leave.

On the other hand, in most organizations there will be a group of people who aren't sure what "*the work*" is. I refer to this group as the 80%, and they will be your target audience. You can't change your organization's practices without this group getting on board. As individuals within the 80% begin to shift their thinking, they will begin to effect the change in others. Who knows, they may even possibly change the thinking of some of the far left 10%.

They may show some resistance, depending on where they fall on the continuum, but they are more likely to be open and curious than the resistant 10%. A few will point out individual examples of success as proof racism no longer exists, e.g., "*Oprah is a billionaire.*" They are unlikely to notice subtle forms of racism and rationalize the overt ones: "*If they followed the law, there wouldn't be an issue.*" Subtle comments and resistance are likely a result of lack of knowledge and understanding more than anything else.

When there are overt acts of racism in your organization, the 80% are more likely to see it as a single incident or question whether it really was what it was. I once worked with an organization where a noose was put in a common area. Rather than using this incident as an indication racism was indeed a problem, some White people in the 80% focused on whether it really was a noose, "*Maybe when the person set the rope down it just looked like a noose.*" These types of comments are usually by White people who don't want to believe there are people in their organization who would do or say such harmful things toward their Colleagues of Color. Brace yourself. I'm going to make a proverbial "It takes time" comment. While people who defend overt acts of racism are closer to the 10% on the far left, they are not in the far left. There is hope so don't give up on them too soon. This work does take time.

Thankfully, there is usually another 10% in your organization who are committed to DEIB and who fall on the far right of the bell curve. This is where you are, and where you will try to move the 80% closer to. This group is doing the work to understand racism and are ready for change within your organization. You don't need to convince them racism is real. They can and will be a great resource to support your organization's DEIB journey if you take a shared leadership approach.

A challenge with this group can be impatience and frustration with the pace and the issues that keep arising. Some will be so far to the right of the bell curve they will have lost hope and take a shaming and blaming approach. How the 10% on the far right engage the 80% in the middle and the 10% on the far left can make all the difference in getting the 80% on board. You may need to guide them in their approach, so you don't lose those in the 80% and they join the 10% on the far left.

Focus your time and attention on those in the middle and those on the far right. As their commitment grows, your organization's culture will begin to shift in how the workplace functions. This won't happen overnight; it will require being strategic in your approach and staying the course. I've heard it said that it can take 10–15 years for an organization to shift from a racist to an antiracist culture. While you may not be in your organization for the duration, you can leave knowing you were a key part in the paradigm shift that is occurring.

Strategies for Engaging

The 10% on the Far Left

Because the 10% on the far left are likely to push your hot buttons and trigger an emotional reaction, be prepared for how you will handle those moments. Setting boundaries will allow you to say something without opening the dialogue up for them to respond. Below are examples of what setting boundaries can look like.

- *"That's not the (name of company) way."*
- *"I'm concerned by that comment, but I'm not going to engage you because I know it's not going to get us anywhere."*
- *"Your comment reminds me of how important this work is and how much more we need to do."*
- *"I'm not open to talking about it with you because, based on past experiences, we got nowhere with it. But I will say…"*

The Middle 80%

- Meet them where they are at in their understanding by normalizing some of their comments. They are not the only ones in the organization who think or feel that way.
- *"I don't hate anyone, and I don't judge people by the color of their skin, I treat everyone the same."* can be met with statements like

"I'm not surprised you believe that to be true. Many people do. It's normal, especially for White people. Most were taught if they did, they were a bad person."

- *What if the opposite were true? What if you discovered that you do judge and you don't treat everyone the same? In your mind, what would that say about you?*
- *I remember when I believed that about myself. It was tough to realize we all stereotype—not just other people, but me too. They have a name for it. It's called blind spot. There's even an entire book on it.*
- *Would you be open to hearing a different way of thinking and why your comment is difficult for PoC to hear?*

Then teach them what you know.
- Help them understand how DEIB work will benefit everyone in your organization. You can even ask them, what is the value of a diverse workforce, so they are doing some of the work. Frances Kendall, a White woman, in her book *Understanding White Privilege: Creating Pathways to Authentic Relationships Across Race* says, "I know that many of us will not begin to grapple with being White until it is clear that it is in our personal best interest."[2]
- Whenever possible, shift the conversation from individual to institutional racism and/or make connections between the two. It can be an easier place for them to start and a great way of meeting them where they are at.
- *"I don't doubt you are a good person; the issue is that our society is set up so that some people are at an unfair advantage because of their identity while others are at an unfair disadvantage."*
- Give an example of your benefit from institutionalisms: *"I have never had to worry if there will be access for me because I'm in a wheelchair. My able body status allows me to navigate society without physical barriers."*
- *"I imagine you've experienced barriers because of one of your identities, i.e., your gender, class, ability, etc. If not you, maybe someone you know has. Would that be a fair assumption?"* Give them a moment to share a marginalized experience then use their example and tie in the similarities, e.g., between sexism and racism and the need to end racism just like there is a need to irradicate sexism.
- Meet with some of them one on one. Check in and find out how

things are going for them as it relates to the DEIB work happening in the organization, learn about any fears or concerns they have and any questions they are left wondering.

- Build relationship with them. Be sure to speak when you pass by, share a meal together, remember something about their family and hobbies to discuss later. In other words, get to know the people in your organization. This helps to alleviate the fears they have about you as a DEIB leader.

The Far Right 10% Who Have Lost Hope

In the section on shaming and blaming, I identified a few reasons why people lash out. If you want those on the extreme end of the far right to engage effectively, if you recognize you need their help, if you value what they bring, they will need to feel some degree of hope, be reminded of some changes that are occurring, and believe you care. Below is an ALERT strategy I often use with the very far right 10% who have lost hope.

- Acknowledge racism is alive and well and give a few examples of where you see it playing out in your organization. Ask them what you are missing. (This helps you to join with them and convey that you see it too.)
- Listen to the experiences of PoC. Give them the opportunity to express how racism has impacted them personally. Sit with their pain, anger, and even rage as they share what it's been like for them in your workplace. (This will convey how they experience the workplace matters to you.)
- Explore what remains the same since they first joined the organization, what has changed for the better (small and big wins), what still needs changing, and any thoughts they may have about how to go about it? (This approach can serve two purposes. One, it helps to mitigate all or no one thinking nothing is different, and second, it indicates their opinion matters to you.)
- Repeat some of the things you've heard them saying that stand out for you.

  "I haven't been here as long as you have. It sounds like some things were tried before, and it got our organization nowhere. I'm also hearing that if there were more People of Color in leadership positions and White people who were invested in change, it

would make a big difference. Thank you for trusting me enough to share the impact this has had on you. It sounds like a lonely and difficult place to work in." (This shows you were listening.)

- Share your Foundational Beliefs that drive how and why you approach the work you do and convey what you hope for and from them. Keep in mind it's normal and healthy for PoC to be skeptical about things changing. And just because you volunteered or were hired to lead DEIB work or even because you are a PoC, it isn't enough proof that things will be different or change will be long-lasting. So don't try to convince them your organization will be transformed because you are there. You are not the magic bullet. In fact, it is why you need them and the majority of the 80% support. This doesn't mean you shouldn't remind them you are moving in the right direction, you are committed, and you need their help.

There Are No Quick Fixes or Cookbook Approaches

As you lead this work in your organization, whether you were hired for the position, you were the one regularly questioning and challenging the status quo, or your understanding of racism made you the go-to person, be careful not to buy into a Eurocentric approach that seeks easy answers. In my twenty plus years of experience, I still don't have all the answers, nor have I ever met anyone who does. There is no organization I can point to and say, *"Do it like they did it."* Each organization is different. There are some approaches that work better than others, Foundational Beliefs that will take you further than others, but there is no one-size-fits-all in equity work. In fact, I'm sharing with you what I've come to understand, but you know your organization better than I do and are likely to have some of your own ideas too.

One reason White people are uncomfortable with DEIB work is they want "the" answers so they can do that thing, and then move on. This is one way that White cultural norms play out and hinder DEIB progress. It's difficult for them to accept and be present in the process that will eventually lead to the "product" they seek. Be ready for leadership to pressure *you* to come up with easy solutions, and some will expect that the change won't necessitate their involvement. The problem with quick fix approaches is that it negates the fact that this work requires collective (vs. individual) effort. Whites in your organization might struggle with the collectivist approach because it is at odds with the Eurocentric individual approach. The best way to diminish institutional racist practices is by pooling together your best thinking, collective understanding, and resources to come up with solutions. No single person should be expected to have all the answers. As a Racial Equity Leader, your role is to lead your organization's effort in addressing institutional racism—not to solve its problems.

In Chapter 2 of *The Theory Behind the Practice: A Brief Introduction to the Adaptive Leadership Framework*, Heifetz, Grashow, and Linsky explain the difference between technical problems (that may be difficult to fix but have a clear solution) and the problem and adaptive problems where the solutions depend more on collective creativity. For example, there is typically a technical solution to repairing your car when it's stopped running. The problem can usually be easily fixed by taking it to the shop. A mechanic will determine what is needed to fix it. You just need the finances to afford the repairs.

While technical problems have a clear solution, adaptive problems are much more complex and have no clear, easy way of solving them. Not having the money to fix your car could be an adaptive problem. It's not as simple as *"just get a job."* Some people have intellectual or physical disabilities making employment a challenging goal. To make matters more complex, even if that person was able to do the job, they must overcome the bias of the potential employer who may not see them as a viable employee. Other people may not have the skills or education to make enough money to cover all their living expenses let alone repair their car. I could name many more possible scenarios. My point is that adaptive situations rarely have a simple solution.

Some problems will require both a technical and adaptive approach. For example, pulling together an Equity Team (ET) (see Chapter 17) is technical. There are important steps you must consider in developing an ET. The work your ET does to address equity and inclusion in the workplace is adaptive. There are many factors involved which can determine the ET's success, e.g., past and present issues in your organization, level of the ET's understanding of racism, work your organization has done in the past, leadership's support, degree of willingness of staff, size of organization, etc.

Strategies for Responding to
the Pressure for a Quick Fix

- Don't look to this author to have all the answers. If you are thinking you are going to find the answers in this book, you won't. Equity work is about working collectively with others in your organization to come up with solutions. This book is a guide to help steer you in the right direction.

- Put questions which rely on you to have all the answers back on the people who asked them. *"Great question. What are your thoughts? What do you recommend?"*

- Joke with them playfully: *"If I had the answers, you would be the first to know."* Or *"I know you're not trying to put the entire burden of solving our problems of institutional racism on my shoulders."* Humor and humility can be disarming and useful tools.

- Help them think through what their role is. If someone says, *"Tell me what to do,"* instead of attempting to answer their question, ask them questions: *"What have you already done to deepen your understanding of racism?"*, *"What new learning have you engaged in to further develop your equity lens?"*, *"How are you applying what you've learned in your work and personal life?"*

- Remember systemic racism existed long before you were born. Because you are committed to DEIB, a magic wand is not going to appear in your hand so you can instantly undo centuries of racist practices.

- Remember the process is the first part of the product. Get people talking about racism as a first step.

- If needed, bring in an outside facilitator who is experienced in getting people to engage in courageous conversations about race. Keep in mind leading the work doesn't mean you must take on every role. When determining an outside consultant and/or facilitator, make sure that how they approach the work aligns with your Foundational Beliefs.

Don't jump into the work with little or no thought to your approach. Avoid a self-righteous attitude of calling White people *out* rather than *in*. Your goal is not to make White people feel some pain. Don't take your anger and frustration out on individuals; instead use it in a productive way to energize and motivate you to change systems. Do the harder work of meeting people where they are, extending an invitation to explore and lean into discomfort as they process new learning around these issues.

Being intentional and relying on your beliefs to guide you in leading this work shapes the types of questions you will ask, particularly when things become challenging. Practice modeling your Foundational Beliefs in all aspects of your life. You can, but you shouldn't, expect others to do what you yourself are not willing to do. When you get off course, which you will, reexamine your approach through the lens of your Foundational Beliefs. Ask yourself, *"Is this approach working?"* Your approach should contribute to bridging the divide not increasing it. Whether you like it or not, you are holding yourself to a higher standard than those you engage when you accept taking on a DEIB leadership role.

Hopefully, effectively engaging will foster insight for both you and those you are engaging, resulting in changes that strengthen how everyone moves forward. What you don't want to do is abandon your beliefs for the sake of being liked, accepted, or approved of by other people. Leading Equity work is not a position for the timid. Be open to the input of others.

Establishing Foundational Beliefs:
Commitment to Change and Be Changed
- Brainstorm a list of Foundational Beliefs you deem as necessary to effectively move DEIB work forward. Include others who are working with you.
- Read Robin DiAngelo's book *White Fragility: Why It's So Hard for White People to Talk about Racism.* If you don't have time, read her article, "White America's Racial Illiteracy: Why Our National Conversation Is Poisoned from the Start." Jot down your thoughts and explore your own opinions about White fragility.
- Generate a few of your own ideas for how to respond when people turn to you for the answers.
- Become grounded in your understanding of the differences between technical versus adaptive problems. Research information on adaptive leadership. This will help you more readily identify what is needed, when it's needed, and when to push back on those who expect you to be the problem solver. If you are not the decision-maker in your organization, invite the decision-makers to read what you've discovered and discuss it together.

FINDING A FRAMEWORK
TO GUIDE YOU

Fighting for our deepest convictions requires relinquishing
control and accepting messy uncertainties. It demands
working as well as we can at efforts that feel morally right,
and then having faith that our labors will bear fruit, perhaps
in our time, or perhaps down the line, for somebody else.

— Paul Rogat Loeb

You know your "*why*" for this work, you're committed to your own
personal growth, you have a better understanding of why these
conversations are challenging, you're becoming grounded in your
Foundational Beliefs, and you've explored your beliefs around PoC
educating White folks. If you don't already have one, it's time to think
about the framework you will use to guide your organization through
their DEIB journey.

There are many points of view regarding what language and structures should be used to approach DEIB work. Cultural humility, undoing institutional racism, antiracism, racial equity, multicultural work,
cultural responsiveness, and more have been put forward to be the
best language to use to guide your approach. In the fourth edition of
Derald and David Sue's *Counseling the Culturally Diverse: Theory and
Practice*, they use the term *Cultural Competence*. Though their framework was initially developed for clinicians working with their clients,
I adapted their model recognizing it applies to anyone and everyone

regardless of their profession. Sue and Sue name three components to effectively working across cultures: Awareness, Knowledge, and Skills. We've added a fourth component, Action/Advocacy,[1] and have given our framework its own name: a *Framework for Social Justice*.

While the word "competence" implicitly implies, we will *arrive*, those who have studied Sue and Sue's model recognize that it speaks to the idea we *all* have work to do, and that Cultural Competence is a journey that keeps us in a constant state of learning, rather than a box we check to indicate completion. In other words, we will never arrive or know all that there is to know, i.e., "*I did awareness work; now I'm done with that part of my learning*." This work is fluid not linear. However, starting with awareness, moving to knowledge and then skills, is a great start to shift people's lenses so they are better equipped to advocate for change. If individuals within an organization don't see or understand the problems, they won't know where and how to implement change. When people say, "*Tell me what to do*," it's because they've not done enough work in the first two areas to see what needs to be done. They are still seeing things through their socialized lenses.

The next several chapters will familiarize you with Awareness, Knowledge, Skills, and Action/Advocacy. These four components often overlap with one another, particularly Awareness and Knowledge. For example, when learning about implicit bias, you can simultaneously deepen awareness of your own bias and develop knowledge of the impact of bias on others. In other words, each component rarely serves as a standalone.

You may want to research different frameworks so you can settle on an approach you can stand behind as you guide your organization. You will need to communicate to staff and leaders what your organization's efforts will involve and promote that framework, so they have a common language and understanding as they move forward. Regardless of where people are in their views, there should be no confusion as to what the work entails. If at some point in your organization's journey, you find a model that better fits the work, adapt and make changes. Remember this work is ever evolving.

5

Be Aware of Yourself as a Racialized Being

Awareness

At the time I submitted my application for graduate school, I didn't really know what was meant by my minor, Multicultural and Community Psychology. It sounded interesting so I applied, and thankfully was accepted. Throughout the entire first year, our professors had us doing Awareness work, unpacking our biases, and looking at parts of our identities where we held privilege. The work was intense, but they knew we would not be effective clinicians if we operated under color-blind thinking or were unaware of how our identities created experiences that shaped our perceptions and formed realities for both us and our clients. They had enough knowledge and experience to know dynamics of differences could and would cause our cultures to clash with our clients', if left unexamined.

Growing up with a White mother, three older White brothers, an older White sister, and a younger sister who is also multiracial, had me convinced I didn't have biases or stereotypes. I certainly didn't believe I had privilege being a Black woman who had grown up in poverty. I knew prejudice existed but was certain it was in everyone else, just not me. I believed I was the exception to the rule. It didn't take long for me to realize not only do I have biases and stereotypes toward those who belong to groups I don't identify with, I also hold them toward people who I share the same identities with. I stereotype women, Christians, Blacks, multiracial people, middle-class people, and so many more individuals, simply because of their real or perceived group identities.

My love for my White mother and older White siblings had me initially resistant to exploring my bias. My family was proof of my truth I didn't do "*that thing*" other people did, especially Whites. I believed that acknowledging my bias meant I was a bad person or didn't love my family the way I knew I did. In truth, we make the people in our lives different from everyone else who shares their same identity. I know my White mother and siblings. My mind has made them the exception. In other words, they become different from other White people. I've come to understand these biases are in all of us, messages we have unconsciously taken in over time, predominantly in our early formative years, through education, media, community, and other sources.

Relationships with PoC won't keep you from having bias, and it is not evidence you don't have work to do. Voting for Obama isn't proof you don't stereotype Blacks. He just becomes different from other Blacks. Even being a PoC won't keep you from stereotyping your own racial group. We all stereotype. We judge people we don't know, immediately and unconsciously in a split second. You are likely to make automatic assumptions about who you perceive to be open or resistant to equity work, who you will like or dislike, who is friendly and who is not, who is smart and who isn't, etc. You don't even need to talk to someone, or even meet them, to hold a preset of assumptions about them. Even their profession will unleash a set of preconceived notions in your mind.

Think about what first pops into your head when you think of teachers, lawyers, custodians, engineers, law enforcement, bus drivers, professors, administrators, therapists, or gardeners. It is likely the images you formed in your head included their gender, age, race, sexual orientation, or some other identity that makes up the person you assume them to be. Our automatic assumptions are based not only on the type of work someone does but also where they do it. Your assumptions about a social worker living in a rural area will be different from your assumption about a social worker in a large city.

The problem isn't that you are judging others or that they are judging you. Sizing people up is, in part, what it means to be human. Problems arise when you are unaware you are stereotyping. When you fail to bring what is in your unconscious to a level of consciousness, you are more likely to unintentionally let your stereotypes get in the way of your decision-making. It's people who believe they "*don't notice race*" that are more likely to do harm because their unconscious stereotypes turn into bias, i.e., how they treat others.

Banaji and Greenwald, in their book *Blindspot: Hidden Biases of Good People*, are among many researchers who have helped society make a shift from seeing bias as intentional acts of bad people to understanding bias can occur unconsciously from good people. "*A quarter century ago, most psychologists believed that human behavior was primarily guided by conscious thoughts and feelings. Nowadays the majority will readily agree that much of human judgment and behavior is produced with little conscious thought.*"[1] Banaji and Greenwald refer to blind spot as recognizing bias in others but not yourself. The fact is, we all have bias. Depending on your role in society, your bias can have a profound impact, especially on the lives of PoC : a judge has a gavel, a psychologist a diagnosis, a teacher a grade book, an HR director the ability to hire and fire, a police officer a gun.

In *Whistling Vivaldi and Other Clues to How Stereotypes Affect Us*, Claude Steele focuses on the research uncovering the impact of stereotypes on PoC in educational settings. One such impact he terms *stereotype threat*:

> When a person knows their group identity, knows how society views it, knows they are doing something for which that view is relevant and know, at some level, that they are in a predicament: their performance could confirm a bad view of their group and of themselves, as a member of that group. Stereotype threat captures the idea of a situational predicament as a contingency of their group identity, a real threat of judgment or treatment in the person's environment that go beyond any limitations within.[2]

Being in the predicament that what you are doing could confirm one of your own stereotypes about another will likely cause that person to underperform, therefore fulfilling the stereotype. For example, Native, Latine, and Blacks are stereotyped as unintelligent. For members of these groups, stereotype threat can occur when taking a test. The person is not just taking the test; they are also worrying about their performance. Taking a test and worrying about confirming a stereotype leads to underperformance because they are doing two things at once, even if they are not aware of it.

As an equity leader, not only will you be engaging in this Awareness work, but you will also be guiding others. Awareness work is the hardest of all four components because people have spent a lifetime developing a sense of who they see themselves to be, and they will resist looking at themselves differently. When you begin leading them through self-exploration, they will uncover within themselves ways in which they have done harm through their behaviors, attitudes, beliefs, values, and assumptions. This will invoke shame, guilt, embarrassment, and anger, along with a host of other emotions.

Not only is Awareness work the hardest work, but it is also the most important of all four components because self-awareness is what is necessary to change how your organization functions. It allows us to be intentional in making sure that how we see ourselves aligns with our actions. Awareness work will produce internal disruptions as new understandings begin to conflict with lifelong beliefs. It requires uncovering what's in our unconscious, how we've been socialized, and unpacking identities where we hold privilege. It is work done to look at our assumptions, beliefs, values, and preconceived notions. It answers the questions *"How have I been socialized? What messages have I taken in about differences? How has my race, gender, sexual orientation, religion, age, class, and abilities put me at an unfair advantage or unfair disadvantage?"* It is not about they, those, or them out there. It is about you and no one else.

The beautiful thing about Awareness work is it's the work that commonly initiates an awakening that leads to personal change. Overtime, as an individual begins to recognize what's in them is in others too, it will normalize their experiences and feelings, making the work less threatening. People will become liberated from the fear, discomfort, and anxiety that comes with pretending that they don't judge, have privilege, or are somehow different from everyone else. It's a lot of work keeping up that façade. When done right, and depending on your audience, most will hunger for more and in the process deepen their commitment to racial justice. It's critical you move slowly in the beginning. No matter the sense of urgency you or others in the organization may feel, allow for a gradual learning process, deepening the personal work overtime.

Becoming Aware of Self:
Commitment to Change and Be Changed

- Go online to www.implicit.harvard.edu and take the Harvard Implicit Association Test on race to deepen your insight about your own racial bias. What surprised you? When you have time, take the same test a couple of times, and some of their other tests on, e.g., gender.

- Read *Blindspot: Hidden Biases of Good People* by Banaji and Greenwald and/or read *Whistling Vivaldi: How Stereotypes Affect Us and What We Can Do* by Steele. Consider ordering multiple copies and holding a book study with several other members of your organization.

6

Develop Knowledge of Others as Racialized Beings

*Understanding without knowledge
is just as dangerous as knowledge
without understanding.*

— Anonymous

Knowledge

The second component Sue and Sue describe is Knowledge. Knowledge work is not as emotionally disruptive as Awareness work because it's about acquiring as much information as you can about diverse groups of people. This includes knowledge of a group's values, beliefs, styles of engaging, and the way society has treated them, past and present. Ask yourself, *"What do I know about the people I work with and was hired to serve?"* While Awareness work is often referred to as heart work, Knowledge work is seen as head work.

I tend to talk loudly. I use my hands when speaking whether to a group or with an individual. I engage through my body, preferring to move around a room rather than stand behind a podium and read notes. I tell stories to make my point and have a habit of interrupting when others are speaking. Though not true of *all* African Americans, they are common styles of communication.

White people, on the other hand, tend to have a more linear style of engaging. They are more likely to remain in one place, take turns when talking, and rely on facts and figures to make a point; they are often agenda bound. While research has revealed similarities in norms within a group, we know that people are also individuals and therefore should not be stereotyped as *all* behaving or acting one way because of their group identity. For example, someone from New

York or who is Italian could have similar styles of engaging to African Americans. There are cultures within cultures. Where someone grew up, when they were born, who they grew up with, and other factors will all influence them culturally.

This work is complex. Human beings cannot easily be placed into a box that defines who they are, how they see the world, or how they interact within it. However, there is plenty of research easily available to assist you in learning common group norms. Having no knowledge of cultural differences is one reason cultures often clash. Imagine a White woman joining a small social circle of her Black colleagues. If she operates from White cultural norms but hasn't taken the time to learn about African American culture, she may leave the experience feeling frustrated that no one gave her the opportunity to speak. It's probable she will view the others as being "rude" for their interrupting behavior rather than understanding that when they inhaled it was her opportunity to jump in.

Most PoC learn White dominant cultural norms early in life. It's one of the gateways to success. Because White norms are the standard from which everyone else must operate, as Ijeoma Oluo points out in her book *So You Want to Talk about Race*, PoC will often know more about Whites than White people do themselves. However, White people rarely take the time to learn about other cultures unless they are preparing to travel to countries where Whites are the minority. It's one of the privileges of being White. White people don't have to learn about Asians, Latine, Natives, or Blacks to get ahead in life.

While PoC may have a great deal of understanding about White culture, it doesn't mean they have knowledge of racial groups different from their own. PoC must also do the work to gain understanding of diverse groups. Knowledge work is necessary for both White people and PoC particularly if one of your goals is to create a work environment where everyone feels they belong rather than having to leave their differences behind.

People of the same ethnic group often have shared experiences, and those experiences can impact why they behave similarly to one another. Their behaviors become implicit cultural norms of their group. When someone's behavior is unfamiliar to you, rather than labeling it as inappropriate, envision yourself becoming curious and wondering if their behavior is tied to their culture. In this way, knowledge of cultural norms becomes a tool for you to explore from a perspective other than your own. The more knowledge you have of different cultures, the more you will be able to effectively engage.

Understanding History

Knowledge work is not just about understanding different groups, it's also about gaining a historical understanding of a group's experience. It seeks to find answers to the question *"How has our nation treated PoC, and what is the current impact?"* History provides context for what might be going on in a given situation. How a racial group has been marginalized informs how they see the privileged group. There is often caution, mistrust, and anger toward individuals who represent the group that has done harm. It can have less to do with who you are as an individual and more to do with what your identity represents to an historically marginalized group. If you understand this, you will be less likely to take cross-cultural tension personally when it arises.

I can still remember sitting on a college campus bench with one of my psychology professors, a Black woman, Dr. Kathy Sanders-Phillips. It was a typical beautiful, sunny California day. I had asked her to meet with me. For as long as I could remember, I wanted to share with someone lifelong experiences I'd been having with darker skin African American girls and, as I got older, women. I needed someone to help me make sense of the dynamics. *Why did I often find myself feeling like they were in a circle, with me on the outside trying to get in, only to have one of them close the space between them the moment I tried to enter? Was it me? Was I doing something wrong?* To my surprise, it was happening again, even in graduate school. I desperately needed someone to talk with who might help me understand these painful experiences.

It felt good to talk with a Black professor, someone who was racially similar, who had studied race relations, and who could possibly shed light on why it was still happening. I felt hope and a sense of safety as I began to confide in her the embarrassing and shameful experiences I'd been keeping a secret since early childhood. I can recall talking a long time, periodically breaking down in tears while she just listened. It felt therapeutic to share my stories and release the pain and confusion of experiences I'd had with Black women my entire life but never understood.

I don't know how long I spent talking and crying. I just remember everything around me seemingly come to a standstill as I heard her say what I had always been feeling with words I will never forget, "*You don't feel Black enough.*" I had never heard those words spoken before, but they described my experiences perfectly. All the years I had tried to fit in, struggling to prove I was the same as they were, seeking acceptance and belonging. I had been striving to prove to Black women my whole life that I was who I already was, Black enough. Those few simple words led me down a new path of discovery.

With this new insight, I was able to not only examine how I showed up in relationships with Black women but also grow in my understanding of the ways in which darker skin women have always been treated in this country. I recognized for the first time that my relationships with darker skinned Black women wasn't about me as an individual but rather our complex history that deemed me more beautiful, more intelligent, less threatening, and more desirable solely because of my light complexion. Colorism was at play, and none of us recognized we were playing our part in maintaining racism. When we were hurting one another, me through my naïveté in thinking my experiences were the same as theirs and them by making me the issue, we weren't focusing on the real problems: institutional and systemic racism.

The more I grew to understand how being light skin granted me certain privileges and how darker skinned Black women are treated, the more pieces of the puzzle began to fall in place. It wasn't me they disliked, it was my naïveté: believing our experiences were the same and the way I unintentionally flaunted my privilege through my innocence. They were angry with White people for creating systems that put Whites and lighter skin people at an unfair advantage and angry with me for not knowing it. My privilege of not having to know, was hurting them.

After my professor and I parted, I went straight home and immediately wrote this poem, continuing to pour out my feelings on paper. This was the true beginning of my journey, and it was liberating.

Listen My Sister

Listen my sister,
can you hear me?
Awake at night,
angry and confused
tears to express my pain, the
*   shame,*
of the way I feel
about the way things are
and have always been.
We fight the same fight,
only you do not see me in your
*   blinded plight*
to fight for what's right.
Why? Because I am not enough
of what you want me to be?
Blinded
because you do not see me
*   for me.*
But I'm standing here
right next to you
waiting to hear what you have
*   to say,*
and hoping
hoping
you too, will listen to me

and not just see
the color of my skin
like they did
when they called me "nigger"
Too young to understand
but old enough to know
they hated me
because of my yellow skin
and yet even they fought
for what they thought
was the right thing.
Though it's not the same
I still hope
that one day
I would prove to them
to you
there's more to me
than the color of my skin.
And so, I turn to you
but you do not listen to me
because I do not understand
what it's like to be you?
My sister
do you understand
what it's like to be me?

— Caprice D. Jones (1995)

My conversation with Dr. Sanders-Phillips opened a door, awakening in me the desire to dive deeper into self-exploration and understanding. Continuing to reexamine my relationships with Black women and what stood between us, I began to accept that I have racial privileges. My misguided belief that the Black experience was the same, no matter the shade of your skin, had begun to fall apart. The more I probed, the more I realized my ideas of "sameness" not only invalidated my darker skin sister's experiences, but those ideas had caused me to collude with racism. It wasn't until I truly understood how White standards of beauty were in my favor that my relationships with Black women shifted to acceptance. This grew into a strong determination to change our ever-present history, which is constantly being fueled by daily oppressions that remind me that race still matters.

Light skin multiracial sisters will sometimes share how bad they had it growing up. Being multiracial for most means being too much of one race and not enough of the other. The rejection is felt from both sides. Multiracial stories need to be honored through listening and acknowledging the pain and hurt that comes with colorism. And, at the same time, recognize that if a lighter skinned person was asked if they would trade their complexion to become dark, most would say "*No.*" Maybe darker, yes. But not dark. Because they know, whether they are willing to admit it, that one common narrative that plays out around the world is the lighter your skin, the more privileges you have, the darker you are, the more inferior you are deemed. The more you look like a PoC, the more stereotypes you will have to navigate.

Understanding history can aid you in your equity leadership role. If you are White leading this work and find yourself experiencing apprehension from a PoC, it could be a result of your race. It's not you as an individual that's likely causing the mistrust, it's what your race represents. People who look like you have done harm to PoC, past and present, probably even in your organization. So, don't expect just because you say you care about their marginalized experiences, or because you are working toward change, you will automatically be granted their trust.

If you are a PoC, apprehension from another PoC could be due to the fact you serve an organization that historically has underserved them. Why should PoC have faith in the changes you say you are invested in bringing about when no meaningful change has occurred so far? Why should PoC believe in you just because you are a Person of Color when throughout history other PoC have colluded with racism making things worse rather than better for them. There is a history in the USA of both Whites and PoC who operate under the guise of being there to "help" but who have intentionally and unintentionally done harm. Mistrust PoC hold of White people, institutions, and other PoC leading within those institutions has been referred to as *healthy paranoia*. When you take on the role of Racial Equity Leader, it will be up to you to do more than *tell* them change will occur, you must *show* them.

When I first became the Director of Equity and Race Relations for Seattle Public Schools, I was anxious and eager to go out into the African American community and engage. I just knew because I was Black and graduated in that very District, I would be received with enthusiasm from the community I had grown up in. To my surprise, this was not the case. The moment I took the position, PoC questioned my motives. They didn't trust I was there to serve them or had their children's best interest at heart. I now represented a system that historically and currently was institutionally racist. I remember an elder in the community saying to me, "*This is not about your goodness, Caprice. How do we know if you will bite the hand that feeds you?*" It would not be wise for him, or anyone else, to automatically trust me just because we were of the same race.

When I accepted the position, I also had to accept I was now part of a system that oppressed. The sooner I figured this out, the sooner I could start listening for understanding without making it about me. This is what you must help White people in your organization under-stand. As they engage in Knowledge work, they will also come to realize it is not about them as individuals: their goodness, how caring they are, or other positive characteristics they possess. This type of thinking invalidates past experiences of marginalized groups. Trust is something that you must build slowly and over time. And keep in mind, because of our history, these dynamics don't just exist between Blacks and Whites. This dynamic occurs across all racial groups.

Whenever you hold a privileged identity or represent an organiza-tion that has historically underserved a group, it is your responsibility as the person with power and/or privilege to be the first one to listen and try to understand. And be mindful, the more you develop knowl-edge of another racial group's experience, the easier it can be to *feel sorry* for that group. That's not what they seek. Work collaboratively with the people you are there to serve and avoid furthering their experiences of marginalization with a savior mentality—thinking they need someone to rescue them.

Beyond Race

Leading racial equity work involves honoring differences beyond race. This means you will need to expand your understanding of diverse cultures and experiences to create a workplace where everyone feels they belong. Years ago, PricewaterhouseCoopers put an advertisement in a magazine that has stayed with me: "*What do people have to leave behind in order to succeed?*" was its headline. It listed aspects of identity people leave behind before going to work, such as religion, background, language, gender, ethnicity, sexual orientation, hair styles, style of dress, etc. At the bottom the ad read, "*A workplace can only be diverse if the people who work there can be themselves.*" It spoke to the notion that counting the diverse number of people in your organization—for example, by race—doesn't make for a diverse workplace. If people can't bring themselves into their schools, communities, and workplaces, you have an organization with diverse people who have learned to function under monocultural, Eurocentric norms and values.

Not only have PoC become skilled, consciously and unconsciously, at making White people feel comfortable being around them, so too have lesbian, gay, bisexual, transgender, and queer (LGBTQ) people with cisgender, heterosexual people. So too have Muslims, Buddhists, Sikhs, and people of other faiths with Christians. Those who have been relegated to the margins pick up on the subtle and not so subtle cues that inform them who and what is accepted by White, male, heterosexual, Christian culture.

When beginning your organization's equity journey, I recommend you start with race. It is the one area White people struggle with the most. If you can get your organization talking about racism, they will be able to have difficult conversations about almost anything. Because Knowledge work is about learning about different groups and understanding history, people will sometimes say, "*We have many different cultures within our workplace, are you saying I have to know about all the difference groups?*" My reply is always the same, "*I'm suggesting you should get started.*" While you will never know all things about all cultures, given there are cultures within cultures, for example, saying you are committed to social justice but not investing time to understand the diversity around you supports a monocultural workplace and colludes with institutional *isms*.

Developing Knowledge of Others:
Commitment to Change and Be Changed

- Observe your own communication style and that of others. Notice eye contact, proximity, hand and body movement, etc. What might be a cultural norm for you and for them?
- Read or listen audibly to either Ronald Takaki's book *A Different Mirror: A History of Multicultural America*, Howard Zinn's *A People's History of the United States*, or some other history book to give you a foundation of the United States' legacy of institutional racism beyond the oversimplified, inaccurate version you likely learned in your K-12 education.

7

Gain Skills to Effectively Engage Across Cultures

Skills

The third component of this work is Skills. Awareness work is from the heart, Knowledge work is head work, and Skills work is our hands. The only way to acquire skills is through practice. Those who are solution focused, outcome based, or who value the product over the process will want to move quickly to Skills. Typically, this is something you will experience from White people who have attended one workshop or are in the earliest stages of their awakening. Questions like "*I get I have bias, but what am I supposed to do?*" are common. As stated earlier, your title or role as a leader of racial equity work may cause you to feel pressure to come up with the answers. Resist the temptation. First, you probably don't have the answers they seek. Secondly, if you gave them ideas for what they could do, they likely wouldn't do them or would tell you they won't work. Third, it's not your job. Your role is in guiding your organization in learning how to have courageous conversations so people can work together toward solutions.

Jumping immediately to skills is problematic in several ways. It's not an institutional change approach. It relies on a few people to have all the answers rather than those within the organization being a part of a solution. It is an oversimplification, like an easy recipe in a cookbook, that ignores the challenges that come with years of institutional racist thinking and practices. It can lead to paternalistic behavior as people within start to do *to* or *for* rather than *with* those pushed to the margins. And it relieves White people of the necessary discomfort they must go through as they embark on their journey. JLove Calderón captures that discomfort perfectly in her book *Occupying Privilege: Conversations on Love, Race, & Liberation*, in an interview with Danny Hoch.

Danny: ...There's a writer named Adrianne Piper, and she talks about something called white people's fatigue, which means that we just want an answer, a quick fix answer that absolves us of our participation in racism. In other words, "So what does that mean? Should I NOT vote for Obama? What should I do? Just TELL me what to do! I don't actually want to do the work; I just want to know what to do. Tell me what to do so I'm not guilty."[1]

In the early stages of Awareness and Knowledge work, you will likely hear another common statement typically made by White people, *"I've already done that."* *That* being taken a diversity workshop, as if one or two workshops is enough to gain skills. This statement usually comes from a place of resistance. When someone asserts this, rather than explain how this workshop is different from the last or why it's important to their ongoing development, follow up with questions such as *"Say more about the work you've done.", "What did you learn from it?", "How has it informed your practice?"* Engaging them with questions rather than responding with answers puts the onus back on them and sheds light on the problems with their assertion. There's an old joke I learned in my first year of graduate school: *"How many psychologists does it take to change a lightbulb? Only one, but the lightbulb has to want to change."* Corny but applicable to this work.

It is likely you are already carrying more than your share of the load. Now you're being asked to do even more when they are required to do so little. Even if you had quick fix answers, you are not the Equity Police. You do not have the capacity to follow people around telling them to do this, change that, say this, convey that. Besides, what happens when you leave? One workshop, a policy, or a diversity position is not enough to undo generations of institutionally racist practices.

Equity work requires a commitment from many people in the organization in their role as manager, sales rep, teacher, accountant, customer service rep, and so on. What needs to be done in one position or department is going to be different in another, depending on their role and responsibility and so much more. You can't do the work for them, and there is no simple recipe or Easy-Bake Oven for equity work. The way to develop skills is by spending a significant amount of time deepening awareness of self and gaining knowledge of others. Skills will come about as a part of the process. Your organization won't change by placing all responsibility on your shoulders.

I remember being at a conference years ago. I had arrived early and so was the first seated at my table. Soon after, a Native American man joined me. I tend to talk a lot and, in situations like this conference, love engaging people I'm meeting for the first time. As soon as this man sat down, I began doing what I do best, asking questions. *"What's your name?"*, *"Where do you work?"*, *"Is this your first time at this conference?"*, *"Did you come with anyone else?"*, *"Which workshops are you signed up for?"*, *"Have you heard the keynoter speak before?"* This one-way conversation went on and on until I suddenly realized there was very little reciprocation.

The White culture within me that values immediately asking questions, to establish relationship, quickly surfaced (Awareness). I imagine my questioning felt like an inquisition to him. When I realized I was dominating the space, I paused long enough to pull from my backpack what I had learned about a common communication style of Indigenous peoples (Knowledge). Native Americans tend to create space for silence after someone has spoken. I became curious. *"Might culture be operating in this moment?"* If I wanted him to engage with me, maybe I needed to stop talking and make room for silence. Yup. Sure enough, our cultures had been clashing. He began speaking once I invited him in through my silence (Skills). If I didn't have that little bit of information about Indigenous peoples, we likely would have left the table with incorrect assumptions about one another.

While the harm done in the above situation may be minimal, the same can't be said for the Gray brothers, two Native Americans who on May of 2018 had campus police called on them while participating in Colorado State University's college tour. These young men had saved their money and driven seven hours from New Mexico to have what should have been an amazing introduction to college life but instead turned into a racist experience. In this case, 19-year-old Thomas Kanewakeron Gray and 17-year-old Lloyd Skanahwati Gray's differences were viewed as a threat. According to a report from several media sources, a White parent on the tour noticed them arrive late. She called campus police because the young men seemed "creepy." Apparently, their clothing, the fact that they were "real quiet," and "wouldn't answer her questions" made her feel nervous. In truth, her racist actions were due to her lack of knowledge of Native culture, and her unawareness of her own bias, power, and White privilege, leading to these two brothers being questioned by campus police.[2]

Again, there are no simple answers or broad brushstrokes we can apply to everyone in all situations. You won't have all the answers and neither do I. If I did, Oprah Winfrey would bring back her show just to put me on it, hopefully. Even when you find a strategy that works for one person, it may not apply to another. Unlike some mathematical equations, people are always complex, and their interactions result in infinite possibilities. What I can tell you is this: the more aware you are of yourself and the more knowledge you have of others, the more effective you will become at engaging across cultures.

It's Not If You Offend, It's When

Do you remember how scary it was learning to drive? You had to pay attention to so many things all at once—your speed, cars next to you, in front of you and behind you, the line in the middle of the road, your side and rearview mirrors, stop signs, the accelerator, the break, pedestrians—you get the point. For those of you who learned to drive using a stick shift like I did, you may recall how extra scary that was! In addition to everything else, you also had to drive with two feet, shift gears at just the right speed, all while hearing the person teaching you scream "*Shift! Shift!*" When on a hill, stopping at a light frightened you with the prospect of rolling backward into the car behind you. You had to drive with one foot on the gas pedal and the other on the brake with just the right amount of pressure. The fear was paralyzing. But over time and with practice, and many mistakes, you eventually were driving with little conscious thought.

Learning to drive is like learning to develop cross-cultural skills. It can feel overwhelming at first. You may think you are never going to learn. However, there is one major difference. With driving you eventually learn how because the rules rarely, if ever, change. I haven't driven a stick shift in twenty years, but I know I could still do it. Maybe I would sputter a little in the beginning, but eventually I'd get the hang of it. However, when engaging across cultures, the rules are always changing. What applies to one person won't always work with another person even within the same group.

Let's examine this using language. You refer to someone as Black and they respond, *"Don't call me Black; I'm African American."* You think to yourself, *"I thought I was supposed to say Black? Well, I won't do that again!"* The next time you engage someone from that same group, you remember what happened the last time, how uncomfortable the interaction made you feel, and how upset the person was for being misidentified. You want to get it *right,* so with a little confidence mixed with uncertainty, you refer to this person as "African American." What happens? They respond by saying, *"Don't call me African American; I'm Black!"* They may even add, *"I was born Black, and I'll be Black 'til the day I die!"* (I'm being funny here, in case you haven't caught on.)

What someone prefers to be referred as, whether it be Hispanic, Chicano, Latino/a, Latinx, Latine, Native American, Indian, or Indigenous, First Nations, Asian, Asian American, or American, etc., will all depend on the person. Trying to get it "right" is a form of political correctness. Don't go there. This work is not about being politically correct; it's about relationships. Certainly, there are words we no longer use, e.g., oriental, just like there are words we could not use but now do, e.g., queer. Rather than being politically correct, developing your skills is about honoring differences and understanding the impact words have on any targeted group.

What if, rather than seeking the "right" terminology, or allowing yourself to be guided by the misconception of political correctness, you became genuinely curious as to why someone held one preference over another? What if, instead of avoiding race conversations or becoming defensive when you've offended and thinking, *"This is why I don't want to have these conversations: 'these' people can't make up their own damn minds!"* you learned to lean in. Imagine what you would learn if you simply became curious and asked, *"I have heard people use both terms, do you mind my asking why you prefer Latino?"* Or *"I've never heard the term Latine before, it is that new?"* And then go home to research it further to deepen your understanding.

With this approach, you are likely to conclude many terms are acceptable in general, but who to use them with, and when, can depend on many factors, including the generation a person is born in, their understanding of the language as it relates to colonization, the evolution of language, as well as their personal preferences. For example, Blacks often refer to themselves as "Black" during in-group conversations but refer to themselves as "African American" in literature and professional settings. Asian Americans tend to be prefer being referred to by their ethnicity, e.g., Korean American, Japanese American, Chinese American rather than being lumped into one group, e.g., Asian. By leaning in and doing a little research, you will improve your knowledge and ability to engage in race conversations, leaving you feeling less frustrated and more excited about your personal growth.

Years ago, while I was facilitating a workshop on implicit bias, a woman became offended when I used the term Latino, stating she was Hispanic. Though she was Mexican American, her preferred term was Hispanic. Many people use these two words interchangeably, but there is a difference between them. In my efforts to learn more about the differences between Hispanic and Latino (later Latinx and now Latine), I've come to understand that Latino is a much broader term, whereas Hispanic is more specific to Spain and comes out of the colonization of Latin and African people. I have met many people like this woman who use the term Hispanic, unaware of where the term comes from, just as I have met Latinos who are unaware of the terms Latinx or Latine.

In situations where someone prefers the use of a term that runs contrary to the knowledge you've acquired, you may or may not want to share your understanding. How you move forward will depend on your relationship with the person, how much time you have, how open the person is, where they are in their Racial/Ethnic Identity Development, and whether it will deter from your overall goal. Be careful not to assume the role of expert and at the same time remember Jamie Washington's quote: "*Just because I am, doesn't mean I do know; just because I'm not, doesn't mean I don't.*"[3] If you determine that how others identify is not inclusive or is embedded in colonization, sometimes it better to honor their preference but only while referring to them individually.

You will come across PoC who are offended by something you've said that is not offensive to the majority members of their group. It is possible their preference has more to do with their understanding or liking than anything you said or did wrong. These are the moments to use your best judgment in how to engage. Don't disregard widely accepted language or new language that is developing just because an individual of that group found it offensive.

> ## Gain Skills to Effectively Engage: Commitment to Change and Be Changed
>
> - There is more to the differences between Hispanic, Latino/a, Latinx, and Latine described above. Watch the YouTube video *"What's the Difference Between Hispanic, Latino, and Latinx."* Write a couple of sentences or share your new understanding with others to help you remember.
> - Identify a cultural norm, value, belief, or communication style you operate under (Awareness). Think about someone who is a member of a different racial group from your own and whom you have struggled to effectively engage with. Research to learn more about that group (Knowledge). List two or three things that are different about their group from your own. Explore how those differences can result in your cultures clashing. Then practice doing at least one thing differently with a member of that same group. (Skills)?

8

Take Action and Advocate for Change

Action/Advocacy

Awareness, Knowledge, and Skills are all areas of work individuals need to do to improve their ability to effectively engage across cultures—it's the interpersonal work that helps you develop your DEIB lens. While doing work in these three areas is key to shifting an organization in becoming a more inclusive culture, it is not enough. *Action/Advocacy* is referred to as the footwork. It's walking the talk whereby organizations collectively address inequity by focusing on institutionally racist practices, policies, and procedures. For example, a teacher in a school could purge antiquated books in his classroom and replace them with multiculturally approved books but this would be an individual act not institutional change. While this is a necessary and worthy practice, it will only impact the students in that one teacher's classroom and would have little influence on the students' overall K-12 educational experience. Once students move on to another grade, they would be exposed to biased curriculum.

Action/Advocacy would require the entire school or school district eliminating any bias materials from its library and classrooms and adding more books, that positively and accurately represented racially diverse group for it to be regarded as institutional or systemic change.

Systemic racism focuses on how institutions work together to maintain racism. For example, a school may decide to purge its outdated books, but if it is in a poorer neighborhood, it won't be properly funded to replace them, given that the value of homes in the school's neighborhood are directly linked to property taxes. Property taxes are directly linked to school resources and therefore superior schools. So, no matter how much the school leadership desires replacing its books, change will have to occur on a state and national level for that school to have the funding to replace its books.

It is essential your organization continuously engage in Awareness, Knowledge, and Skills work so individuals within your organization develop the lens to identify where and how racism is operating. Together you can commit to taking on the larger issues that create barriers to institutional change.

Because systems intersect with one another to sustain racism, it sometimes will require a social movement for change to occur. Begin by focusing on what's in your locus of control. While none of us are to blame for the beginnings of racism, and maybe it's true when someone says, "*My ancestors didn't own slaves*," we are still responsible for playing an active part in undoing systems of oppression. Our schools, health care, judicial, housing, and economic structures were all designed by White people for White people, and continually favor them while keeping PoC at an unfair disadvantage.

Measuring Success

As your organization takes action to change institutionally, there will be some things that won't be easily quantifiable. While you can more easily measure the increase in number of PoC in leadership roles, retention of PoC, high rates of suspensions, and graduation rates, many of your efforts will also require you value qualitative data to assess progress. Numbers are valuable in many ways, e.g., in that they can inform your organization where change needs to happen, sometimes even compel the people within to change. For example, the high suspension rates of Black, Brown, and Indigenous students can bring a sense of urgency to address discipline issues in a school.

However, quantitative data should not be the only measure driving your organization's equity work. Look for indicators where change is occurring. Listen to the PoC in your organization and create a survey to find out about their workplace experiences. Conduct exit interviews with PoC who have decided to leave and find out why. It is likely you won't always be able to say, "*Fifteen percent of PoC feel...*" Just because it's not measurable doesn't mean what you hear from one PoC or notice happening in your organization isn't of value.

Qualitative data is also a powerful tool to find out what's working and what's not. It can lead to institutional change practices like creating a position for a Director of Equity, developing a diversity policy, standardizing your hiring procedures to increase diversity, multicultural content infused into your curriculum, and ongoing culturally relevant professional development for staff. These can be valuable indicators your organization is transforming even though the evidence is not quantifiable.

I worked for several years as a consultant providing culturally relevant professional development for an organization whose primary goal was to serve children in foster care. This organization had been giving the same amount of money to children and youth to get their hair done (Equality). They realized this practice wasn't fair to all the children they served. For some children, particularly African American girls, going to a beautician cost more than it does for a male child to go to a barber. As a result, this organization changed their institutional practice and began providing different amounts based on need (Equity). While you could measure how many families no longer put off getting their child's hair done due to costs, the policy change is one act. These examples of Action and Advocacy illustrate that some equity components are quantifiable, and others are better suited for qualitative data. The organization developed the lens to be able to identify where institutional change needed to occur and moved forward without getting stuck in the common idea that everything must be measured quantitatively for change in practice to be funded.

Changing Culture Takes Time

It is not impossible to change culture, but it does take time. I'm a smoker. Yes, I said it. It's not something I say with pride. It's an unhealthy addiction I've been struggling with most of my life. Usually when people learn I smoke, there is an apparent change in their facial expression and demeaner. They seemly go from *"I like you"* to looking at me as if to say, *"I liked you until I knew you smoked."* If I had said I smoked 30, 40, or 50 years ago, it wouldn't have been an issue because smoking was a cultural norm. Most everyone did it. The question wasn't *"Where can you smoke?"* It was *"Where can't you smoke?"* People smoked in their offices, on airplanes, in elevators, in restaurants, in schools, and even in hospitals! Today, we live in a culture where smoking is no longer socially acceptable.

The Clean Air Act banning smoking in public places first passed in California in 1995. Fast-forward to today, and our attitude toward smoking has changed significantly. Those who still smoke often do so in secrecy, for fear of how they will be perceived by nonsmokers or those who kicked the habit and feel the need to talk at us from a place of superiority. As I said, I'm not proud of smoking, but it does amaze me how many people will look at me with disdain and the comments they feel free to make. Two of the most common questions I hear from nonsmokers are, *"You know smoking is bad for your health, right?"* and *"Have you ever tried quitting?"* Yes, I do know this fact, and yes, I've tried quitting many times. I typically don't answer these questions because they aren't really questions asked with curiosity. They are disguised as questions meant to educate me about the need to quit.

What I want to say but don't is, *"You know racism is bad for PoC's health, right?"* and, *"Have you ever tried quitting racism or at least tried to stop it?"* What I can't understand is why people are committed to ensuring the health and safety of people when it comes to smoking but not when it's due to racism. Why won't these same people get involved in changing how acceptable racism is in our country to one where people no longer tolerate it? Just saying.

Like with public smoking or anything in our country that was at one time the norm, taking action and advocating for change requires an active effort from committed individuals who are willing to work together and speak up to oppose policies and practices that are harmful. Just like with the Clean Air Act. Taking down our long history of racism will take time.

Practice Advocating in Your Everyday Life

Just because your individual act doesn't lead to institutional change does mean it's not worthy of your efforts. A friend of mine, an African American single parent of two children who I will call Liz, worked for a small private medical doctor's office. The doctor and his wife, the office manager, had a few staff including Liz. The husband unjustly fired Liz after she had been working for them for several years. As Liz, still in shock, was leaving with her box of personal belongings in hand, the wife walked her down the hallway to the door, in tears. As she was crying, she conveyed to Liz how unfair it was she was fired. Who's the one who should be crying in this situation? Who is the one who can act?

These situations are common for PoC. White people unknowingly end up making it about them. Her tears conveyed to Liz many things, *"Don't be mad at me, I didn't make the decision. I'm not like him. I feel bad for you, that counts for something right? You don't think bad of me, do you? You still see me as a good person, right?*" I have no doubt this woman felt guilt and shame for what had happened to Liz. But rather than use her guilt to propel her to advocate on behalf of Liz, who now must worry about how she will provide for her children and keep a roof over their heads, she centered on her own needs to be seen as a good person. In this situation, the woman was asking Liz to take care of her. I once read somewhere shame and guilt serve no other purpose than to let us know something is wrong. Shame and guilt don't make the wrongs right. Our actions do. While a White person may feel bad about the treatment of PoC, PoC are often left to deal with the impact of the injustices on their own. We need White people to speak up in the face of injustice and advocate on our behalf when we are the target of unfair practices.

I recognize there is a lot we don't know about the husband and his wife in the above example for me to assume she had the type of relationship with her husband or the power to make a difference. However, what I'm suggesting is that there are many instances where each of us can advocate for change. Rather than going to a PoC after a meeting and saying, *"I'm glad you spoke up, I was thinking the same thing"* or *"I'm so sorry they said that to you,"* take the risk to have your voice heard even if it doesn't immediately change the situation. As an Equity Leader, there will be many occasions where you will have to speak up and interrupt the status quo. So, start practicing.

If enough people speak up, it makes it more difficult for our united voices to be ignored. One voice is singular, but add in your voice, and it becomes plural, plus his voice and her voice, their voice and ours, the effort gains momentum with each added voice. Small wins turn to big wins, whether the action you take impacts one person's life, leads to new and revised policy, or turns into a movement for justice.

Action and Advocacy is noticing, naming, and taking action to change policies and practices that support and maintain the unfair treatment of people who are marginalized because of their group identity. These are the same practices that trick heterosexual, Christian, able-bodied middle-class, White women and men into believing they are where they are, solely due to their hard work. Following are some ways to take action and advocate for institutional change within your organization.

- Include PoC and other marginalized voices in decision-making.
- Develop an Equity Team to devise action plans to address institutional isms (See Chapter 19).
- Voice your concerns with people in power when you notice unfair practices.
- Develop a safe way and effective process where individuals can have their concerns addressed when they experience unfair practices.
- Advocate for culturally relevant professional development so staff and leaders can grow in their understanding of power, privilege, and racism and its impact.
- Invest in creating a library of culturally relevant resources for ongoing learning of staff.
- Start a caucus or affinity group so PoC and White people can process their experiences without fear of retribution.
- Identify where your organization's resources are being allocated. Reallocate to promote equity, inclusion, and belonging for groups who have historically been marginalized.
- Survey staff to assess their experiences in the workplace and advocate for changes that address the issues that surface.
- Advocate for accountability measures when racist, sexist, homophobic, and other disparaging jokes, comments, and behaviors occur within the workplace.
- Identify workplace cultural norms that exclude diverse groups.
- Examine policies within your organization and make necessary changes to address the needs of diverse staff and communities your organization is designed to serve.
- Craft a diversity policy that speaks to your organizations commitment to equity, inclusion, and belonging.
- Review and change hiring practices to include diversity beyond legal jargon.
- Include your commitment to equity and inclusion in your mission and vision statement.
- Include information informing new hires of policies and practices that address DEIB during the hiring orientation process.
- Develop a mentoring program for newly hired PoC.
- Examine your organization's evaluations and assessment tools to ensure they take into consideration racism, power, and privilege.

- Analyze curricular materials to ensure cultural relevance and anti-bias qualities.

Sue and Sue's Cultural Competence framework we've adapted is one of several approaches to this work and may not be the one you choose to adopt. Whichever model you do decide to use, it will be critical your organization understands that Action and Advocacy are needed to change systems of oppression. Any work people in your organization engage in to increase their understanding of bias, privilege, micro-aggressions, and other important work is ultimately to help them develop a lens whereby they are able connect to their learning to institutional and systemic racism and other forms of isms.

The work of Awareness, Knowledge, Skills, Action and Advocacy is not linear. It's important you move staff back and forth continuously engaging your organization in all four areas. You will have to decide how long to stay in one area and when to move to the next, sometimes simultaneously focusing on two or three areas, sometimes going back to the place you began.

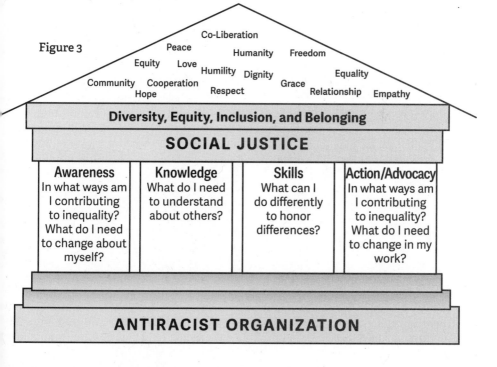

Figure 3

Co-Liberation

Peace   Humanity   Freedom
Equity   Love   Humility   Dignity
Community   Cooperation   Respect   Grace   Equality
Hope   Relationship   Empathy

Diversity, Equity, Inclusion, and Belonging

SOCIAL JUSTICE

Awareness	**Knowledge**	**Skills**	**Action/Advocacy**
In what ways am I contributing to inequality? What do I need to change about myself?	What do I need to understand about others?	What can I do differently to honor differences?	In what ways am I contributing to inequality? What do I need to change in my work?

ANTIRACIST ORGANIZATION

Finding a Framework to Guide You:
Commitment to Change and Be Changed

- Search the internet for "Equality versus Equity" images. Invite others to unpack the image with you. For example, if you look at the image with the baseball field, examine what the field, the fence, the boxes, and height metaphorically represent. As a Racial Equity Leader, it's important you are clear about the differences between these two terms. This will become language you commonly use and rely on to guide your organization through its transformation.

- Research other approaches to this work to determine which framework you will use to help your workplace understand the journey you will be embarking on together. If it lacks important components, adapt it to make it work for your organization.

- Once you've chosen your organization's framework, figure out how you will teach it to the rest of your organization. Because this work is a collective effort, have at least one other person work on developing the training and co-facilitate with you.

- Take twenty minutes to complete the Antiracist Leadership Practices survey in the Appendix.

9

Plan for the Journey,
Not an Event

DEIB WORK IS NOT JUST about honoring Dr. Martin Luther King
Jr.'s birthday or recognizing Indigenous Day. It is the way your
organization continually works to develop a culture that values differences, is equitable in its approach, inclusive of its diverse staff
and those it serves, and manifests practices that convey a feeling of
belonging. DEIB work necessitates organizations constantly assess
their culture and adapt an ever-changing approach. There will be no
point of arrival in DEIB work. You are leading your organization on a
journey, not taking them to an event.

One way to think about this journey—in addition to the Social Justice Framework—is with the model *Four Stages of Competence*. While
there is some confusion around who first developed this model, the
earliest findings come from Martin M. Broadwell in an article he published in 1969, "Teaching for Learning." In it, Broadwell describes four
stages teachers go through as they move from a state of unknowing
to knowing their profession: Unconscious Incompetence, Conscious
Incompetence, Conscious Competence, and Unconscious Competence.[1] These same stages can similarly be applied to individuals as
they grow in their understanding of race, racism, and race relations.

Unconscious Incompetence

In this first stage of Unconscious Incompetence, you don't know
what you don't know. This is when a fish doesn't know it's wet. This
person is unaware of inequities that exist between White people and
PoC and will likely attribute any disparities to the PoC—e.g., laziness,
lack of effort, or intelligence— rather than racist systems. A person in

Unconscious Incompetence is looking solely through the lens of their own experiences, efforts, values, and beliefs to comprehend another person's life experiences; there is no effort to understanding another. It is common for a person in this stage to take the Universal Approach *"We are all the same,"* or the Individual Approach *"What matters is what's on the inside."* They blame the individual rather than systems, for oppression. People in this stage typically have little or no exposure to research or literature that runs contrary to their way of thinking. Genuine relationships with people who are different from them are minimal or nonexistent.

When White people are confronted with evidence that opposes their beliefs, they may maintain their resolve and refute it. Such a person lacks genuine curiosity and knows what they know just because they know. They will dig their heels deeper into the ground and maintain their uninformed beliefs with shallow examples. Check out this e-mail I received, after delivering a keynote address, from a White woman who was Unconsciously Incompetent:

> Deanne: My concern with your lecture is how you seemed to single out 2 groups specifically, whites and People of Color and if I am incorrect, I apologize as I am just commenting on what I heard. While I know that discrimination has occurred toward People of Color more frequently, I'm sure it happens to white people as well (though we probably just don't hear about it as much).

What Deanne heard was partially correct. The focus of my keynote was not on discrimination. It was on racism. So, yes. I did indeed single out White people and the experiences of PoC. One cannot talk about racism without discussing who manifests it, who benefits from it—White people—and who it negatively impacts. Instead, her true intent is revealed as she attempts to defend the discrimination that White people experience but which *"we probably just don't hear about..."* because people like me are not talking about it.

By shifting my keynote from racism to discrimination, it prevented her from leaning into the impact of racism on PoC and also allowed her a window of opportunity to derail the conversation. I can't negate the fact that White people can and do experience discrimination.

> Deanne: I hear about White conservatives being silenced be-
> cause of who they voted for, or white Christians being per-
> secuted because of their beliefs or White people being called
> "supremacists or nationalists" simply because they are defend-
> ing their God-given Constitutional Second Amendment rights.
> I guess my question is, can racism go both ways?

Deanne seems to use discrimination and racism as if they are the
same and asks if racism can go both ways versus can discrimination
go both ways. The answer would be different depending on which
question she is asking. She also minimizes how supremacists and
nationalists abuse their Second Amendment rights to keep PoC and
other groups oppressed, and not surprisingly she uses God to back her
up. As you read further, you will continue to see how Deanne is not
really coming from a place of curiosity, but rather has an opinion she
wants to share (disguised as curiosity, i.e., "can racism go both ways?")

> Deanne: I know the history of America has never been perfect
> and slavery did exist. I also know a great man, a Republican,
> named Abraham Lincoln signed an Emancipation Proclama-
> tion (and eventually pushed the Thirteenth Amendment) while
> leading a bloody Civil War with over 600K casualties. I want to
> be sure people know the facts and not just spurious informa-
> tion that is being fed to us daily. I don't believe there is systemic
> racism in our country, but there are racist people of all colors.
> Another great man, Martin Luther King Jr., said he hoped one
> day his children would be judged by the content of their char-
> acter as opposed to their skin color. So that's what we should
> be teaching our children instead of blaming racism on "White
> privilege."

Like many Whites who are resistant to entertaining realities that
exist for PoC, Deanne goes to three common examples used to prove
why racism against PoC is a non-issue: Abraham Lincoln, the Civil
War, and Dr. Martin Luther King Jr. While Deanne is quick to exclaim
the importance of "people" knowing the facts, she is not willing to
do her own fact-finding beyond her surface level examples. In fact,
what she *knows* to be true is more than the *people* or this Person of

Color who holds a doctorate degree on the subject matter. Instead, she relies on limited information as the full source of her understanding. She also speaks to supremacists and nationalists as if they don't exist then quotes Dr. King as if judging by content of character is what is needed when that's not what PoC, the LGBTQ+ community, or Jews experience. There are many more things that could be unpacked in the above scenario; however, my goal here is to illustrate Unconscious Incompetence and the common resistance Racial Equity Leaders face.

Thankfully not all Whites in the Unconscious Incompetence stage are resistant to new learning when presented with the idea that inequities exist between their racial group and PoC. There are many who are naïve and who will lean in with curiosity and want to know more once they are invited to explore race through a different lens. This is the hope of Racial Equity Leaders and personally one of my *whys* for leading this work. When White people are open to reexamining what they've been taught, it will launch them into the next stage: Conscious Incompetence, related to a particular issue or group.

I have on occasion come across a PoC who has assimilated into White dominant cultures beliefs as it relates to race, racism, and race relations. Oftentimes this person will not identify themselves as a PoC and/or see hard work as the solution to the problems other PoC face. While I have met PoC who are Unconsciously Incompetent, when it comes to racism, it isn't very often. They are more likely to be Unconsciously Incompetent when it comes to PoC who belong to a group different from their own. When they do have an awakening and realize they have been duped into thinking racism isn't an issue, they typically take on racial justice issues with a vengeance.

Lack of education, denial of White privilege, color-blind thinking, focusing on similarities rather than differences, and naming individual examples of success are some of the signs that a person is operating in Unconscious Incompetence.

Conscious Incompetence

Conscious Incompetence is a tough stage to be in. You are aware that how you interact with others needs some changing, but you don't know what to say or how to engage differently. A person in this stage is usually just beginning to develop Awareness of themselves and Knowledge of another group's experiences. Early on in their learning, they are typically eager. Their lack of skills generally comes from minimal experience and exposure to the culture they are newly engaging. Though the best way to grow your skills is to practice, it can sometimes lead to harming the person you are interacting with.

While preparing for a workshop, I arrived early to set up the room just as I always do. My audience was residents of an assisted living complex. Informed in advance that one participant would be in a wheelchair, I set the room up so that they would be able to sit anywhere they chose. I had learned years prior that people in wheelchairs often experience being forced to sit in one location rather than having the option to sit where they want. I was determined this participant would have that freedom in my workshop.

As he arrived, I greeted him just as I did the other participants. However, I was so proud (and not the good kind) of my level of competence that I felt the need to tell him what I'd done. "*Hello, my name is Caprice. Welcome. What's your name? Nice to meet you, Larry. Come on in. I made sure there are multiple places for your wheelchair.*" With a hint of anger in his voice, he responded, "*You didn't make a space for my wheelchair, you made space for me!*" Ouch! Did I really just say that? I had never in my life thought of it in this way. How many times have people seen him as his chair rather than a person sitting in a chair with wheels? I was not off to a good start.

Being Consciously Incompetent generates a lot of mistakes while learning and growing. Unfortunately, it often comes at the expense of those you are learning about. When people don't respond favorably because your action impacted them negatively, it can cause the Consciously Incompetent person to give up trying again. Rather than seeking grace from the person you've harmed, or thinking "*Gosh, at least I tried,*" or even making yourself the victim, try becoming genuinely curious as to why the person reacted the way they did. To become Consciously Competent with different groups, you will need a lot more practice, which means making many more mistakes. So, get used to it.

Conscious Competence

Conscious Competence involves intentionality. The person in this stage knows what they need to do differently, but because they don't have a lot of practice, engaging feels awkward like a baby taking steps for the first time. In this stage, your actions are methodical, you are careful and aware of your words and actions. As you practice new skills of engagement, sometimes you will do it well, other times you will fumble, stumble, and fall. In this stage, you take things slow as your conscious mind tries to navigate the cross-cultural interaction.

A few years ago, I made a commitment to myself that I would open all my workshops and keynotes by first recognizing which tribal lands we were on, and their ongoing cultural and geographical legacy. Whenever I witnessed someone doing a land acknowledgment, it felt right to me, and I wanted to be a part of it. But even though I told myself this was something I would start doing, I often forgot to do it or felt too anxious. The truth is, I was downright afraid. As easily and as often that I speak about this work being *a journey not an event*," that "*none of us are experts*," or that "*the very definition of Cultural Competence is our willingness to continue to grow and learn*," I rarely enjoy the process of my own development. I have so many worries when putting what I've learned into practice. "*What if I get it wrong, mispronounce a tribal name, or offend? What if I appear inauthentic?*" I could go on and on, but I think you get the point.

One day I confessed my fears to Canadian colleagues, Kaleb Childs, a member of the Kwakiutl First Nation, and Cygnia Rapp, a White woman who has been intentional in understanding Indigenous cultures. They were both supportive and encouraging. Cygnia followed up with an e-mail and shared some of her own learning. She included a helpful resource, published by the Department of Arts and Culture, *Honor Native Land: A Guide and Call to Acknowledgment*. It was just what I needed to move forward in my commitment. The simplicity in which it is written, the resources it offers, and the examples of ways to do a land acknowledgment left me with no more excuses and a renewed sense of commitment.

Around the time Cygnia sent me the guide, I was preparing for a keynote for hundreds of people in Detroit, Michigan. With the help of the guide, I researched whose land we would be on, wrote notes on a 3 × 5 card, and began memorizing what I would say in the land acknowledgment. But when the day came, I was so nervous I could barely pay attention to the speakers before me. I kept checking and rechecking my notes, repeating in my head the correct pronunciation of tribal names, and committing the acknowledgment to memory.

When they called my name, I walked on stage with my *"fake it 'til you make it"* pseudo confidence. I immediately tried to bring up the land acknowledgment slide, but the wrong one appeared. I panicked, *"Did I forget to include it?"*, *"Did I download the wrong PowerPoint?"*, *"I thought I had tripled checked!"* Taking a deep breath and flying solo, I did my best to acknowledge whose land we were on without the PowerPoint, but my mind froze. I glanced at my notecard, but everything seemed a blur. This wasn't turning out like I had rehearsed when no one was listening. I rambled as I tend to do when nervous, saying more than was needed. I eventually got through it, finding my groove as I moved on to the more familiar parts of my presentation.

Afterwards people waited in line to talk with me. That's always a good sign. Maybe they forgot about my mishap at the start. As people moved through the line, my confidence grew with each person's praise, that is until I spotted a Indigenous man several people back. Thoughts like *"I guess not everyone forgot. I really messed things up"* and fears of what he would say began to surface. While I can't recall anything anyone else said to me that day, I will never forget his words. With tears in his eyes, he told me, *"This is the first time I've ever been at a conference where the speaker acknowledged whose land we are on. Thank you. I'm going to tell my friends what you did."* He thanked me again, said a few other things, and walked away. I was flooded with relief and joy. He didn't care that it wasn't perfect. He only cared that I had tried.

Being mindful of what you say and how you interact with people around you are not bad things to do. They are a sign you care and are working at being inclusive. Notice the subtle worries trying to push their way to the surface so you don't allow them to keep you from trying new things. While I'm not at the next stage of Unconscious Competence as it relates to land acknowledgment, I am improving, and I know that, with enough practice, I will eventually get there.

Unconscious Competence

In Unconscious Competence, the person is familiar enough when interacting with a group, they can relax and just be present in a conversation. They no longer think about how to act or what to say. They just do it. Unconscious Competence does not mean you will never make mistakes. However, you will find yourself less focused on avoiding making mistakes or constantly worried about doing or saying the wrong thing, and more present in the interaction. I'm not there yet as it relates to people with visible disabilities, land acknowledgment, and many other groups, but I am getting better and so will you, with commitment and practice.

It's Like Recycling

In the same way Cultural Competence is ongoing work, you will never be Unconsciously Competent with all groups because, for one, the groups with whom you are Unconsciously Competent will change over time. I liken it to recycling. Before we started recycling on a large scale like we do now, we were Unconsciously Incompetent. We didn't know we were destroying the one planet we have to live on due to the amount of waste.

Environmental scientists sought ways to save our planet. The questioned remained, "*How?*" Up to this point, recycling was limited to taking your bottles, cans, and newspapers to recycling centers located in various parts of your city. The motivation for this practice was usually money rather than a concern for our planet. Scientists were Consciously Incompetent as they sought answers to our world's waste dilemma.

One day everyone received bins for their homes. If I recall correctly, there were four blue bins and you had to rinse and sort. While this information is irrelevant, it speaks to the details that stand out when doing something new and unfamiliar. Cities were entering the Conscious Competence stage as it relates to recycling. You would start to put something in one bin and then quickly pull away not quite sure which bin it belonged in. Eventually, you would throw it in any bin and think to yourself, "*Well, at least I tried.*"

With some practice, experience, and mistakes along the way, those of us who stayed committed to saving our planet entered Unconscious Competence where recycling became second nature. It is now so automatic that when I can't find a recycle bin I will hold on to the item until I do; some people will even take recyclable items home. That person recognizes that even one piece of plastic can make a difference in saving our planet, so they will endure a bit of inconvenience and carry it around refusing to put it in with landfill waste.

Just when we became familiar enough with the recycling process to the point of no longer having to think about what goes where, environmental scientists realized there was more we could do. Composting was added to the process, and we were right back to Conscious Competence, unsure of what goes where.

Like recycling, in race work you can be Unconsciously Incompetent with one group, Consciously Incompetent with another, Consciously Competent or Unconsciously Competent with yet another. It will all depend on your Awareness of self, Knowledge of others, and how much practice you've had. Even when you've mastered something, culture will change, and you will have to acquire new learning. Staying with it even when things change or become difficult will require your steadfast commitment. When it comes to recycling, you don't hear people say, "*People are being too sensitive*" or "*This is too hard*" or "*Everything was fine the way it was.*" Doing nothing or giving up won't end racism, just like ignoring the harm waste is creating for our planet won't make it go away.

10

Be Mindful of the Language You Use

THE LANGUAGE YOU DECIDE to use will be critical in guiding you as you move the work forward in your organization. There will be people who will become resistant at the mere mention of "diversity" or "race." The moment they get a hint that things are changing, and that equity and inclusion are focus, they will begin huffing and puffing, eye rolling, followed by statements like, *"We don't have race issues in this organization."* So be prepared.

Some White people will tell you the number of years they've been in the organization, their profession, and how they have been doing their job just fine, as evidence that race has never been an issue before. This is their proof that race does not need to be discussed and professional development is not necessary, even though they have never talked with their Colleagues of Color about their experiences or noticed how few are in leadership positions. Others will blame PoC for not being where they themselves are: *"I worked hard to get where I'm at, no one gave me any handouts"* and *"I treat people how I want to be treated"* or *"I don't have time for this, I have real work to do."* Even if these types of statements are not stated overtly, there will be some, maybe many (depending on your organization), who will resist.

As mentioned earlier, some PoC may feel they don't have work to do because they are a PoC. If they are one of a few or the only Person of Color in their organization, they may fear it will make them the center of attention in a way they'd rather not be. Others will worry it won't make a difference, or the mental toll it will take to engage their White colleagues will be too much. And then there will be those who have assimilated into White culture and don't see the need.

The framework you use to help everyone grow in their understanding will be key to your organization's success, and so will the language you use. Language will either exacerbate fears or encourage a commitment. You will need to find language that initially is less threatening and meets people where they are at. This isn't to say people won't feel discomfort, that there isn't risk involved, or the conversations won't get intense. In fact, that is exactly what will happen because it is a natural part of the process.

My husband was the Director of Sales at a small, mostly White telecommunications company. At least once a year, they would have a party where family and friends were invited. I didn't look forward to these celebrations. While I want to support him, I don't usually enjoy mingling with people with whom I have little in common. They are nice enough, and I'm the friendly type who knows how to engage diverse groups of people, but I find the conversations boring, just like I do when talking about sports. A common way in which our society initially interacts with one another upon first meeting is to ask, "*What do you do?*" This question always causes me to pause whenever White people ask. Whether it is with my husband's coworkers, my dentists, a party, with a neighbor, in these moments I will pause and quickly determine whether I am in the mood to talk about it.

I have two responses to this question. One I use when I'm open to talking about racism, have the mental capacity, and want to play nice. "*I do race relations work.*" This less threatening response makes White people feel more comfortable. Typically, it produces stories of their *close* relationships with a PoC, their Children of Color, their children's Friends of Color, how they rescued a PoC from a life of despair (Just think of the movie *The Blind Side* with Sandra Bullock and Quinton Aaron), maids they had growing up, and other ways they unconsciously try to verify how different they are from other Whites. And yes, on many occasions White people will tell me stories of their childhood and the close relationship they had with their Black maid who they loved dearly and who loved them. Their stories inevitably result in at least one microaggression.

My husband was one of many who were selected to participate in his company's President's Club for reaching their annual sales goal. Each year those selected travel somewhere different and can bring a guest, all expenses paid. I'm sitting at the dinner table with my husband and a few other couples when one of the spouses and I start conversation. I learned she is a CEO of a large corporation. When I tell her I do race relations work, she becomes enthusiastic and tells me that her company has done some diversity training and one thing she learned was to bow when meeting Japanese people and how she now does that with her gardener. I refrain from rolling my eyes, and my only response is *"That's not the kind of work I do."*

We are getting along quite nicely until we are standing in line to get our food. This is when she informs me about a time she was at an event where everyone in the room was Black except her. She seems pleased with herself when she says, *"And I wasn't even scared."* Still in line getting our food, I respond, *"Remember when I said, that's not the type of work I do. One thing I do is teach about stereotypes and bias. What did you mean when you said you weren't scared?"* I don't remember how she responded, but I do recall trying to help her understand the stereotypes embedded in her comment. She didn't speak to me the rest of the evening and avoided me the remainder of our stay. Heavy sigh. I guess it was too much too soon upon our meeting. White fragility is real.

So, when I'm not in the mood to talk about my work, because most times it will require work, I will casually reply, *"I do antiracism work."* Nothing will cease the conversation with an uninformed White person quicker than mentioning the word racism. While both responses are true regarding the work I do, the former invites White people into the conversation initiating curiosity and conversation, while the latter shuts them down.

Some Racial Equity Leaders are adamant we need to use language that speaks to the experiences of PoC and not try to make White people feel *"safe"* or *"comfortable"* in the process. They are rightfully frustrated with White people's fragility and their derailment of these crucial conversations. However, changing the language is not softening some necessary blow; it's meeting White people where they are at so we can move into the more difficult conversations together.

Because most White people are just beginning to enter race conversations, they often react to the language before knowing its meaning. Your goal is to get these conversations happening in your organization so people within can develop a lens where they are able to identify practices, policies, behaviors, and systems that need changing. That won't happen if you can't get White people to the table.

Another example of language that easily ruffles White people's feathers is the term *White privilege*. When first engaging, I find starting out with the term *privilege*, or even *racial privilege*, helps them to become more open to exploring their White privilege. The far-right 10% who were already on board from the start will be the only ones you have ready to engage if you start with "White" privilege. Dr. Kimberlé Crenshaw, Professor of Law at UCLA and Columbia Law School, also cofounder and Executive Director of the African American Policy Forum, gifted us with the term *intersectionality* in 1989.[1] This term has become a tool, particularly in race discourse, to examine and convey just how much more complicated and difficult the lives of PoC become when we hold other marginalized and stigmatized identities. For example, to be Black, and queer, with a disability holds more challenges than someone who is Black, cisgender, and has no disability...[2] When engaging White people around the concepts of privilege, it can make the conversation more palpable by first introducing them to other marginalized identities they can identify with, e.g., class, gender, ability, age, and so on. The idea of White privilege becomes less threatening. You will get them there. It's when and how you get them there that's critical in the early stages of their work.

Keep in mind that it won't just be White people who struggle with the term *White privilege*. PoC who have assimilated into White dominant culture, and who have left their own racial identity unexplored to be accepted by White people, will also find these conversations unnerving. If you use language that pushes them too fast, too far, it can cause them to retreat. Awakening PoC to how hard they've worked to make White people feel comfortable being around them and the price they've paid will need to be done with care and consideration of the emotional unraveling that is likely to arise.

A gradual process increases the likelihood people in your organization will let you lead them deeper into the work. Some organizations we've worked with have shared their journey of starting by doing what they called "diversity" work, then graduating to "diversity, equity, and inclusion," transitioning to "racial equity," and later naming it for what it is: antiracism work.

You will need to be intentional about the language you use depending on where your organization is in this process. Being mindful can prevent you from having to spend most of your time defending the need for the work when the 10% on the far left try to use it as an excuse to derail the conversation, "*You're trying to tell me I'm a racist,*" and "*You don't even know my story and you're trying to tell me I have privilege.*" If not thoughtful in your approach, you also risk losing some of the 80% who hear certain words and jump to conclusions before understanding what you mean. Like it or not, fair, or otherwise, the language you choose will either call people in or out of the conversation.

PRACTICING STRATEGIES FOR ENGAGING IN RACE CONVERSATIONS

How do we hold people accountable for wrongdoing and yet at the same time remain in touch with their humanity enough to believe their capacity to be transformed?

—bell hooks

11

PoC Fatigue—
Knowing When to Walk Away
and When to Engage

IT IS NOT UNCOMMON, at least here in the Northwest, to hear PoC say, "*It's not my job to educate White people.*" This statement is generally made in response to the fatigue PoC are undergoing from a lifetime of being bombarded with questions and comments White people make related to race. It has become a quick way for PoC to respond, without having to engage—and an attempt to circumvent the mental labor involved when White people offend. In essence it is a practice of self-care.

Racial Microaggressions Committed by White Folks

The most common encounters PoC have with White people that lead to the response, "*It's not my job to educate White people*" are when White people commit *microaggressions*. A Black psychiatrist named Chester Pierce coined this term in 1970. Few were familiar with the term until 37 years later when Sue, Capodilupo, Torino, Bucceri, Holder, Nadal, and Esquilin wrote an article, "Racial Microaggressions in the Life Experience of Black Americans," based on Pierce's work, that the term microaggressions became well-known.[1]

There are three types of microaggressions, but the two most common are microinsults and microinvalidations. *Microinsults* are subtle, often unintentional, are sometimes meant to compliment the person but usually convey a hidden, demeaning message embedded in a stereotype about their racial group. It results in an insult toward the PoC. Some examples include assuming Asians are good at math ("*I'm sure it's easy for you*"), that the Latine person you see in a restaurant is a service provider ("*Excuse me, where are the bathrooms?*"), reaching out to touch a Black person's hair while saying, "*I really like your hair, is this your real hair?"* and to a woman dressed in a burka, *"How do you use the bathroom?"*

Microinvalidations invalidate or minimize a PoC's racial experiences. *"We don't judge people based on race; we treat everyone the same here," "This is America, anyone who works hard can succeed," "This is America, speak English," "It all just comes down to loving one another."* In reference to using Indigenous people's culture as a mascot, *"It's been our mascot for years"* or *"You should feel honored."* These types of comments cause PoC to feel unheard, marginalized, and frustrated that our history can so easily be justified and ignored.

Anyone can be insulted, disrespected, or slighted due to an identity they hold. However, there is one distinguishing factor that makes a microaggression a microaggression, and it isn't the one time the insulting comment is made, or the seemingly innocent question asked. It is the many times the person and their racial group have heard and experienced racial slights that lead some PoC to saying, *"It's not my job to educate White people."* Microaggressions have been likened to a thousand small cuts and experiencing many mosquito bites.

Questions Disguised as Curiosity

Other common encounters PoC have with White people that lead to *"It's not my job to educate White people"* are the questions asked that aren't innocent. These insincere questions are often meant to either negate a PoC's perspectives and experiences or indirectly validate racist perspectives: *"If Blacks can say the N word, why can't we?"* and *"Shouldn't All Lives Matter?"* or *"It's fine if Black people want to protest, but do they really have to vandalize their community?"* If the PoC doesn't quickly identify these remarks as ploys to refute anything they have to say, they may end up wasting their time and energy attempting to educate that person with one example of racism after another. This will likely turn into a power struggle, resulting in the PoC becoming frustrated and exhausted as they realize that they've been deceived. I know because this has happened to me on several occasions.

Not too long ago, I was providing a keynote address to students in a predominantly White high school. The presentation was on standing up when their peers are the target of bullying because of differences. I was intentional about including numerous examples, e.g., gender, ability, race, religion, and sexual orientation. When I was finished, I was pleased so many students came up to speak with me. Students thanked me and shared stories of their experiences. As I was talking with students one on one, I notice a group of about six White male students standing in a cluster waiting. One stepped forward and asked, *"Do you think it's OK for someone to call a White person a cracker?"* I responded with, *"I hope you heard in my message it's not OK to put anyone down or call someone names, especially, because of their differences, regardless of their race."* He followed up with a second question, *"Do you believe in freedom of speech?"*

Initially I wasn't sure where he was going with his questions. We went back and forth a couple of times, him asking me questions, me asking him, when I realized what he was doing. He wasn't asking questions. He was making a point. He didn't believe what I had to say held value, and he wasn't interested in listening to another person's perspectives. He wanted me to know that freedom of speech was more important than anything else even if it meant dehumanizing someone because of their differences. I thought if I shifted the conversation from race to disability, which usually works, that I would get somewhere with him.

I pointed to the area where students who had different types of disabilities had sat during my presentation. I asked him if he believed that freedom of speech included the freedom to call his peers names and put them down due to their disability, and gave specific examples, *"I'm talking about the ones with intellectual disabilities? Your peers who struggle to communicate? The ones who are in wheelchairs or those who can't defend themselves?"* His response was simply *"yes."* In his mind freedom of speech took precedence over the well-being of any and all students' sense of belonging.

There were several times before this moment where I had tried to end the conversation, having realized he and his entourage were in the far left 10%. There was not going to be any planting of seeds with them. Unfortunately, I let this young man keep hooking me back in as he made the case for his First Amendment rights. Before I knew it, we were in a power struggle. I had fallen for his trap. It wasn't until he responded yes to my earlier question that I ended the conversation with my rendition of a James Baldwin quote, "If your freedom of speech is tied up in someone else's oppression, you don't get the freedom to speak." In case you're wondering, I'm referring to Baldwin's statement, "*We can disagree and still love each other unless your dis-agreement is rooted in my oppression and denial of my humanity and right to exist.*"[2]

I wish I would've ended the conversation sooner. Not because I felt embarrassed that I was doing the very thing I teach others not to do, or because I let a seventeen-year-old take me down a rabbit hole that would never see light. Well, maybe those were some of my reasons. But the real reason I regret engaging for as long as I did was because, when I turned around, there stood two Black students who had been waiting patiently for me, one who was in tears. She heard our conversation. I'm certain they weren't naïve about the attitudes some White people have about Black people. But there's a different impact when hearing it said out loud, and by people you share the same space with. Though they weren't speaking about Black people directly, she knew they were using freedom of speech to argue for the right to oppress anyone who wasn't White, heterosexual, able-bodied, cisgender, male, and Christian, and that included her. All I could do in that moment was wrap my arms around her and hold her as she sobbed. I had given racism a platform to hurt the very people I live my life trying to pro-tect. This is something those two young women will never forget, and for that reason, I will always regret.

When White people ask questions meant to debate or disprove the need for equity, inclusion, or belonging, try not to waste your time and energy as I did. Shut the conversation down immediately. The authen-ticity of someone's question can sometimes be discerned from their tone and the questions they ask, but if you're not sure, ask, "*Are you asking me because you're curious and really want to know, or have you already made up your mind?*"

Questions White People Ask to Show They Know More than PoC

"*It's not my job to educate White people*" is also said when White people make statements or ask questions that position them as the expert of PoC's experiences. Similar to questions asked that are dis-guised as curiosity, these questions are not intended to bring about understanding. They are different from the above example in that their questions and comments are disguised as concern for the PoC, but they really serve to demonstrate that PoC are the problem. "*Do *you really believe...?", "Have you tried...?", "Have you considered looking at this way?", "I have a friend who is* (same race), *and he says he doesn't have that experience. Do you think maybe...?" "Don't you think it's about having a positive attitude?"* In these interactions, the PoC receives the message that their life would improve if they just responded or thought about their experience differently. Racism is completely omitted as a possibility, and it is the PoC who is doing something wrong because if life worked for them (the White person), it should work for you (the PoC) too.

These frequent encounters with White people leave many PoC feeling like they don't have the mental capacity to engage with one more White person about racism. Because when they do try to convey how racism is real, it often requires sharing how racism has impacted them and their families. And each time a PoC shares their stories, they relive a little bit of that experience. So, whether it is in a workshop or a one-on-one conversation, PoC know there will be an emotional and mental toll they will likely have to pay. *"It's not my job to educate White people"* is one way to protect themselves from further harm. This is where I need to pause and take a deep breath. PoC are understandably tired, worn-out, exhausted, fatigued, drained, spent, depleted, sapped, and expended from trying to teach White people. It's even exhausting writing about it.

Questions Expecting PoC to Speak for Their Entire Race

"It's not my job to educate White people" not only stems from the endless, tiresome encounters PoC have with White people, it also derives from encounters PoC have where they are expected to represent their entire race. While this may not be the intent of the person questioning, it implies PoC have the expertise to speak about their racial group's culture, thoughts, attitudes, values, beliefs, impact of racism, etc. Rather than taking the time to research, study, and learn these things on their own, it becomes the PoC's *job* to educate. White people unknowingly exercise their White privilege with these types of expectations. It conveys a subtle message of entitlement that what White people want to know should be answered by whomever they ask to educate them, at whatever costs.

Being asked so many questions requires additional mental and emotional labor on top of the energy PoC must expend living, working, surviving, and navigating predominantly White spaces. Subsequently, PoC feel the need to push back or risk submitting to yet another form of superiority. *"It's not my job to educate White people"* has become a quick and easy, go-to response to say to White people *"Back off, I'm not your walking Wikipedia!"* or *"I don't have the mental capacity to engage you right now."*

White People Policing Other White People Around "Rules" of Antiracism

When Ilsa first posted on Facebook her excitement about the publication of her and Tilman's book *What's Up with White Women? Unpacking Sexism and White Privilege in Pursuit of Racial Justice*, she received what I would consider a disturbing response from someone who I imagine sees themselves as an ally for racial justice.

> E: Is this book written by exclusively white women?
> IG: Hey E! The authors are both White women and the forward is by Shakti Butler, a Black woman. We include lots of insights and quotes from PoC whose work we read and who we've talked with over the years as we were developing the book content and facilitating workshops on this topic.
>
> Proceeds from sales benefit two PoC-led organizations, Delbert Richardson's award-winning American History Museum: The Unspoken Truths, and Tsuru for Solidarity. Please join us in supporting their important work.
> E: I don't generally support books on antiracism written by white folks since PoC still have to scrape for recognition for their work. (Cough...Robin DiAngelo). But I'm at least glad you aren't profiting off this.
> IG: I hear you around the ways institutional white supremacy leads to the differential uplifting of white voices, even in the space of antiracism. At the same time, I've learned a ton from reading antiracism books by white people and People of Color. I love Robin's work and Paul Kivel's and Tema Okun's, and I love Angela Davis's and Melissa V. Harris-Perry's and Audre Lorde's (just to name a few whom we quote in our book).
>
> I look forward to all of the conversation that comes from the critique of our work—I'm sure I'll continue to grow in my

understanding as a result. And I'm looking forward to hearing from those who read the book and find it a useful tool for their growth.

E: I 100% disagree, respectfully. It's not our place as White folks to take up space in the antiracism education sphere. It doesn't matter how long we have been doing the work. We need to prioritize PoC voices and make space for them. White folks like Robin are part of the problem. We will NEVER be authorities on racial issues as white colonizers. Period. I will never purchase a book on antiracism by a white period. Ever.

While E makes a good point about White folks not taking up space, she fails to recognize the nuances of this work. Her belief that Whites don't have something to offer, nor should they at least when it comes to publishing books on racism, puts the burden solely on the shoulders of PoC. Absolutely, PoC are often asked to teach White people about racism without being compensated, or they are expected to give discounts to organizations led by White people. I've experienced this myself. We don't have to look far to see the research on the disparities in pay between PoC and their White counterparts even when we hold degrees. But can't both be true? Can we fight for equal pay for PoC *and* learn from White people? Can we support Authors of Color *and* at the same time read books by White authors? Isn't there a win-win in there somewhere?

E is doing what many White people have done and continue to do in race discourse. They learn statements like, *"It's not PoC's job to educate White people"* or gain information on how PoC voices are constantly marginalized, then they swallow the information whole without chewing on it. They find a quick fix that makes them feel like they are contributing to racial equity, they hold on tight, and then they don't hold back in letting other White people (who are also trying to contribute to the change) know they are the problem. Let me just pause to say, I for one, have greatly benefitted from the work of Robin DiAngelo, Tim Wise, Frances Kendall, and many other White authors. And of course, I have learned a great deal from PoC authors. It's not one or the other.

No wonder so many White people are left confused. If White people aren't supposed to learn from PoC, and they're not supposed to read books written by White people, how are they to learn? Why does E believe that White people won't have any insight into the harm that they themselves and other White people have caused and continue to cause? Why does she believe the very institutional racist structures, intentionally designed by White people to benefit White people, can't be talked about by White people?

I'm probably reading more into it than is relayed in her post, but that's because far too often I have come across White people who stop doing their personal work once they've reached a certain point of understanding. And quite frankly, this intransigence can be a big part of the problem.

Why This Statement Can Be Problematic

In some areas of the US, "*It's not PoC's job to educate White people*" has become a mantra synonymous with racial equity work. I am concerned that, while it is true, this statement is being universally used without distinguishing when it is a necessary response to White people's insincere or entitled inquisitiveness and when we need to be educating White people. Without understanding why PoC make this statement, unpacking it, and discerning between when and when not to educate, it easily becomes an automatic response to all and any inquiry about race, racism, and race relations. This statement holds a lot of power in that it prevents White people from engaging PoC for fear they are doing something wrong by asking questions, and therefore impedes progress.

Take a moment and just imagine: what would happen if PoC stopped educating White people? How would White people learn about PoC's experience of racism without the stories of those impacted by it? They would have to solely rely on other White people, literature written by White people, social media sources from White people, and research by White people, on the experiences of PoC. If PoC were not educating White people, Whites' perspectives would come from theory based on other White people's understanding, without the stories, insights, and knowledge of PoC to inform the conversation. I may be going a little far with my suggestion, but it's important we recognize that PoC are essential in irradicating institutional and systemic racism, just as White people are. In fact, we should all be very afraid of racism being addressed without the voices of PoC. While this isn't what is intended by "*It's not my job to teach White people,*" the statement can be used unintendedly to disengage White people.

Become clear about the power and impact of this statement, when to use it, and when not to. This statement is commonly felt because of PoC experiences with Whites, yet it is often made at times when White people are truly open to learning and would most benefit from hearing about racism from PoC instead of another White person. Rather than opening the dialogue up and engaging in much needed discourse, the conversation gets shut down with those eight words.

The Roles People of Color Can Play

PoC are correct. It isn't a PoC's *job* to educate another person, no matter that person's race. So, if it's not PoC's *job*, then what is it? What role do PoC play in race conversations? Is it the meaning of the word "job" that is the problem? And if it's not the *job* of PoC to educate Whites, whose job is it? Surely, PoC see themselves as playing a role in teaching White people about racism and helping them to understand it's not a thing of the past. How will Whites understand the impact past and present racism is having on the lives of PoC if we don't help them understand?

Perhaps *commitment* to end racism is a better term. Changing the language can help PoC distinguish between when to educate and when not to. When it's their *job*, PoC have little say in when, how, or what their education of White people looks like. But if we see our commitment to the work and our role in ending racism, the question isn't *if* we will educate White people but rather when, how, who, and why.

Most likely, people who were active during the Civil Rights Movement felt they were making a commitment to a collective effort to change existing racial narratives. The many injustices they experienced daily likely fueled their commitment to stay the course even when the risk was so high it could cost them their lives. The choice of action wasn't what they necessarily wanted to do; it was what they believed they must do. The movement wasn't fueled by White people's expectations but by those who acted in their resolve for racial justice. They saw it as their responsibility to be a part of the change they sought. Our role today, in part, is to tell our stories when it is safe to do so, continue marching for Black Lives, voting, running for political office, preparing our children, speaking up when we see injustices, serving on DEIB committees in our organizations, educating ourselves, supporting one another, taking care of our well-being, and so on.

When It Is and Isn't OK to Ask PoC Questions

When White people ask questions, like "*What is the Black Lives Matter Movement, who started it and why?*", this is a technical question that can easily be answered with an internet search. Such seemingly innocent questions burden PoC with being the experts. Some people grew up in an era where encyclopedias, usually 26 separate books, were the main source of learning new information. That's what my family had, and it wasn't even a full set. Today most people have the internet at their disposal where they can find answers to just about anything they are interested in learning about. And when they don't feel like reading, they can easily access two- or three-minute videos which will teach them what they want to know. This doesn't even include the countless books, podcasts, documentaries, and other means for learning. In other words, there is no excuse for White people not to invest in in their own learning. So dear White People, stop asking PoC to educate you on systems designed by your people, when they have had to find ways to educate themselves on something they did not construct.

On the other hand, when a White person takes the time to do their own work to learn about an issue, even if it's occurring in the moment and then asks questions about the PoC opinion, experiences, or preferences, this is an opportunity to deepen their understanding. Personal inquiries are adaptive in their approach in that the person inquiring is likely to get a different response depending on the PoC they are speaking to. This is an opportunity for the PoC to share their perspectives and experiences that can help a White person grow their understanding even though it may come at a cost to the PoC. Consider the following asked by a White person: "*White privilege is a new concept I'm learning. It has me thinking about how it relates to my parenting. I've never ever worried about teaching my son what to do if he is pulled over by the police. I've always been able to experience the police as there to protect me and my family. Would you be open to sharing your experiences as a parent of a Black son?*"

The PoC in this situation is likely to have many thoughts and opinions of their own about it, as well as unique experiences that will be different from other PoC. They will need to decide if they want to risk being vulnerable. They will also need to consider if it's the right time and place and whether they have the bandwidth to give of themselves in this way. How a PoC responds won't always be simple or clear-cut either. As they share, it is likely to bring up emotions depending on their experiences and how much they are willing to divulge. There can be a lot of intellectual distancing when White people hear or read about another Black person being racially profiled. However, a PoC's personal experiences brings it closer to a White person's heart, particularly if the two have a relationship with one another.

As someone who is trying to lead equity work, be prepared to hear, "*It's not a PoC's job to educate White people*" from both PoC and Whites. As with Foundational Beliefs, get clear about your own thinking around any issue. Explore the implications of PoC not educating White people and move forward with empathy knowing PoC will be the ones to pay the price of White people's ignorance. Distinguishing the differences between a PoC *job* versus their *commitment* can help you avoid thinking in binary terms, "*It is or it isn't my job.*"

For Equity Leaders of Color to Consider

- First and foremost, be sure you have a support system in place. There will be times when you will need to draw upon your community of colleagues to help you get through triggering moments. You will need to have loving spaces, shared with those who understand, to help you process the challenges so you can further your work.
- Approach DEIB work not as a job but as a commitment to end racism, which will often require educating White people and will usually come at a cost. Determine if and when you are willing to make the sacrifice.
- Pace yourself. When you are tired and exhausted, give yourself a break. It's fatiguing carrying this burden of commitment. Racism should be a thing of the past by now, but it's not; in fact, more overt forms of racism are once again more commonplace. Taking intermittent breaks is key and will support your overall health and well-being.

- When you feel like giving up, imagine what would happen if all PoC stopped educating White people. Whom would they gain their understanding of racism from? How will White people benefit if we stop educating them? While White people most certainly can learn from other White people and the books they read, deepening their understanding of the impacts will require the stories and experiences of PoC.

- When you are asked technical questions that insinuate you are the expert or it's your job to educate them, ask them what research they've done to find the answers to their own questions. Put the work back on them.

- If a White person is doing the work to learn about racism and wants to better understand how you are personally being impacted, when you have the mental capacity and inclination to do so, be willing to give of yourself in this way.

- When you need to step out of the conversation for a while to rejuvenate, know that there will be other PoC carrying the load. There will be times when you need to hit the pause button, and that's OK. But get back in the work as soon as you can.

- If it helps, think about the sacrifices of the people who came before you. Imagine how difficult it must have been to walk miles to work every day for an entire year during the Montgomery Bus Boycott.

- Whatever you do, don't let the weight of this burden fall on the shoulders of a few PoC. We need as many people as possible in these conversations to create a critical mass for meaningful change to take place.

- When another PoC says "*It's not my job to educate White people*," don't immediately agree or correct them. Give them the space to share their frustrations and experiences of White people who have believed it was their job to educate them. Ask questions to better understand what they mean by it. After you've listened, share your own thoughts, understanding, and beliefs. The more you talk about it with other PoC, the deeper understanding you will both gain.

- When a White person says "*It's not the job of PoC to educate White people*," ask them how they came to know what they know and what their statement means to them. It is likely their learning was, in part, from stories of PoC. Ask them what they learned and how it impacted them in developing an equity lens.

For White Equity Leaders to Consider

- Form a relationship with the PoC before engaging them in conversations about their experiences of racism.
- When you do engage PoC, start the conversation with, *"Would you mind if I asked you a question about…?" "How would you feel about sharing with me your experiences of…?"*
- Don't expect PoC to respond in a way that makes you feel comfortable. Allow them to express their experiences with whatever emotions surface for them as they share. Anger can be a shield to protect PoC from further hurt and harm.
- Talk to your White friends, families, and coworkers. Help them understand racism as you've come to understand it. Educate them as much as they are open to learning. Bring more potential White allies into the conversation and model for them that their learning doesn't have to come solely from conversations with PoC.
- Call White people "in" not "out." Meet them where they're at and invite them to explore the impact on PoC when they expect PoC to teach them.
- Help White people understand the differences between being a job versus a commitment or responsibility to change. Refrain from making this a catchall phrase the minute another White person asks questions of a PoC.
- Don't assume PoC can't advocate for themselves. I recognize it is challenging to discern when to step in and when not to. I don't have the answer to this. Unfortunately, the best way to learn will be through trial and error.
- Invite other White people to think about what they will do with the stories of PoC that are gifted to them. Are Whites willing to act and advocate for change when PoC share their experiences? PoC are not looking for White people to feel sorry for them. We share our stories with the hope and expectation Whites will commit to changing not only themselves but the systems that were designed to benefit them.
- When a PoC says *"It's not my job to educate White people,"* don't just immediately agree. Give them the space to share their frustrations

and experiences of White people who believe it is their job to educate them. Take the risk to ask questions to better understand what they mean by it and what their experiences are. This can aid you in understanding before responding or sharing your concerns or fears about that statement.

- When a PoC says *"It's not my job to educate White people,"* sometimes you will need to just accept their response without question.
- Recognize that it is, in part, due to the willingness of PoC who shared their experiences that you grew in your understanding.
- There are plenty of books, blogs, documentaries, podcasts, and even the internet at your fingertips to help you learn about racism. Do your homework to find out as much as you can so you don't solely rely on PoC for your learning. Once you have at least a foundational knowledge, try engaging a Friend or Colleague of Color if they are open to sharing their experiences.
- Right now, you've been reading about how PoC are often expected to be the experts of their group's racial experiences. Try engaging a PoC you are in relationship with about what you've just learned. Ask them their thoughts about this issue. This gives the PoC the opportunity to speak from their own experiences without needing to have all the answers or carry the burden of representing their entire race.

In my daughter Makena's experience, her peers persisted in turning to her as if she had all the answers or was the expert on the Black experience; this inadvertently conveyed it was her *job* to educate them. These same students, who long before tenth grade discovered the internet, books, social media, and other means of finding answers to their questions, probably never even considered they might have valid thoughts and ideas of their own on race, or that there were other ways to learn besides from my daughter, who is also learning about racism. It probably never occurred to the teacher that this type of expectation places too much weight on the one Black student at the table. This will not be the last time Makena will experience the pressure of representing her race. This is something White people rarely, if ever, face.

○ ● ○ ●

Regardless of your race, research strategies for effective caucusing and/or affinity groups and consider putting them in place. This provides opportunities for PoC to speak freely and support one another without worrying about taking care of White people. They provide spaces for White people to teach one another and practice talking about race, without having to worry about offending PoC in the process. As I've heard it said, group work allows people to "speak in draft" so they don't have to do the mental labor of filtering their thoughts while trying to learn and process their experiences and understanding.

How and Why People of Color Benefit from Talking about Race

Another Foundational Belief Cultures Connecting holds is that *"This is everyone's work."* It is not uncommon to hear in a workshop a PoC say, *"Why do I have to be there? I live this* (racism) *every day."* While PoC work can look different from White people's work, it is not just for White people's benefit. PoC have been impacted by racism, internalizing a lifetime of inferiority messages in ways they don't always recognize. And while PoC experience racism daily, this doesn't mean that there isn't learning that needs to occur, particularly as it relates to institutional and systemic racism. Also, the more they understand how racism operates and is impacting them, the more tools they gain to talk about and fight against its impact. In other words, PoC must externalize what has unconsciously become internalized.

Unfortunately, one impact of racism is colorism. Colorism, a term coined by Alice Walker in the early eighties, refers to a racial group favoring lighter skin over darker skin. Many PoC have internalized this message and collude with racism by adopting White standards, values, and beliefs around their own group's intelligence, worth, and beauty simply due to skin color. As I mention this, I'm tempted to go deeper, but recognize this issue could easily be a chapter or book of its own. I imagine that some individuals are saying "Not me. I prefer darker skin." That may be true. However, your preference does not negate the negative experiences that dark skin people have experienced from their own racial group since early childhood. My husband and many other dark skin people have countless stories that attest to this fact.

Years ago, I attended a conference my colleague was organizing. While walking to our next session, we were approached by a Black man who had questions about the conference. My colleague and I teach similar courses, and we both hold doctorate degrees. The most prominent difference about us was that she is darker where I am of lighter complexion. Even though I told him she was the one he needed to talk to, he looked at me the entire time as if she wasn't there. I tried looking in her direction whenever he spoke, hoping he would pick up on my nonverbal cues and speak directly to her. If you've ever done this before, you know how awkward it is. It's like trying to point your head in someone else's direction. But even when I stayed silent allowing her time to respond, he never addressed my colleague directly.

These and other types of subtle experiences render darker skin PoC invisible. Whether PoC experience colorism or racism, it takes a psychological, physical, and mental toll on us. We experience a roller coaster of emotions that vacillate between sadness, anger, frustration, hopelessness, hope, confusions, and so on. Sadly, many PoC have learned to keep their emotions bottled up inside in ways that ultimately exacerbate the impact on their health. Talking about our experiences of racism with other PoC through caucusing and with White people in workshops and healing circles can be beneficial in many ways.

- Gives PoC the opportunity to voice and express our feelings about how racism has impacted us and our families and friends.
- When done solely with other PoC, it allows us to be in community and a space to be heard without being told how to express ourselves, i.e., tone policed.
- Putting words to the harm caused by racism and speaking that truth to White people can be an important step in our healing process.
- Develops our skills in engaging more effectively across cultures.
- Centers the conversation around our experiences rather than the needs and feelings of White people.
- Normalizes our experiences when we hear other PoC share theirs.
- Helps us to identify ways in which we ourselves may have internalized racism.
- Allows PoC to support one another and recognize we are not alone.
- Helps White people understand what needs to be changed and why. When White people get on board, it benefits us. We cannot

pull ourselves up by our bootstraps. We must collectively work for change.

- We develop new language that becomes a tool to help articulate our experiences and identify the problems that exist within our organization, e.g., microaggressions, privilege, equity, bias, and White fragility are just a few. Having language to describe the problems can help decrease stress and feelings of frustration.

- Through conversations, PoC become more skilled in identifying how and where more subtle forms of racism play out the workplace; these conversations can assist them in identifying where change needs to occur.

- Talking about experiences of racism aids PoC in bringing to a level of consciousness ways in which they have unconsciously internalized oppressive messages so they can then shift the paradigm from us being the problem to externalizing the institutions as the problem. When we engage conversations about race, we can begin to heal from our individual and collective past trauma.

When a PoC Says They Don't Want to Attend DEIB Workshops

It's always tricky when engaging PoC who don't want to attend DEIB workshops. Typically, they will say either "Why do I have to attend that workshop, I live this every day?" or "Why do I have to attend this workshop so White people can learn?" It's particularly challenging when other PoC are going to be attending or when White people are expected to attend and PoC don't show up. It conveys messages that run contrary to the work, AND at the same time, we must acknowledge and honor the fact that the impact of these workshops on PoC is different from that of their White colleagues.

Engaging in Conversations

When a PoC requests not to attend, explain that you need to know more before you can decide whether they can opt out of the workshop(s). Don't make an immediate decision. Help them to understand, as a leader, it's not as simple as just saying yes or no. See below some ways you might approach the conversation.

- Before I can determine how to proceed with your request, I need to understand more. This may not be easy for you, particularly given I'm asking you to share your experiences with me, someone who is (describe differences between you, e.g., your boss, a White person, in a position of power, you don't know).

- Thank you for letting me know you do not want to attend our DEIB sessions. I have a tough decision to make. Because I've made it mandatory for all staff, I need to have a clear understanding of why you don't want to attend. Do know that I won't share with your colleagues what you share with me. I need to know so that whatever I decide, I can feel like my decision aligns with my Foundational Beliefs about DEIB work.
- I didn't think that a PoC would not want to attend. I just assumed that you would be glad that we are finally having DEIB trainings. I now realize my assumptions were wrong. It's important I understand your why for not wanting to attend so I can make an informed decision.

Get Clear About Why They Don't Want to Attend

Make sure you have a clear understanding as to why they are requesting not to attend, before deciding. Ask questions with genuine curiosity to find out about past workshop experiences. Were they negatively impacted? What do they worry will happen if they attended? Or worry that won't happen, i.e., nothing will change. What do they think the workshop is about?

- Please help me understand what worries, concerns, or fears you have about attending our DEIB trainings?
- What have your past experiences been like when participating in these types of workshops?
- Help me understand why you don't want to attend?
- If they say they don't want to go because they feel like it is White people's work, share a few of your Foundational Beliefs that speak to why you see it differently.
- Are you saying you don't have anything to learn? Help me understand what you mean by "*Why do I have to attend just so White people can learn?*"

Summarize

Whatever they are willing to share, convey how what they are saying makes sense to you, so they feel you are listening and doing your best to understand.

- It sounds like you've been through this before and nothing changed.
- It sounds like the last time you participated in a DEIB training the facilitator handled it badly when a White person said something racist.
- I can't imagine what it must have been like for you to go through (what they shared). Did I miss anything?
- If I'm hearing you correctly, the last training you went through caused you to feel more isolated and alone, even sometimes on the spot.

What They Can Do Instead of Attending

If you determine that they do not want to attend because, for example, they have unresolved trauma from past trainings, or the training is happening right after a major public incident like the murder of George Floyd, or something traumatic is currently happening in their life, it is likely they don't have the emotional capacity or bandwidth to engage in these difficult conversations. Do not make them attend. Not attending may be the best way for them to take care of themselves.

- Ask them to connect with one or two other people they feel safe with, who did attend, to discuss what they learned and their experiences. This also serves to give the person who attended the opportunity to share with someone what they learned and therefore will be more likely to retain important information.
- I want to make sure that you are still growing in your understanding of DEIB. I will ask the facilitator if they have articles, videos, or other things you might watch, read, or listen to so that you have the similar vocabulary and information the rest of the organization has as we collectively move along in our DEIB journey. I know it won't be the same.
- Be sure and check in with them later about how they are doing given everything they previously shared with you. Find out what they've heard about the workshop.
- What would you like me to convey to your colleagues if they ask why you are absent. I want to be careful to honor what you've shared with me, and we both need to be prepared for questions that might come up.

Highly Encouraging Them to Attend

Unless their reason for not attending is due to negative past experiences or trauma, convey that you *highly encourage* them to attend at least the first session and why. I don't recommend you make it mandatory for them. No one can fully determine the impact of racism on a PoC's life.

However, hopefully they left the conversation with you feeling heard, understood, and that their well-being is a priority. By letting them know the choice is theirs to make, and with your explanation of why you want them to attend, maybe they will. If they choose not to attend, through no fault of yours, maybe the workshop will be so well done that they will hear great things about it and elect to attend future sessions.

- I've heard a lot of great things about (the company or facilitators name) approach to these conversations and about their style. It's why we chose their company. Have you ever heard of _____?
  - If yes, ask what they heard or experienced.
  - If no, share what you've heard about the speaker and/or organization and why you chose them.
- I'd like you to experience how (the facilitator) approaches these conversations. One thing this might offer for you, in addition to new insight and learning, is help you to heal from your past workshops (or help you move forward from your past experiences with these types of trainings).
- When you hear what I've shared, what are your thoughts?
- I'm not trying to change your mind at this point. It makes sense to me why you wouldn't want to attend. With that said, I do have an ask of you. Would you be open to at least attending the first session? You are not required to verbally participate; I understand if you need to get a sense of everything and everyone first.
- Encourage them to watch any videos of the speaker, e.g., TEDx Talk, YouTube videos, etc., and have them go to the presenter's website to learn more. You want them to make an informed decision that is not just based on their assumptions or past experiences.
- If after the first session, you still do not want to participate, let's talk about it. At least I will know you have given it a chance.

Explain Why You Hope They Will Attend

Why do they matter to you? What would they bring to the sessions? Why do you care if they don't attend?

- We can't embark on this journey without you.
- You are an essential part of our organization.
- If White people are the only ones participating in these conversations, how will we ever get to a place of making effective change? Your voice, perspectives, and experiences matter.
- We all have something to learn.
- I want all our Staff of Color to feel like they have each other's support. It's hard enough to be one of few PoC in our organization. Being one of few PoC in race conversations can be even more challenging.
- You are someone who (name things about them that they will bring to the table, e.g., empathetic, a good listener, caring person, someone people respect, or trust).
- My thought is we will build trust amongst ourselves as we embark on our DEIB journey together. I don't want the bus to leave if you're not on it.

Hopes for Your Everyone in Your Organization

- Staff learn how to have difficult conversations about race and racism with one another.
- Provide staff with the tools so they can work together to dismantle institutional racism together.
- Do the work together so the burden doesn't all fall on the shoulders of PoC.
- Hope that the workshops will help address some of the issues your organization has been experiencing.

Support Them

Offer to support them if they decide to attend the workshop. Be careful not to overpromise and underdeliver. Anything you say should be things you can follow through on.

- How can I support you if you do attend?
- I will make myself available if you'd like to debrief with me after the session?

- Is there someone you trust that you'd like to debrief with after the session? I would be glad to do it with you, and I also want to acknowledge that you may not feel safe with me (or have the connection with me, or that I will understand).
- Would it be helpful for you to connect with the facilitator before the session? I can arrange for you to talk with her so you get a better sense of what the session will involve and what will be expected of participants.
- Give them permission to not attend. They should have the final say in their own well-being.

Follow-Up

Check in or have someone else check in. Whether they do or don't attend, it is likely you learned some things about their experiences as a PoC. Don't just drop it.

- Schedule a date and time to follow up. Give them a couple days to think about it and check back in with you so you know what they decide.
- Check back in with them after the first session. If they did attend, how was it for them? If they didn't attend, what did they hear? Was there anything they heard from colleagues that has them considering attending the next session?
- After several sessions, check in and find out are they noticing any small changes, e.g., staff are talking more about race.

○ ● ○ ● ○

Lastly, when you do have workshops on race, let White people know they should not go to the PoC and start bombarding them with questions. If they don't have a relationship with them, they shouldn't try to start one now by asking questions about their racial experiences. PoC are doing their work too, and they don't need to feel like they must take care of White people, particularly when they may be raw with their own emotions or new insights. In other words, give them space.
    Consider

- Reflect on your reactions to what you've read about PoC's job to educate White people.
- Identify at least one other way PoC benefit by sharing their experiences of racism with White people.

12

Taking a Collective, Universal, or Individual Approach

The Universal Approach

When you try and engage some people in conversations about race, they will take what Sue and Sue refer to as the *Universal Approach*. This is typically an approach White people will take to sidestep race conversations. They will commonly say things like, *"We are all human,"* *"We all bleed,"* *"Why do we need to talk about differences? Talking about differences just divide us,"* and *"Respect is universal."* Yes, we are all human, and we do all bleed. In fact, this should be a given. In other words, why are people even talking about something we already know to be true? When was the last time you were in a room full of people and questioned whether they were human?

At the same time, we shouldn't lose sight of the fact that people are human beings who bleed and have feelings. Unfortunately, we don't treat everyone as if they are human. For example, separating thousands of Latine children from their parents and locking them up in cages is not humane. It is inhumane. This isn't about whether you are a democrat or republican, and it isn't about immigration reform, it is about treating our fellow human beings with dignity and respect. You don't need to be a parent to imagine what this must be like for those families.

Another common argument to avoid race conversations is *"Respect is universal."* This saying is meant to reinforce the golden rule, *"Treat other people the way you want to be treated."* It is true that every-one wants to be shown respect. However, what respect looks like for one person may differ for another, often depending on cultural dif-ferences. Instead practice the platinum rule, *"Treat other people the way they want to be treated."* Learn what different groups value as a show of respect. For example, some groups prefer to be acknowledged with their title (Mr. Mrs. Ms. Dr., etc.). Develop knowledge of different groups and honor their preference. Don't assume respect looks the same for everyone.

Lastly, talking about differences isn't what is dividing us. It's the racist systems and our avoidance in talking about them that is divisive. Intentional or not, statements like these keep White people comfortable by minimizing the impact of racism on PoC and ignores how they benefit from being White.

The Individual Approach

More commonly in conversations about race, White people will take the Individual Approach. Statements like, "*I don't notice race*" and "*My best friend is Asian*" or—one of my favorites—"*I don't care if you're black, brown, purple or green, I hate all people equally*" are readily spoken as a defense to prove they somehow don't notice race. These types of comments allow White people to avoid being accountable to their actions and prevent them from having to critically examine their stereotypes and racist behaviors. As with the Universal Approach, it is important to keep in mind not only are we all human but we are also all individuals. Recognizing same group identity does not mean ignoring the fact that we can have different values, beliefs, or ways of engaging. People within a group can have different experiences and ways of interacting in the world.

Let me pause here for a moment to address color-blind ideology. When a White person says they don't notice race, the most common message they are trying to convey to a PoC is that they won't judge them or treat them unfairly because they are Black, Indigenous, Asian, or Latine. Basically, that they aren't racist. Essentially, they want PoC to see them as one of the *good* Whites. If you are White reading this and have made similar statements, I want to let you in on a secret. The moment you tell a PoC you don't notice their race, you are actually letting them know that you do notice. Think about it. When was the last time upon meeting another White person you said, "*I don't notice your race?*" It just doesn't happen.

I'm not proposing that White people start walking up to strangers pointing out their differences, "*Excuse me sir, I notice you are in a wheelchair*" or "*I just want you to know I can see you are Latina.*" What

I am suggesting is that they become curious about those moments when they go out of their way to profess to *not* see differences. Why is that? Whom does it benefit? Whom does it impact?

There are times when race doesn't need to be named because it has nothing to do with anything. Saying "*I have a friend who is Indigenous*" serves no purpose. In this case, why would someone feel the need to say their friend's race? What do they want that friend—or other friends—to believe about them? How does it provide needed context? It doesn't. In this case, their race doesn't tell me anything other than you have one friend who is Native American. However, when race provides context, it is essential to name it. If you were discussing something going on between staff members in a workplace, their race can change how the story is heard, understood, and interpreted.

When my husband, Gary, and I were out walking the other day, he shared he was in the process of hiring. He interviewed a candidate he thought was promising. According to Gary, the only problem was, "*He couldn't sell himself, and if he can't sell himself how is he going to be able to sell our product?*" I asked him the race of this candidate. When I heard he was Asian, not speaking to his own strengths made sense. Some cultures are collectivistic versus individualistic. In this case, meaning they will speak highly of their group or team accomplishments but not their own. Naming someone's race in this case, can help understand how culture may be playing a role.

When identifying the only Person of Color in a group, Whites will often go out of their way to say anything about the person other than their race, "*You know, the one wearing the purple hat, blue shoes, green coat, orange shirt....*" PoC will often think, "*Oh, the Black person. Why didn't you just say so?*" After all, Black people know they are Black. Your noticing their race in this situation isn't a bad thing. In fact, in this case not naming race implies there is something wrong with being Black. If there wasn't anything wrong with it, why wouldn't you just say, "*the Black person*"?

There are White people in our society who are overtly racist. They see differences as negative and inferior and will spew racial epithets when talking about PoC. White people who know this is wrong will work to be different from the overt racist, which can result in their taking a color-blind approach. One component of race work in the

twenty-first century is to notice differences and to see those differences as positive rather than noticing differences and seeing them as
negative or "invisible."

While White people are typically the ones who take a Universal
Approach to conversations about race, there are some PoC who will
also take this stance. In these rare situations, it is likely they have
bought into White attitudes, values, and beliefs and have yet to
explore how the Universal and Individual Approaches are forms of
colluding with racism.

The Collective Approach

While maintaining we are all human and that we are all individuals
is a necessary part of race conversation, the third approach, the Collective Approach, is where these conversations need to be positioned.
This approach recognizes a common collective experience that people
have because they belong to a group. It allows for the examination of
a group's experiences. For example, what would it be like to be Indigenous, provide research to non-Natives on the harm mascots have
on children's and adolescent's self-worth, produce videos beseeching
schools and sports teams to change their mascots, stand outside the
stadium before a Redskin (name has since changed) game imploring
fans not to support the team, only to be told, "It's been this way for
years, it's tradition" or "We're honoring you, you should feel proud."

These types of microinvalidations are another way in which White
people see themselves as the experts of someone else's reality, in this
case, Indigenous peoples. What would it be like to be second-, third-,
even fourth-generation Asian or Latine American and have people say
to you, "Where did you learn to speak English so well?" or "Where are
you really from?" or "You speak such good English." My stepmother,
who came from Thailand as an adult, would understandably hear
these comments and questions as compliments. However, they are
all too often said to American-born Asians, conveying a presumption
that they not "from here." A workshop participant once told me when
people tell her she speaks good English, she replies by saying, "Thank
you, you do too."

Above are just a few examples of daily experiences PoC have as
members of their racial group. White people frequently become upset,
even angry, when referred to in terms of their racial group member-

ship, i.e., "*White people.*" This is because they are not used to being lumped in with other Whites. They've had the privilege of being perceived as individuals their entire lives, whereas PoC are seen for their group membership rather than who they are as individuals. When White people are grouped with other Whites, in race conversations they will quickly speak to who they are as individuals to uphold their individuality. "*I'm not like that!*" or "*I treat everyone the same*" and "*Why are you trying to make me feel bad for being White!*"

Racism cannot be confronted or dismantled through a Universal or Individual Approach. Take, for instance, the Black Lives Matter Movement founded by activists Alicia Garza, Patrisse Cullors, and Opal Tometi in response to racial profiling and police brutality. Many White people, in their discomfort to address this serious issue, responded with "*All Lives Matter.*" All Lives Matter is a Universal Approach. While it is true all lives matter, as mentioned earlier, this should be a given. "*Black Lives Matter*" will also evoke in a White person the need to share positive attributes of someone they know in law enforcement. The underlying messages are "*because I know a person in law enforcement who is good, you are wrong that police can do bad things*" along with denial that the law enforcement system needs changing. Blacks too have friends and family members in law enforcement, but it doesn't take away from the fact that, as a group, something is seriously problematic in how the police commonly treat Black people.

White people pointing to someone they know as proof that the collective experiences of People of Color aren't real is all too common. We typically see this play out in media. Some issue will arise for PoC, usually in politics, and then White people will find one or two Voices of Color (sometimes even just a face) whose perspective runs contrary to their collective group's beliefs and experiences. This serves the purpose of saying, "*See? Kevin doesn't think that way, therefore everyone else from that group must be wrong in their thinking.*"

Another approach to "*Black Lives Matter*" is "*Blue Lives Matter.*" This is a Group Approach, but it is *another* group. Of course, the lives of police matter. For me, that important point was addressed in "*All Lives Matters.*" Those in law enforcement risk their lives whenever they respond to a call. It's not a job everyone could handle. It is a profession that has high suicide rates due to the stressors that come with their work. The problem with "*Blue Lives Matter*" is that it is in reaction to "*Black Lives Matter*." No one was wearing t-shirts or holding signs that read "*Blue Lives Matter*" until Black people began calling attention to the disproportionate number of Blacks being killed by police.

When White people go to the Universal, Individual, or another Group in race conversations, they derail the conversation and therefore aid in maintaining institutionally racist practices. PoC end up wasting precious time defending what they mean or don't mean by "Black Lives Matter." All the while, innocent Black people are being killed.

Strategies

When engaging a White person who is taking a Universal or Individual Approach to racism, your goal is to try and get them to understand the collective experience. Sometimes this can effectively be done by approaching the conversation through a marginalized group identity they have where they have suffered oppression. For example, talking about the collective experience women have in this country of getting paid less than their male counterparts for doing the same jobs can help a woman become more open to listening to experiences of racism. Listening to stories of someone who experiences ableism can help them to make connections to racism. This is one of the more difficult and painful strategies to use with White people, particularly if you are a PoC, because it requires centering White people's experiences in the conversation first.

Because this strategy requires leaning into White people's experiences, you will need to make sure you have the emotional capacity and bandwidth. If you can give of yourself in this way, keep in mind the reward in many cases is that it will lessen their defensiveness and their inclination to argue against the need for racial justice when it's your turn to talk about racism. This strategy requires a great deal of patience on your part. It involves paraphrasing to show understanding and asking numerous questions with genuine curiosity to gain insight about their marginalized experiences. Once they feel heard and understood, it opens a door for you to invite them to listen and learn about the impact of racism. Asking them if they would be "willing," "open," or "curious" to hearing about racism is one way to transition the focus away from them and onto the subject of race. Hopefully, they will learn what it looks like to be open to leaning into another group's experiences from your modeling.

If those you engage are operating from the Individual or Universal Approach while you are speaking to the collective experience, the conversation will not go anywhere. At every turn you will find yourself defending with, "*I don't mean you*" and "*I don't mean all*" and "*I never mean every White, Black, Asian, Indigenous or Latine person.*" This will slow things down significantly as White people become defensive and blame you for "dividing your organization." Take the time to explain your approach and why the other two approaches are not helpful in race conversations. Some White people still won't get it even after all your efforts. However, keep focused on the 80% and move forward with race work.

13

Adopt Norms for Engaging in Courageous Conversations

UNDERSTANDING THE NEED for a Group Approach when addressing racism is just part of what's needed to effectively engage in race conversations. When everyone at the table is talking about collective experiences of racism, it is likely things will get heated, emotional, and tense. You'll need tools to guide you and your organization so you can hold one another and yourselves accountable for *how* you engage. This will help your organization stay in the work no matter how challenging the conversation becomes. Leaving people to their own methods of discourse is likely to increase the probability of divisiveness, and feelings of hopelessness.

Some organizations will brainstorm with their staff agreed upon norms to utilize. The idea is to have everyone give input about what they need or want, in order to participate in the discussion. The thought behind this strategy is that staff are more likely to participate because they were included in the process. I recognize that this runs contrary to everything I've been saying about the importance of inclusivity of voice and perspective. However, when it comes to courageous conversations about race, the opposite is true. In this case, it is best not to involve the group in the decision-making process. Instead, you will rely on those with expertise and experience who have already thought through what is needed to effectively engage in difficult conversations and then teach what you have learned to your colleagues.

One problem with letting the group decide is inevitably someone will suggest a norm that runs counter to DEIB work. One example of this is the common request for "safety" as a norm. White people often seek safety because they worry a Person of Color will become angry or label them racist if they use the wrong language or hurt a PoC while talking about racism. They want to know they can process out loud their thinking and learning without any pushback or big emotions from PoC. One way this shows up is, *"Don't take this the wrong way, but..."*

PoC often seek safety to ensure their experiences won't be invalidated by their White colleagues when they share their experiences. They want to know if they say something that makes White people in the room feel uncomfortable, they won't face retaliation for speaking their truth or their experiences won't be minimized. Agreeing on "safety" as a norm won't guarantee that the space will be safe. How staff treat one another, how they hold one another's stories, and how they handle the mishaps and offenses is what will determine whether people in the room feel safe enough to share. In other words, safety is something they must create together and that will evolve over time. It requires people taking risk to speak and practicing the other norms of engagement that will create a safe space.

Glenn Singleton is a person with experience and expertise in race conversations we can rely on. In his book, *Courageous Conversations About Race: A Field Guide for Achieving Equity in Schools and Beyond,* Singleton lists four Agreements for Courageous Conversation: *Stay Engaged, Speak Your Truth, Experience Discomfort,* and *Expect and Accept Non-closure.* My company, Cultures Connecting, adapted Singleton's agreements and expanded on them to include *Listen for Understanding, Take Risks,* and *No Fixing.* Singleton refers to them as agreements; we think of them as norms or tools for courageous conversations.

Below are explanations of each of the norms to help guide you and your organization in courageous conversations. Once you become familiar with the norms, you will recognize how they are interconnected with one another and can be used as tools in any conversation, not just race. However, the reverse is not true. If you are not explicit about the norms your organization practices when engaging in race conversations, you will unconsciously default to White dominant cultures norms (for example, assume positive intent, which I will explain later in this chapter) for engaging. Also, be clear that these norms will not work with the 10% on the far left of the bell curve who are not open to learning about racism.

Experience Discomfort

Given most of us were not taught to have conversations about racism, it makes sense as adults we would feel extreme discomfort in cross-cultural dialogue. Sweating, increased heart rate, fear of making a mistake, risking relationships, further marginalization, and so on can keep us from leaning into a conversation. It wouldn't take courage if it was easy. But if you wait until you become comfortable, what will happen? You probably answered correctly. Nothing. Nothing will happen. White people's discomfort with talking about racism is one of the many reasons why we are not further along than we could be. Instead of seeking safety or comfort, one thing you and your organization will need to learn is to become comfortable with the discomfort. Rather than allowing discomfort to create a reoccurring cycle of avoidance behavior, normalize your discomfort, identify your fears, and engage despite them. If you don't, the conversations will never occur, and our organizations will never change.

Take Risks

Taking risks is probably one of the hardest things many in your organization will wrestle with. While there are different risks involved for PoC versus White staff, taking risks is scary business for all involved. PoC risk losing their jobs, feeling invisible, having their experiences downplayed, and so much more. When White people take risks to engage across differences, the question they typically ask themselves is, *"How do I risk, without offending?"* rather than asking *"How can I engage when I do offend?"* In addition, people don't like to appear incompetent—but in truth, racial equity work will reveal our ineptitude. Being certain that you and others will benefit from taking risks isn't taking a risk. What makes it a risk is that things won't always turn out the way you hope, no matter how much risk-taking you do.

Like it or not, it's through the risks you take, and the mistakes that follow, that learning occurs. If you and others in your organization want to dismantle institutional racist practices, you must first learn to have courageous conversations with one another through practice. Your organization can and will improve over time, even if you never perfect it. I once heard a speaker say he knows he will always sin. However, he doesn't say to himself, *"Well, I guess since I will always be a sinner, I'll stop trying not to sin."* The point is, we should all work toward being our best selves, even when we know we will never achieve perfection.

Stay Engaged

Daniel Wile in his workshop, Collaborative Couples Therapy: Turning Fights into Intimate Conversations, described three ways a conversation can go when conflict exists. One such approach he refers to as *attack* mode. When couples get into arguments, rather than being present in the conversation or attempting to resolve the conflict, they build their defenses, ready to pounce the moment they hear something triggering. This type of lashing out often takes place in race conversations. Those who tend to lean toward this style when offended or in response to being told they've offended probably know it doesn't work. In other words, lashing out doesn't move race conversations forward. There have been occasions when I've lashed out at people who've said or done things that pushed my hot buttons, but never once has anyone responded with, "*Dr. Hollins, I want to thank you for the way you attacked me. I learned so much as a result.*" When attacked, fight, flight, or freeze kicks in, and the person will either attack back or shut down. Dr. Wile advised that attacking creates a cycle resulting in becoming enemies.

Another common style Dr. Wile shared when couples are in conflict is to *avoid*. This is no more helpful in moving race conversations forward than attacking. Avoiders don't talk with the person who has offended them, they talk with someone they are close with about that thing the person did or said that was offensive. The person who was offended misses out on the opportunity to practice engaging, and the offender continues to offend because they were likely unaware that what they said or did was offensive. Hopefully, you believe most people are good, kind, loving, moral, ethical people. I don't want you to be naïve and believe this about all people. However, when most people offend, they don't wake up in the morning thinking, "*Who can I hurt, harm, or belittle today?*" Wile explained that avoiding behavior distances us from one another, turning us into strangers.

The third response to being offended or offending, and the one that will increase the likelihood growth will occur, is what Wile refers to as *engage*. He says this approach leads to becoming allies. It requires shifting your thinking from "*You're wrong and I'm right*" to pursuit of deepening your understanding. This begins when people lean in and ask questions with genuine curiosity. In Courage and Renewal retreats, developed by Parker Palmer, facilitators use a quote that nicely captures this approach: "*When the going gets tough, turn to wonder, wonder what's going on with you, wonder what's going on with me.*"[1] Though not easy, often because of the emotions from all sides, engaging is a critical tool necessary to have courageous conversations about race. What follows suggests how to ask questions that lead to engaging (rather than lashing out or avoiding).

Listen for Understanding

This may be the most difficult of all the norms to practice, particularly when you are the one who did the offending. Listening for understanding is about your "*impact*" not your "*intent.*" As stated earlier in this book, because you've spent a lifetime developing a sense of who you see yourself to be, the moment someone calls you *in* or *out* on something you've said or done that was offensive, your automatic response is likely to defend. When defense is the reaction, the offending person will quickly turn it around and make it about the way the person offended is looking at it. Common retorts include, "*That's not what I meant,*" "*It was just a joke,*" "*Why do you have to take everything so personally?*" and "*That's why I don't like having these conversations; you are way too sensitive.*" These statements convey to the person you offended that your intentions matter more than the impact they had. Intent can revictimize the victim. It also sends the message that not only are you unwilling to listen but you are also not the one who needs to change.

PoC have learned avoidant and lashing out behavior from years of interacting with White people who became defensive when they were told they offended. Though PoC don't have to share with White people how they have harmed, they take a risk anyway. And often when they do, rather than White people receiving this as a gift, they invalidate or minimize PoC experiences. PoC will get knocked down and eventually get up again, hoping the next interaction will result in a different outcome, i.e., change in White people's words and actions. However, PoC can only do this so much. Eventually some of us will become so fatigued that they will lash out or find someone who does understand, usually another PoC or a White ally. In frustration they will say, "You're not going to believe what this White woman said to me today!" The White woman in this case likely has no clue that she offended. Styles of engaging can also be a result of how you were raised. If conflict was avoided when you were a child, it is likely you are a conflict avoider as an adult.

As a Racial Equity Leader, your role will be to help your organization understand why "assume positive intent" doesn't work in race conversations. It puts the responsibility on the PoC who was offended to do all the work and to assume the other person's goodness, leaving the harm unexplored. Not only is it likely that the goodness of the person who offended was never in question; "assume positive intent" is a White dominant cultural norm that serves to protect the offender and does not lead to new learning. In race conversations, when you offend, rather than have the offended assume positive intent, assume they assume you intended well, and focus on your impact.

Expect/Accept Non-Closure

Things will not always turn out the way you and your organization hope simply because you're engaging in courageous conversations about race. In fact, things are likely to get more challenging before they get easier. Accept this. PoC have been hurt and harmed by White people for generations. Just because someone wants to work through things, the person who is wounded may not be in a place where they can talk about it. Let it go and let them be. In an ideal situation, the person offended will be open to discussing the situation further. Unfortunately, sometimes this won't be the case. Expecting and accepting non-closure is a tool to help in these moments when you want to talk about it but the other person doesn't.

Help your organization understand when you persist in trying to get the other person to engage you, it may not be what they are wanting or needing. It isn't easy to let go, yet sometimes that is the most caring thing you can do for the person harmed.

Speak Your Truth

Being a leader in this work means sometimes you will be the only one that sees things the way you do. You may be the only voice advocating on behalf of another person or the only one initially seeking to change your organization from within. The questions you ask of your organization and the concerns you bring up are likely to leave your colleagues or staff viewing you unfavorably. Speaking your truth goes hand in hand with taking risk or, as some say, being brave in the space. Practice getting used to hearing your own voice speak out for justice. Don't remain silent because no one else is speaking up. At a workshop put on by Larry Bell, he said something I will never forget, "*On your worst day on the job, you are still some child's best hope.*" Though his words were meant for K-12 educators, you may be the best hope for PoC within your organization.

Encourage others in the organization to speak their truths too. Rather than speaking from a universal "we," shift to "I." This approach helps others in the room personally connect with the speaker. For example, when someone says, "*People are afraid of taking risks for fear of being misunderstood.*" "People" makes it sound like everyone, which may not be the case for everyone. Even if everyone does have that fear, the speaker needs to create room for others to share their truths. Redirect the person to speak "their" truth. Have them repeat what they said only this time by locating themselves in the story. It would sound like, "*I'm afraid of taking risks for fear I might be misunderstood.*" Speaking one's own truth is a powerful tool for connecting. It requires taking risks and coming out from under cover by showing vulnerability. It invites others to do the same. This is another way safety will come about.

No Fixing

Anyone who believes we can have conversations about race, racism, and race relations free of emotion is really conveying unwillingness to get messy in the work. People will cry, they will become angry, they will feel. Every time a PoC tells a personal story of oppression; they are reliving a bit of their story often so White People can learn. Whenever a White person cries because they realize harm they've done, they are revealing their humanity. The emotions people feel are real and necessary for the work. Whether you are the one expressing the emotion or a witness, give yourself permission to feel. Allow what is happening to be a part of the experience rather than trying to fix it or make it go away.

We must lean into this work with both our heads and our hearts, enough to motivate us to want to be changed and to make changes around us. Leading this work means showing people the way. It requires letting go of old ways of thinking about what it means to lead. Leading is authentic, relational, messy, unclear, and it is risky. Because many people don't see the workplace as a place to be vulnerable, they will quickly become uneasy when others show emotion. One response to such discomfort is an attempt to fix another person's pain. The dynamics of fixing, as stated earlier in this book, commonly occur when a PoC has an emotional reaction to something a White person said; when the White person feels shame or becomes defensive, the PoC will often unknowingly attempt to comfort them by saying things like, "*That's OK. Don't worry about it. I know you didn't mean it.*" But fixing doesn't just occur in cross-cultural interactions.

I once witnessed fixing occur between two Black male firefighters. One of the firefighters began to cry as he shared a story about his experience of racism. His colleague sitting next to him began giving him the "man pat." The man pat is a heavy, slow pat you can hear from a distance. While the intent was likely meant to convey "*I care for you,*" "*I'm here for you*" and "*It will be OK,*" it can have the impact of conveying "*Stop crying,*" "*Man up,*" or "*I'm not comfortable with your display of emotions.*" Think instead about how "*Listening is a form of action.*" During the times you want to fix, remember that sometimes there is nothing you can do with the pain of someone you care about other than be there for them by listening. I'm not suggesting that people never pat someone on the back when they are upset. What I am suggesting is you first ask yourself "*Whose needs are being met?*"

As you lead this work, your organization will struggle with not being able to make the pain or upset of their colleagues go away. As you teach them this norm, they may even become defensive. When using rubbing people on the back when they are crying, a woman who was listening predatorily said to me, "*Oh come on, now you're telling us we can't even rub someone on the back when they are hurting?*" She didn't mean it as a question with genuine curiosity. This work rarely involves either you do or don't. The more you lead this work, the more you will notice other ways in which people try to fix. These are just two examples.

With a set of norms to guide staff through race conversation, you'll need to explain each of them, give examples so they understand how they apply to DEIB work, and remind people of them when conversa-

tions get messy or go sideways. This will be one of the most important things you do for your organization. Norms need to be stated out
loud, practiced, followed with check-ins to see how staff are doing
practicing these norms. Norms are what will help shape your culture
and lead to effective conversations as you identify where and how
racism exists within your organization and what change is needed.

**Adopt Norms for Courageous Conversations:
Commitment to Change and Be Changed**

- In the workplace, do you tend to lean toward attack, avoid or
engage when you are offended or are the offender?
- Choose one of the above-mentioned norms that is difficult for
you and practice it until it becomes a way of being. Once you
have some practice and skill at developing this skill, add another
one and begin practicing it until you are in the habit of practicing
all of them.
- Identify which of the norms described in this chapter you think
will be helpful in your organization? What's missing that you'd like
to add?

14

Strategies for Engaging
When You Offend

WHEN ILL-INFORMED White people engage in conversations about racism, they are drawing conclusions about racism from their very narrow perspective. How they know what they know will come from the news they watch, what other White people have told them, or by comparing their own experiences of marginalization. How PoC know what they know will derive from their own experiences, incidents occurring with friends and families, what others have taught them, research, literature, media, and other sources. Because of the different ways racial groups have come to understand racism, cross-cultural conversations between White people and PoC are frequently emotionally charged. It is common to experience avoiding, lashing out, minimizing, othering, blaming, and shaming behaviors from both groups. It also means that White people offend PoC a lot!

Effective race discourse requires listening and trying to understand a situation from the perspective of the marginalized group rather than the privileged. My husband is African American, over 6'5", has dark skin, and has been in sales for most of his life. And though I'm not happy about it, he has only taken three workshops on diversity in his life, and two of them were led by me. He is in his 60s, so I doubt at this point there is much I can do about his lack of training. While I have studied racism, facilitate workshops several times a week, and am writing this book on the topic, he will sometimes see racism where I don't. These are those moments when I'm stopped in my tracks with another aha moment, recognizing the privileges my skin color afford me.

One day we were in the mall walking through Macy's. A White woman was walking toward us with the insert of a cash register in the crook of her arm. There is a second where we all made eye contact at the exact same time. In that instant, she grasped the register with both arms. My husband leaned down and whispered, "*Did you see that?*" I instantly thought to myself, "*Now come on Gary. You don't think she thinks you're going to rob her, we're in Macy's.*" And because these thoughts only take a split second to enter our minds, I also thought, "*You know Gary, it could have been a coincidence.*" To this day I still believe it could have been a coincidence. My husband and I have been married over twenty years, I'm a psychologist, I know how to preserve a marriage. So rather than say what I was thinking, I simply responded with "*Yes, I saw that.*"

My response bothered me for a while. I continued to contemplate why I essentially agreed with him when really, I disagreed. Eventually I came to realize that when he asked "*Did you see that?*", it didn't matter what was happening in that moment. It doesn't matter if it was a coincidence, if her arm was tired, or if she was stereotyping my husband. This is not the point nor is it something that can easily be proved. If I had been so bold as to walk up to her and say, "*Excuse me ma'am, we were just wondering if you might have been stereotyping my husband as a dangerous Black man?*" How might she have responded? "*No of course not, I dated a Black guy once.*" She's not likely to have been aware if she were stereotyping.

Without being aware of it, I said to my husband, "*Yes, I saw that,*" to convey to him an understanding that he is frequently profiled by White women as a threat. It was less about whether his race was playing out in that very moment and more about acknowledging the way in which White women often view Black men, i.e., dangerous, threatening, untrustworthy. No one has ever crossed the street when they saw me coming. I have never in my life experienced a White woman clutch her purse when I walked by. I have never stepped onto an elevator and had a White woman tense up. Even though, between the two of us, I'm the one people should be afraid of, these things don't happen to me. But because these are not my personal experiences doesn't make them untrue for him.

Whenever I have shared this story when facilitating workshops, there are two common responses from White people. Some will say, "*Well maybe it's his height that caused the woman to feel afraid.*" I don't disagree with this thought. We know the stature of a man, regardless of race, can cause women to feel intimidated. The most frequent response I hear is, "*Maybe it's his gender that caused the woman to put the register in both arms.*" I also don't disagree that gender differences can elicit fear in women. But what if it was true? What if race did matter? What if my husband was being racially profiled? One thing that is tiresome for PoC is engaging White people who are willing to recognize class, gender, and other groups marginalized experiences but will refuse to acknowledge that racism is real. They come up with any reason other than race as a possibility.

It's not just the right-wing conservative who is resistant; it's also White people who see themselves as good, kind, loving, moral, ethical liberals. And it's the latter that produces the most fatigue for PoC. Leaning into the racial realities that exist for PoC surface guilt and shame in White people. I believe it is from a sense of goodness that they begin to feel bad. To avoid these feelings, they make it about something else. If they allowed themselves to see the world through a racial lens, in order to maintain how they view themselves, they would have to advocate for change. You cannot be a good, kind, loving, moral, ethical person and ignore injustices right in front of you.

The next three chapters are strategies to assist you during those times when you are the one who offends, you are offended, or you witness an offense. Just as with the norms in the previous chapter, these strategies are for the 80% and those on the far right in your organization who may be defensive but are also more open to learning. Though these strategies are listed for specific scenarios, keep in mind that any of the ideas shared can be used in any of the situations. For example, apologize is described under "When You Offend," however, you may need to apologize if you were the one offended, or who witnessed an offense if you handled it poorly. They are grouped where they commonly fit, but there is no set rule. Also, at the end of Chapter 16 (Strategies for Engaging when you Witness an Offense), additional strategies are included to help you in your skill development.

When You Offend

When it comes to race conversations, typically it is White people who most often offend PoC, usually in the form of microaggressions. However, it is not uncommon for PoC to offend other PoC within their own racial group and other racial groups. Regardless of your race, no matter how long you've been doing this work, how many strategies you've practiced, or how much knowledge you hold, you will offend. So, when you do, you will need to have some strategies in place for leaning into the conversation. No strategy is easy. Like with the norms, they may sound simple as you read them, but they are not. There will be times when you find yourself stumbling, rambling, and sometimes even making things worse. Each time you offend, learn from it, and try again.

Listen and Believe

The first step to effectively engaging when you have offended is to listen to what the person is telling you and believe it as their truth without defending yourself. Like the situation in Macy's with my husband, Gary, don't reveal your thoughts as to why you think the other person's perspective is wrong. Unlike the workshop participants who tried to make it about his height or gender, don't make it about something else. Give the person you offended the opportunity to share their experience while showing you are listening, believing, and doing your best to understand. When PoC engage White people, much of the problems stem from White people not believing our experiences. Showing you are listening and believing can be done by simply nodding your head, eye contact, inserting a word or two in between the conversation ("um hum," "yeah," "yes," "I hear you") and by just being silent.

While it can be extremely uncomfortable to hear how you've done harm, displaying an openness to listening encourages the person to continue sharing. It does not mean you agree with what is being said, you are, however, recognizing how it landed on them.

Invite Feedback on Impact

When you offend someone from a marginalized group, like the norm Listen for Understanding (see Chapter 13), focus on your impact rather than your intent. You should essentially be saying, "*Tell me more about the harm I did to you.*" When I offend, I call them "*Hurt so good moments.*" It hurts to know I've offended you, but it's good you told me so I can learn from it. You need to show the person you offended that you are genuinely curious about what you did that was offensive by asking questions that seek to understand. After all, if you didn't know it was offensive, now's a good time to find out how and why.

Even if you instantly realize how and why it was harmful, you can still focus on your impact. This gives the person harmed the opportunity to process what they are feeling, feel heard, and enhances your learning. It can also help to repair the relationship.

Learning Conversation Stems: Inviting Feedback

- Can you say more about what you mean by _____?
- I'm not sure I'm understanding you clearly. Are you saying _____?
- Is it when I said _____ that was offensive, or was it something else?
- Have I ever done something like this before? What made you decide to open up and take the risk to share this with me? I imagine it wasn't easy.
- I'm really trying to understand. What are your thoughts if I would have worded it this way?
- I'm still struggling with understanding _____ would you mind sharing _____?

The person who was impacted is likely to have many thoughts and feelings tied to your offense based on numerous experiences, not just the one that occurred with you. Be prepared that they may not convey it in a way that makes you feel comfortable hearing it. Create space for whatever emotions come up for them. This doesn't mean the person harmed has the right to dehumanize you, call you names, or intentionally hurt. It does mean, however, that their feelings of anger, frustration, or hurt is normal. When this is the case, focus on the message not their affect. Try and remain open and curious and avoid fixing statements (discussed in Chapter 13) or tone policing, e.g., *"You could have said it more nicely"* or *"You don't have to get so upset"* or *"If you just calm down, we can talk about it rationally."* Tone policing is an experience PoC have when engaging White people around the harm they did. It tells PoC how they need to talk to the White person, and it typically centers on White cultural communication norms, values, and beliefs.

On the following page is a chart outlining two different directions a conversation can go when the focus is on impact and intent.

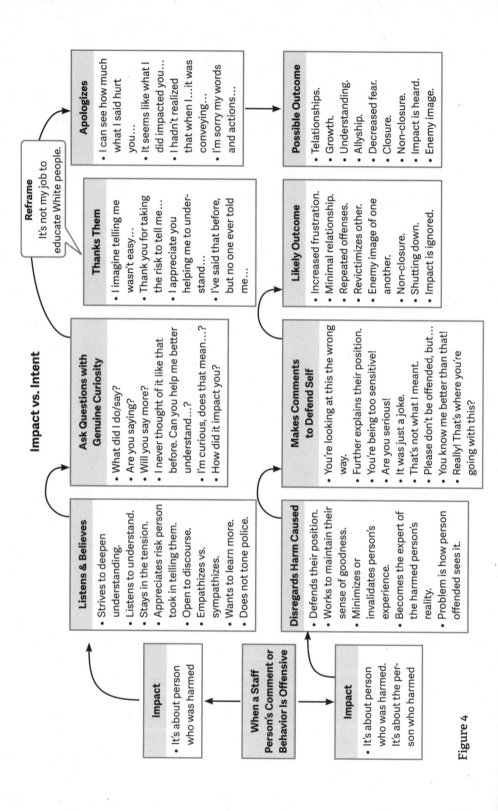

Impact vs. Intent

Reframe
It's not my job to educate White people.

When a Staff Person's Comment or Behavior Is Offensive

Impact
- It's about person who was harmed

Impact
- It's about person who was harmed.
- It's about the person who harmed

Listens & Believes
- Strives to deepen understanding.
- Listens to understand.
- Stays in the tension.
- Appreciates risk person took in telling them.
- Open to discourse.
- Empathizes vs. sympathizes.
- Wants to learn more.
- Does not tone police.

Disregards Harm Caused
- Defends their position.
- Works to maintain their sense of goodness.
- Minimizes or invalidates person's experience.
- Becomes the expert of the harmed person's reality.
- Problem is how person offended sees it.

Ask Questions with Genuine Curiosity
- What did I do/say?
- Are you saying?
- Will you say more?
- I never thought of it like that before. Can you help me better understand...?
- I'm curious, does that mean...?
- How did it impact you?

Makes Comments to Defend Self
- You're looking at this the wrong way.
- Further explains their position.
- You're being too sensitive!
- Are you serious!
- It was just a joke.
- That's not what I meant.
- Please don't be offended, but...
- You know me better than that!
- Really! That's where you're going with this?

Thanks Them
- I imagine telling me wasn't easy...
- Thank you for taking the risk to tell me...
- I appreciate you helping me to understand...
- I've said that before, but no one ever told me...

Apologizes
- I can see how much what I said hurt you...
- It seems like what I did impacted you...
- I hadn't realized that when I...it was conveying...
- I'm sorry my words and actions...

Likely Outcome
- Increased frustration.
- Minimal relationship.
- Repeated offenses.
- Revictimizes other.
- Enemy image of one another.
- Non-closure.
- Shutting down.
- Impact is ignored.

Possible Outcome
- Relationships.
- Growth.
- Understanding.
- Allyship.
- Decreased fear.
- Closure.
- Non-closure.
- Impact is heard.
- Enemy image.

Figure 4

Thank Them

Though it won't feel like it in the moment, when someone tells you how you've impacted them, it is a gift. They didn't have to divulge how you hurt or harmed them, so when they do, appreciate that they took a risk by telling you. They may be risking their job when telling someone in a position of power that they've offended. With their colleagues and friends, there is a risk of losing the relationship. In addition, when PoC tells a White person they've offended, e.g., committed a microaggression or said something racist, they also risk the offending person making it about the way they are looking at it, being seen as the angry PoC, and having their voice marginalized.

So let them speak their truth. Once they have had an opportunity to offer you feedback, and you've listened and asked questions for better understanding, thank them. State specifically what was helpful and any new learning that occurred because of the gift they gave you.

Apologize

Now it's time to apologize. A sincere apology requires your knowing what you are apologizing for. It includes conveying back to the person you harmed any insight and understanding you gained from the courageous conversation they had with you. Simply saying, *"I'm sorry,"* or apologizing as soon as the person tells you that you've offended them—without listening to why or how it was offensive—can feel shallow to the person harmed. Immediate apologies typically convey you want to quickly end the conversation and are unwilling to sit in the discomfort and tension.

Apologies like *"I'm sorry you feel that way"* blame the person offended for feeling upset that you've harmed them. Adding the word *but* after the apology followed by a statement—e.g., *"I'm sorry I said what I did, but I was frustrated at the time"*—conveys it wasn't your fault, it was theirs for frustrating you. It also justifies the behavior. Make sure when you apologize, the person feels you were listening, you understand, and you mean it.

Learn More

I once heard my business partner Ilsa Govan ask participants in a room, "How will you allow yourselves to be changed by the story (PoC) just shared?" It's a powerful question and one I now ask of others and myself. Over the years, I have hurt many people while trying to lead DEIB work. I've come to realize that my learning always comes at someone else's expense. While there is little I can do once the harm is done, that doesn't mean that I can't be different moving forward. I can, and you can too. As stated before, whatever you learn from the person you harmed, do some research to grow your understanding rather than relying solely on what you learned from them. Find multiple sources to enhance your learning. The more you understand, the more likely you won't make the same mistake.

Take Action and Advocate

Talk to other people about what you've learned so they can avoid adding another cut to an already painful wound. People are often more open to learning when they aren't offending in the moment. If what you learned is common practice or policy within your workplace or community, advocate for change. For example, if you no longer say nonwhite when referring to PoC because you learned it centers the conversation around White people, share your learning with others in your organization and change the language in documents.

Listen and Believe, Invite Feedback, Thank Them, Apologize, Learn More, and Take Action and Advocate are a series of steps you can take when you offend. The situation won't always require you do each one of these steps, and it's certainly not the only strategy, but it is one way to get the conversation going in a way that is more likely to leave the person you offended feeling like you care.

15

Strategies for Engaging
When Someone Offends You

ONE OF THE MORE CHALLENGING things about being an Equity Leader of Color is that you will experience microaggressions while trying to make change in your organization. It is not easy to lead when you are also a frequent target. Personally, I am better at engaging when I have done the offending than when I am the one being offended. Early on in my role as an Equity Leader, I tended to lean more toward reacting when offended rather than responding. My reacting was usually in the form of lashing out. If you are like I was, when you are offended, old wounds are resurfacing, and before you know it, you have lost emotional control and end up harming the person who harmed you. For me it wouldn't be until after I had time to gather myself that I would realize I've made things worse rather than better. On top of everything, the other person was able to make my reaction the focus rather than why I reacted the way I did. When you experience racism, you want the conversation to end in a way that has the other person lying awake at night, not you. Though White people can use the strategies in this chapter, it is geared toward PoC. It provides you with strategies to help train your brain to respond in new ways rather than allowing your old brain to react out of hurt, anger, or frustration. The following strategies are not in any order. Some will be more helpful than others, depending on your level of comfort with each one and what most closely fits your style.

Stop, Take a Breath (STAB)

In *What's Up with White Women: Unpacking Sexism and White Privilege in Pursuit of Racial Justice*, Govan and Smith refer to the STAB acronym that they and their colleague MG came up with. It's a simple way to remember to breathe in triggering moments. Hopefully, you don't find yourself so angry you feel like stabbing the other person. Instead, Stop and Take a Breath.

Mindful breathing slows your heart rate and creates a calming experience as oxygen is released into your brain. Try it. Place both feet flat on the ground, sit up straight, and lean your back against your chair. Relax your arms and shoulders. Close your mouth and take a deep breath inhaling through your nose while slowly counting to four. Now hold your breath while counting to four again. Slowly exhale through your mouth while counting to ten. Repeat this three times. Can you feel yourself calm? If not, try it a couple more times and practice during triggering moments standing up or sitting down. The great thing is you can practice this 4-10-4 breathing exercise, and no one has to know.

Ask Questions with Genuine Curiosity

When PoC begin to share with White people what it's like for them as a PoC, it's common for White people to offend by inserting their own experiences of marginalization into the conversation which will have nothing to do with race. Before the Me Too Movement, I referred to this as the "*Me Too Phenomenon.*" White people will take this approach to either connect with the PoC, by suggesting they understand, "*I know what you mean, I grew up poor,*" or to deflect from the PoC experiences, "*I grew up poor, and I made it.*"

When White people interject their "*Me Too*" experience into the conversation, regardless of the reason, it leaves PoC feeling unheard, minimized, and invalidated. This can quickly lead to the PoC feeling angry and frustrated. As a result, the PoC may try to further educate the naïve White person or share additional stories of racism to convince them of the differences and the fact that racism is real. On the other hand, the PoC may shut down altogether, tired of educating White people, and doubtful talking about it will make a difference.

Not only can questioning with curiosity open dialogue but it can also help the offender think more deeply about their words. Imagine a PoC and White woman are talking. The PoC shares an experience she's had around race. The White woman responds by saying, "*I understand, I grew up poor.*" There was probably no ill intent in the White woman's comparison of class and race. She may have simply been trying to connect. Regardless of intent, the Woman of Color becomes offended because the White woman has invalidated her racial experiences by making their experiences out to be the same when they are not.

Of all the strategies, asking questions with genuine curiosity is the most effective because it opens dialogue between people rather than shutting conversation down. Like all the strategies in this book, no single approach will work every time. It's essential you put as many tools in your backpack as you can. The secret to this strategy's success is to ask questions with *genuine* curiosity. Not easy to do after a White person has committed a microaggression or some other offense towards a PoC. Saying to your child "*Now do you know why I told you not to run in the house?*" is technically a question, but it isn't asked with genuine curiosity. You aren't curious as to whether your child understands why running in the house is dangerous and therefore not permissible. Likely you told your child over and over to stop running. When they run in the house and hurt themselves, it becomes an opportunity for you to prove your point.

As a PoC leading equity work, when you encounter situations where you are offended, it can become an opportunity to help the other person grow. While you may be tempted to immediately educate them on what they did wrong, that approach leaves the person who experienced the offense having to do all the work. However, if you ask questions with genuine curiosity, it puts the responsibility on the person who offended to do most of the work. Through your questions, they are called in to reexamine the impact of their words and actions. Following are some examples of Conversation Stems to help PoC help White people do their own work.

**Learning Conversation Stems for People of Color:
Ask Questions with Genuine Curiosity**

- What do you mean when you say "*I understand*"?
- Help me understand how you see them as being the same?
- What is your understanding about the differences between race and poverty?
- Repeat a key word or statement they've said and wait in silence for a response. "*You don't notice differences?*"

- I'm not sure I'm understanding what it is you want me to know or understand about you when you tell me *"You grew up poor."* I wasn't talking about class.
- Help me understand how race and poverty are the same in your mind?
- I understand you have Children of Color and that it gives you some insight. What I'm unclear about is how having children who are Black is the same as being Black.

What's most challenging about this strategy is determining what questions to ask. Open-ended questions tend to work best in getting the dialogue going. Close-ended questions allow the person to respond with yes or no answers, require no effort on their part, and will end the conversation quickly. Remember, the purpose of this strategy is to open dialogue so the person who offended develops insight about the impact of their words and grows in their understanding of racism. Your first few questions may fall flat and not take the conversation very far initially. Keep trying. The more questions you ask, the more the conversation gets going. The more the conversation unfolds, the more naturally your questions will flow.

It would be great if these types of things weren't common encounters PoC have with White people. Imagine how differently the conversation would go if instead the White woman asked questions with genuine curiosity about the Woman of Color's racial experiences rather than inserting her own class experiences into the dialogue.

Learning Conversation Stems for White People:
Ask Questions with Genuine Curiosity

- What's that like for you?
- How does it impact you emotionally?
- How do you cope with it?
- What would you like to have happened instead?
- I can't imagine what that must have felt like. Are you OK?

Share Impact

Sharing the impact of another person's words or actions can be risky for PoC. When they share impact, they risk having their voice further marginalized if the offending person tries to defend themselves. On the other hand, if the White person has no idea what or how they have offended and if they are genuinely open to learning, when impact is specified, they are more likely to take what you share to heart.

Learning Conversation Stems:
Sharing Impact

- When I'm followed around the store suspected of being a thief, it's not because the salesclerk sees me as poor. It's because I'm Black. When I didn't do anything wrong and yet I'm thrown to the ground in the mall, it isn't because I'm seen as not having money. It's because I'm Black. It frustrates me when you and other White people view racism and classism as the same. What are you implying?

- I realize I'm reacting to your use of the word "*same.*" It's something I commonly hear White people saying in race conversations. I know what it's like to grow up without money, and I know what it's like to be a Latina woman in this country. There are significant differences. When you say you "*understand,*" it minimizes racism and makes me feel like you're not open to hearing my experiences. What did you mean by "*same*"?

- I don't know if you intended it this way, but when I hear you say you understand because you grew up poor, it seems like you're saying, "*White people who grew up poor understand what it's like to experience racism.*" They are two very different things. I can have money, but because I'm Black, White people assume I don't belong in the neighborhood I live in. I guess I don't understand why you are comparing the two.

- Maybe you didn't mean it that way, but as soon as you said you understand, it made me feel like shutting down. It sounded like you're saying you know what it's like to be in my skin. What are you saying?

It's not fair that PoC should have to find ways to carefully strategize so they are heard, and so their experiences of racism are taken seriously. I don't always do this well, and truth be told, in my personal life, I'm often exhausted from having to work so hard to find ways to meet White people where they are. If you are a PoC reading this and feel this is more than you are willing to take on, go back to your *why* for this work. White people play a critical role in dismantling racism. See your engagement with them as a part of your work as a Racial Equity Leader. What am I saying? Learning to engage White people is the work. Or at least an important part of it. It's far easier to lash out or avoid when White people offend than it is to engage. Unfortunately, these are challenges PoC still must endure, even in the twenty-first century.

Build a Platform

Building a Platform (also referred to as setting the stage) is a helpful technique for more difficult conversations.[1] It can serve to inform the other person how much what you are about to share matters to you. Some of you are likely to use this strategy naturally, having no idea there is a name for it.

When my daughter, Makena, was about six or seven, she would sometimes say, "*Mommy, I want to tell you something, but I'm worried you'll get mad at me.*" She was building a platform without knowing it. She was telling me what she was worried would happen if she told me what happened. She conveyed her fears first. If I wasn't the type of parent that got mad, I would see this as manipulative. If I thought I was being manipulated, I'd be doubly mad. But because there was truth in her worry (I do tend to get mad), it made me mindful of my behavior. Because I care about her and didn't want her to grow up seeing me as a parent who always reacted with anger, her worry caused me to pay attention to how I handled the situation rather than respond automatically.

A platform can be long or short depending on the level of your fears, how much the offense bothers you, and the relationship between you and the person you are engaging. There are three parts to this strategy. First, name your fears or worries. (What do you worry will happen if you share your concern with the other person?) Second, build a bridge. This is a statement that bridges the gap between your worry and the thing they did wrong. If you worry or fear, e.g., they will become defensive, then why are you telling them? Third, tell them what they said or did and why it impacted you. Below are examples of platforms. The italicized sentence is an example of the bridge statement that sits between naming your worries and the problem.

Examples for Building a Platform

- Out of everyone we work with, you are the only White person I feel close to. I've been wanting to talk with you for a while about something but have been hesitant. I've worried it will create tension in our relationship if I were to be honest with you. However, *I realize one of the reasons I feel close to you is because I can talk with you about racism. If I'm not truthful, then I'm not really being a friend.* I need to trust you'll be able to hear what I have to say. (Then share what they did or said and wait for their response.)

- Because you're my supervisor, it's difficult to talk with you about this. You have power and authority so it's hard for me to trust that if I tell you what's been bothering me, it won't end up being reflected in my performance review. *However, I realize by not telling you, I'm not giving you the opportunity to explain or even correct the situation, and that's not fair to you.* (Then share what they did or said and wait for their response.)

- Something you said earlier has been on my mind. I've thought about whether I should tell you. In the past when I've talked to White people about racism, they've become defensive and made it about the way I was looking at the situation, rather than trying to understand the impact from my point of view. *I realize that not all White people are the same and not every White person has responded with their good intensions, and so I decided to take the risk and tell you.* (Then share what they did or said and wait for their response.)

The above examples may not be something you would say, but hopefully you get the point. Building a Platform is one of the more vulnerable strategies. Depending on the situation and how much you are willing to reveal, it can leave you feeling like you turned yourself inside out. If you tell the person your fears and they do the very thing you worried would happen, you will likely wish you never revealed your thoughts and feelings. To help you get a sense of how this strategy works, practice in low-stake situations first. Also, keep in mind African Americans tend to be more direct in their style of communicating. If you are speaking to someone who shares this cultural style, it can feel to them like you are beating around the bush. They will want you to just get to the point. This indirect approach can cause them to feel frustrated with how long you are taking to speak what's on your mind.

Try to be as vulnerable as you can. It will look different for everyone. When you do, include letting the person know how hard it is to talk about the issue, how much thought you've put into it, and your fears about what you worry will happen due to voicing your concerns. The more honest you are, the more likely it is that the offender will see how much what they did or said matters to you. Though, unfortunately, there is never a guarantee when you take this type of risk.

16

Strategies for Engaging
When You Witness an Offense

WITNESSING IS LIKE BEING a bystander. You overhear someone doing or saying something offensive that is not directed at you. It could happen during a staff meeting, while walking down the hall, getting your lunch, standing in line at the grocery store, in virtual breakout groups, etc. It can be scary to interject, particularly when you are not originally a part of the conversation. When hearing someone do or say something you know is not OK, you will have to determine when to involve yourself and when not to. The quote "*Is my comfort more important than someone else's pain?*" may help to launch you into action. I don't know who said it, but this question helps me to get out of the way of justice and be an agent for change when I feel worried about how others may perceive me when I call them in. You can also ask yourself, "*Why am I not stepping in?*" If your answer is because you are tired and just want to enjoy the meal, you may need to give yourself that break. The more your equity lens develops, the more you will see all forms of isms everywhere you go. If you leaned in every time you witnessed an injustice, you'd be advocating nonstop. Just know that when it comes to isms, your silence is not silent. You're saying something, just not with your words.

If the answer to my earlier question as to why you are not stepping in is because you worry about how others will perceive you or not doing it perfectly, then take the risk and lean in. These are heart-palpitating moments in which you will play out a half dozen different outcomes in a matter of minutes. Keep in mind that if you don't do anything, you're actually doing something. When we avoid calling someone in, the silent message conveyed is that what they said or did was OK. Not only will you help shape the culture because of leaning into your discomfort, working to overcome your fears will bring about personal growth. Not only will you learn more about yourself and others, but you will also be able to practice turning strategies into skills.

I was at a Black owned and operated hair salon several years ago, sitting at the shampoo bowl while waiting for the dye to kick in. I haven't yet come to terms with the greying of my hair, so I head to the salon every few months to get it cut and colored. There was an older client sitting to the left of me when another client about my age joined us on my right. As we began talking, the woman on my right shared a conversation she recently had with her 10-year-old daughter.

> Nia told me to stop referring to a kid at her school as "she." She told me I'm supposed to say "they." I told her there is no "they"— there's "she" and "he," period.

I imagined when she shared this with us, she assumed because we are Black and maybe due to our ages, we'd agree with her point of view. This was one of those moments when I didn't want to say anything. I feared not being accepted. What if I said something and it created the awkward tension I so vividly remember as a child? What if she thought I thought that I was better than her? What if, what if, what if, someone else's pain became more important than my comfort.

So I leaned in with, "*I used to think that way too.*" I recall ever so gently explaining what I was taught about gender growing up and then shared my new understanding. To my surprise, the older woman joined in and agreed with me. (Note: Surprise is an emotion that surfaces when you have stereotyped someone. I had stereotyped the woman on my left as being too old to think in new ways.) As a result, all three of us engaged in a conversation about gender identity. In the end I think the person who made the comment shifted slightly in her thinking or at least some seeds may have been planted. At a minimum I was able to practice my skills, and the worst-case scenario did not play out.

This isn't always how courageous conversations end. But even if it doesn't go well, you've said something that hopefully has others thinking differently, and at the very least, you've let them know you disagree. On the other hand, if I just listened and didn't say anything, it is likely they would assume I agreed. While I didn't use the following strategies in my above example, it speaks to the idea that there is no one right way to have difficult conversations. When you hear or see something happening that is not OK, step up, lean in, and approach the conversation with humility.

Ask Questions with Genuine Curiosity

Asking questions when you witness an offense gives the person an opportunity to explain, clarify, or even correct themselves. Social justice allies and advocates are sometimes quick to react by jumping in to educate as soon as they hear an offending remark. It's as though they're thinking, "*I already know why you said what you said.*" Immediately educating someone can carry a tone of shaming and self-righteousness and can send the message "I'm good, you're bad." This often shuts the other person down.

Asking questions with genuine curiosity before educating invites the person who offended into conversation by calling them in rather than out. (I reserve calling out strategies for those who deliberately harm people from marginalized groups.) In the process of asking questions, you will gain insight into the other person's thinking. Once you have collected some information, you will better ascertain where they lack understanding and need educating. This is one way to meet people where they are at.

Learning Conversation Stems:
Ask Question with Genuine Curiosity

- Where did you learn that?
- What do you mean by _____?
- What are your thoughts about why some people may find that offensive?
- I'm trying to understand where you're coming from when you say _____. Will you say more?
- I couldn't help but overhear your conversation with Dina during lunch. When you said _____ should go back to where they came from if they don't like it here, what did you mean by that?
- I walked by just when you were telling Ned anyone should be able to say the N word. Why do you think that? Or, why would you want to say that word?
- What do you mean by "*they should get over it?*"

Connection Before Redirection

This is an opportunity to share a time when you thought that same way, made similar comments, or offended someone from a marginalized group. This approach can lower the other person's defenses by conveying that you are learning too, and that you too have said or done offensive things. It requires your showing humility. It can communicate you are truly invested in their learning and don't want them to continue making the same mistakes, particularly with someone who may not be as gracious as you are trying to be.

Whenever I'm driving and I've done something on the road that I shouldn't have, I hate it when another driver lays on the horn. It's as if they are saying, "*Hey idiot, can't you see the light's turned green!*" or "*Don't you know how to drive?*" It's as if, in all their years of driving, the other driver has never done improper road etiquette. Approach these conversations as if you are saying, yes, me too. You're not the only one who is learning or who has gotten it wrong.

Educate Them

After asking questions, you should have a better sense as to whether they were intentional in using harmful words. If they meant to do harm, and know why it is harmful, call them out on it. Let them know it wasn't OK and set boundaries. However, if like many of us, they had little understanding of their impact, thought they were being funny, or were speaking without thinking, take the opportunity to educate them. Your insight gained from asking questions provides an opportunity for you to help shift their thinking even if it's just planting seeds. Educate them about what you understand about the issue and how you came to understand it the way you do.

Thank Them

When you were the one who committed the offense, you thanked them for their willingness to tell you. When you witness the offense, you are thanking the person involved for staying engaged in a difficult conversation. Even if the person doesn't seem open, try to find something to appreciate about their engagement. Thanking them is not only appreciating the conversation but also about reinforcing positive behaviors.

> **Learning Conversation Stems: Thank Them**
> - Thank you for staying curious, even though I imagine it was difficult at times to hear.
> - I appreciate how open you remained in the conversation. Many people become defensive when told they've done something offensive, including me sometimes.
> - I'm grateful to you for really trying to understand why what you said was offensive. I know from experience it's often not easy to do.
> - Thank you for hearing me out. I wish more people were open to learning.
> - Some people will turn their cameras off when the conversation gets challenging, particularly when they are the focus of discussion. Thank you for doing your best to remain open to what I was trying to help you understand.

As said many times before, there's no guarantee any of these strategies will work. Sometimes they will, and sometimes they won't. These are just additional strategies meant to aid you in your skill development as you practice engaging in courageous conversations about race. Whether you commit, experience, or witness an offense, the central idea is to try and work through the tension. The strategies in Chapters 14, 15, 16 are, of course, adaptive, and while they may be grouped under certain sections, remember they can all be used in any given situation, and not just with race.

Calling People Out

Typically, intentional offensive comments are made by friends, family, and even strangers you interact with who think it's OK to tell you exactly what they think of *those* people. There are plenty of people who are perfectly fine with making hurtful and hateful comments and who, since the last major election in the US, have recently become more emboldened spewing racist, sexist, antisemitic, and homophobic thoughts. This book is not written for how to engage them. In other words, I'm not suggesting you call people in or ask questions with genuine curiosity when they know what they are doing or saying is not OK. What I do recommend is that you call them out and set boundaries.

Several summers ago, my husband learned that a friend he hadn't seen since high school was visiting Seattle for the first time with his wife. Gary asked if we could have them over to our home. I'm an extremely busy person in a public role, and so entertaining rarely appeals to me. I don't want to clean my house, I'm not interested in learning how to prepare gluten-free meals, and frankly I have red wine in my home, not white. But Gary seldom asks this of me, so I agreed.

After a few moments of general introductions, the friend's wife and I went out on the patio where we could get to know one another while our husbands talked. I ended up having a really great time getting to know her to the point where I thought, "*Why don't I do this more often?*" I appreciated the visit and realized how nice it was to just sit and relax in good company.

We eventually went into the house and joined our husbands at the dinner table. We easily fell into common Black cultural norms of engaging. At times there were two different conversations happening at once, and our voices would rise as we laughed, talked over, and interrupted one another. Suddenly, I couldn't believe my ears, "*Did my new friend just say something about Asian people?*" Maybe I wasn't hearing her correctly because I have no idea what led up to this.

My new brain started kicking in. "*You gotta say something!*" "*What do I say?*" "*How do I say it?*" Before I could say anything, the opportunity had passed. Maybe I heard her wrong. We were having such a good time. Why did she think it was OK to say these things in front of me? Maybe it was the wine, who knows? But then she said it again. This time I was ready. In a calm voice, I said, "*You know, there are people who will say negative things about Black people too.*" This was my attempt at getting her to think about the adage that two wrongs don't make a right.

Unfortunately, it didn't work. She immediately replied, "*I don't care what people say about Black people.*" Her husband was across from me. I vaguely heard him saying something to the effect of, "*She always talks about Asian people*" as if to tell me not to get upset or take it too seriously.

We all continued talking, and before I knew it, she started moving her hands toward her eyes to pull them back in the same way elementary school children do to mock Asians. Before she could get her hands to her eyes, I threw my hand out inches from her face bringing her gesture to a stop, and with a firm voice said, "*Uh, yeah, you're not going to want to do that with me!*" Everyone went silent. I quickly got up and went to the kitchen. Gary knew what that meant. Follow me. I started rapidly speaking at him without pausing, "*Who does that? Did you see that? Oh, my goodness, I can't believe it. Am I imagining things?*" Keep in mind my house is not very big, I'm quite certain they were able to hear us. We then walked back in the dining room to join them and continued with another conversation as if nothing had happened.

When my subtle attempt at letting her know what she said was not OK failed, I resorted to a more assertive approach. It wasn't easy for me given all my fears. But I acted on my core values, no longer caring what she thought, or if it was ruining a great time, or if she left my home feeling I wasn't a good host. Someone else's pain, in this case the racism Asians experience, became more important than any fears I held.

When I share this story, some people will ask, "*Didn't she know about the work you do?*" I'm sure I had told her. However, when people share the same identity as you do, they may believe it's OK to let lose in inappropriate ways, especially when no one from the group being targeted is in the room. Other times people will ask, "*Why didn't you try to educate her?*" I didn't call her in because it was clear she already knew what she was doing wasn't OK. She needed to be called out. I don't hold ill feelings toward her. I just needed her to know "*I'm not for play play*"[1] when it comes to putting people down because of their differences. She eventually understood I'm not the one to behave that way in front of, so we were able to move on.

There will be times in this work when trying to engage people in courageous conversations is not the best approach. In situations like the one I just described, the best you may be able to do is set boundaries by calling someone out on their words and actions. Setting boundaries lets the offending person know you disagree, are not going to allow those things said in your presence, and that you don't find joking at someone else's expense funny. When calling people out, share your thoughts firmly, and when you ask questions, do it in a way that lets them know you are not really asking. The last thing you want to do with people who are not open to learning is to try and engage. You are likely to end up in tears or increasingly frustrated.

Stop trying to educate people who refuse to learn. I imagine you may have already tried before and discovered it doesn't work. When people know what they are doing is wrong, they find spaces where it is acceptable or, at the very least, tolerated. You are wasting your time thinking "*Maybe if I said it this way or that way, they would change their thinking.*" It's not that you are not doing a good job or that it's your approach that is lacking. It's them.

And stop saying people are too old to learn. You are making excuses for them. There is no age at which people stop learning. If your grandparents can operate a cell phone, they can learn. In these moments, be clear about what is nonnegotiable and set boundaries by conveying, in a matter-of-fact way, that saying _____ around you is unacceptable. When your colleague makes disparaging remarks about *those* people, let them know those types of remarks are not permitted in our workplace and what will happen if he/she/they continue. As you do practice leaning in, remember, this is what it means to advocate for racial justice.

Learning Conversation Stems: Calling People Out
- I don't find that funny.
- If you continue saying things about _____, we are going to have to leave.
- What makes you think that's OK to say in my presence?
- That's a very hurtful thing to do.
- That's racist!

Naming the Elephant

There were many times, in my past profession as a therapist, that I worked with clients who held different identities from me. Whether it be due to their age, race, gender, sexual orientation, religion, ability, class, etc., or some combination of these, I knew it was imperative to engage them in conversation about our differences if therapy were to progress. It is difficult to know when to talk about these differences. Do I name them immediately, wait until I sense tension, or when differences appear to be getting in the way of our work together?

Right after graduating, I started working for a mental health organization. One of my roles was to facilitate a grandparents' group. This was a group of about twenty grandparents, primarily African American, who were raising their grandchildren. We met in the evenings once a week. Initially I was excited about working with them. After about the third meeting, I started to dread going. Things were not progressing as I had hoped. I could easily sense we lacked a connection with one another. They would not trust me with their stories, and I was doing all the work.

One day I decided to take risk and name the elephant in the room. I was already uncomfortable, and things weren't progressing as I had hoped, so I figured it was worth the risk of naming what I thought might be getting in our way. During our fourth meeting, I opened the conversation by asking, "*What has it been like for you having me come into this room each week with a doctorate degree, no children of my own, telling you how to raise your grandchildren, when you've raised children who are probably my age?*" I don't recall what they said in response. I can only tell you everything shifted from that moment on. It was like a bubble popped. The tension immediately went out of the room. It was as if they had been saying, "*We won't trust you until you show us that you are worthy of being trusted with our stories. If you won't be courageous and name some truths, why should we share with you the painful parts of our lives?*"

I have applied this same strategy in other therapeutic settings as well as in my role as a facilitator, and I can't recall a time it hasn't worked. You will feel afraid to the name the dynamics of your differences. You will concern yourself with the possibility of suggesting something that the other person isn't feeling or thinking. You will worry you will make things worse. But if you're willing to take risk, you'll also discover you have gained the person's respect by showing your ability to talk about difficult things. The worst thing that can happen is the person will become confused as to why you are bringing up something that isn't a concern for them.

> ### Learning Conversation Stems: Naming the Elephant
> - I'm wondering what it's like for you to have someone who is White talking to you about your experiences as a PoC in this organization. I can't help but wonder if it's difficult for you to trust me with your experiences?
> - As a White woman, I've come to understand some of the reasons it isn't easy for PoC to trust us. It makes sense to me, given the

harm we have done past and present. My guess is it will take time for you to be able to share openly and honestly about your experiences in our organization.

- I'm sensing some tension between us. As a light skin Black woman who has racial privilege, I'm wondering if you might be worried that I've adopted White cultural norms as the standard, making it hard to believe I'm concerned about your experiences.

- It seems like every time I turn on the news or look at social media, there's another situation where a Black person has been murdered or a White person has called the police on them while they're just living their lives. Now here I am, a White man who shares the same identity with White people who have done harm, asking you to have courageous conversations with me about the situation that occurred last week. I imagine that can't be easy.

- Given that there are so few Students of Color here at Brown Elementary, I imagine you must have some concerns about your child's experience here. Would you be open to sharing what it's been like for you and Jordan?

- I recognize not only am I a White woman but that I also hold a lot of power in my position in our company. So, asking you to talk about your racial experiences may feel risky. I respect any hesitation you may have in talking with me, and at the same time, I hope to develop a relationship with you enough for you to trust that I take racism very seriously.

- I don't expect that just because I'm also a PoC that you will automatically trust that I have your best interest at heart. I recognize there are many instances where PoC have been in leadership positions and made decisions for their own gains.

How you approach these conversations will be adaptive not technical. A lot will depend on your role, relationship, your race, their race, their experiences of racism, and the environment you work in. Though not easy, try not to ramble through your anxiety as you speak. Pause for silence and allow for the other person or group to respond. You will have to use your own best judgment on when to use this strategy. The above examples are meant to give you a sense of what talking about the dynamics of difference might sound like.

Circle Back Around

Circling Back Around can be used when you make thing worse in your first attempt or when you need more time to think clearly about your response. When the conversation becomes heated, it gives both people the opportunity to cool down, reflect on how they each handled the situation, collect their thoughts, and then revisit the conversation later in a way that is responsive rather than reactive. Talking with a friend or colleague who you can process the situation with is a great way to critically reflect on how you are feeling and ways to engage. Find a critical friend who can help you discern what the other person's issues are and what are yours. This way when you engage, you won't own what you're not responsible for. Circling Back Around can happen minutes, hours, days, or even weeks later, depending on you, the other person, and the situation.

Learning Conversation Stems: Circle Back Around

- When you shared with me that I had offended you, I didn't say much at the time because I didn't know what to say. Now that I've had some time to think about it, I realize...
- When you said my joke was hurtful, I reacted defensively. I didn't give you the time to explain. My apologies for not doing a better job of listening. I'm wondering if you would be open to talking with me about it again.
- Our initial conversation didn't go so well. I realize that I was triggered and so wasn't open in the moment to hearing my impact on you. I want to try again. If you are still willing to share, I'd like to better understand...
- I appreciate your taking the risk to share with me how what was problematic about my choice of words. I've been thinking about it some more and realize...
- When we were talking, I said it made sense to me why what I did was cultural appropriation. I was nervous at the time and said I understood when I really didn't. I did some research and now have a better understanding of how my actions were harmful to Indigenous peoples. Would you be willing to talk about it some more?

Reflect on Identity Issues

This is a way to move forward after you've reacted poorly when the person harmed first brought it to your attention. This strategy requires your stepping back and critically reflecting on why you reacted the way you did and then owning that your response had more to do with you than anything they said or did. If you are left feeling embarrassed or ashamed about how you handled the situation, were highly defensive during the interaction, or find yourself searching for people who will take your side, it's likely you need to explore why this is. Reflecting on your identity issues is about being open and honest not only with the other person but with yourself.

It is not uncommon for people to react versus respond when initially being made aware of their harmful words, actions, or behaviors. Our reactions can often tie into experiences from our childhood, the ways we perceive ourselves, or how we want to be viewed by others. I know this has been the case for me on numerous occasions. After an incident that occurred with my teenage son, I reflected on my identity issues and came to realize I had been raising my children to be perfect. I was unconsciously driven by the desire to be seen by others as a *good* psychologist. In my mind, the proof was dependent upon my children's *good* behavior.

My insight came one day when I had lost emotional control with Matae during his sophomore year in high school. I was livid when he was late showing up after a game at the time I had told him to meet me. As I waited for him in the parking lot, every minute he was late, my anger grew. The moment he opened the car door, I unleashed my fury. My reaction felt over the top even to me, but while it was unraveling, I couldn't seem to stop myself. As I later reflected, I realized something deeper was going on—my need for him to be perfect. This insight gave me the opportunity not only to apologize but to explain to him what was going on for me and how unwarranted my reaction was. It wasn't OK for him to show up late, and at the same time, his lateness did not justify my excessive reaction. At fifteen, Matae had no trouble understanding once I explained. If I had not reflected on my identity issues and shared the deeper reason for the degree of my anger, he likely would have been left confused. My discernment also gave me the opportunity to shift in other ways I parented.

If you react defensively to someone telling you you've offended them, or you say or do something that is beyond what the situation necessitates, take some time to reflect on where it comes from and then share it with the person you offended. They will likely appreciate your openness and honesty if you don't do it to defend or justify your actions. Not only can it potentially repair the relationship, but the insight can also benefit you personally in the long run.

Learning Conversation Stems: Share Your Identity Issues

- (When you offend) I understand if you no longer want to talk with me about what happened between us the other day, but I would like to at least offer you a sincere apology for how I handled it. Growing up I would hear my dad using racial epithets about Asians. He was clearly racist in his thinking. Most of my life, I've tried to be different from him in that way. When you said that my asking you *"Where are you really from?"* was racist, I became angry and defensive. In my mind I heard you saying I was racist just like my dad. I'm sorry for shutting you down. I now realize you were not saying I was racist, but that my words were.

- (When you are offended) I owe you an apology. I was upset because I felt my experiences of racism were invalidated when you suggested that I just needed to change my attitude. It reminded me of other times my experiences have been invalidated, and I emitted my pent-up anger on to you. You didn't deserve to be called names. I apologize for calling you _____. It wasn't appropriate or fair.

Strategies for Engaging the Tension: Commitment to Change and Be Changed

- List three to four fears you have in talking about race. What do you worry will happen if you engage in these conversations? How do you fear being seen or labeled? What do you worry will happen? How is it different when at work, with family, or strangers?

- Reflect on a situation where you either committed, experienced, or witnessed an offense. It doesn't have to be related to race if you can't think of one. What went well? What didn't? Identify a strategy from this chapter that you used that led to it going well, or one you could have used that might have improved the interaction. Reflecting and identifying skills that worked or didn't work will help prepare you for the next time something similar happens.

- Think of a family member or friend who frequently makes inappropriate comments about other groups. Come up with an anchor, a statement you will be prepared to say the next time they make a similar comment. Remember, this isn't a lecture or an opportunity to educate. It's simply your setting boundaries about what they can't say or do in your presence.

17

I'm Not Passionate,
I'm Angry

WHEN PoC EXPRESS ANGER or lash out at their White coworkers when they are wronged by them, it's common for White people to focus on their emotions and *how* they engaged rather than being curious as to *why* they were angry or behaved the way they did. "*It's your tone.*" "*You made them feel unsafe.*" "*It's your attitude.*" In situations like these, the PoC is quickly perceived as the problem, and their voices and experiences are easily marginalized. PoC are then labeled the angry Black, Brown, Indigenous, or Asian in the office. When you focus on how a PoC engages rather than why, it can create a cycle where the PoC feels more anger, more frustration, and more hopelessness. It can also lead to their physical, emotional, and psychological disengagement from work. "*My heart just isn't in it anymore.*"

Supervisors, managers, and others in leadership positions often encounter race-related situations that need to be addressed immediately. I have observed organizations bring in diversity trainers, create DEIB initiatives, develop DEIB policies, and even hire a DEIB leader, but fail miserably at addressing racism in a timely and effective manner. It's as if leadership are unable to connect how their DEIB initiatives, the very ones they helped to create, apply to them as leaders or the real-life workplace situation taking place. They will minimize what is happening, become too busy to give it attention when most needed, ignore the situation altogether, or mishandle it because they don't consult, think it through, or check their automatic assumptions. Losing sight of the importance of taking race issues seriously, handling them inefficiently, or taking too long to address them can lead PoC in your organization to have little faith that DEIB initiatives will change their daily work-life experiences. These are common reasons why it can be difficult to retain PoC or get them involved in DEIB initiatives.

PoC, particularly Black employees, will frequently describe instances where a situation between them and their White coworker was handled poorly by leadership. It usually goes something like this. The White coworker, often a woman, has conflict with their Black coworker over some issue typically related to work, though not always. The White coworker seeks out their supervisor and reports feeling afraid, threatened, uncomfortable, unsafe, or a host of other stereotypical language that suggests potentially being harmed by the Black coworker. The Black coworker automatically becomes labeled as the problem. Probably not as angry as the White woman insinuated, the Black coworker is now truly angered due to how they are being characterized. Rather than the supervisor or manager viewing their emotions as a normal healthy response to the situation that occurred, the Black coworker is reprimanded or given a corrective action. The Black coworker suffers yet another injustice and becomes even more incensed at how things were handled. They now are labeled the "angry Black person" in the office.

Because there is a worldwide fear of Black people perpetuated by stereotypes of being aggressive and dangerous, even when Black people calmly present themselves, they are often perceived as a threat. White people on the other hand can express their angry emotions freely without being labeled negatively and with little if any repercussions despite displaying alarming behaviors. For fear of being labeled the "angry" Black person, Black men, women, and gender diverse will often work hard to manage their emotions even when a situation warrants anger. When some level of anger is present, it is usually not to the degree described by their White colleagues, and rarely are they threatening.

Because PoC risk being dismissed, invalidated, reprimanded, or even fired, PoC will consciously and unconsciously minimize their own emotions to make White people feel comfortable: *"I wasn't even angry," "You'll know when I'm angry," "I wasn't angry, I was passionate."* While passion may be a part of what they were feeling, this coping strategy denies Blacks the right to voice valid feelings and allows the institution to maintain racist practices by denying anger as a healthy response to racism. As a person in a leadership position, one way you can affect real cultural change is to address these situations in a way that that explores racial conflict from multiple perspectives rather than jumping into an either/or dichotomy. Consider the following situation that has been slightly modified to protect the identity of the people involved.

When Cultures Clash

Two Black women were talking from their cubicle, discussing their perspectives on Colin Kaepernick kneeling during the National Anthem. Simone said she agreed with his decision because in her opinion *"He stood up for what he believed in."* Kim, a White woman, was walking by and overheard the conversation. She decided to join in stating, *"I think his kneeling was rude and disrespectful to Veterans."* The conversation quickly grew heated. Simone tried to end the conversation by stating *"OK. That's your opinion. We can agree to disagree."* Kim continued to convey her opinion. Frustrated with Kim for many reasons, Simone again attempted to end the conversation with Kim by stating, *"If you want to continue this conversation, we can take it off the floor. You keep trying to talk about it. I don't want to talk with you right now."*

Kim immediately went to their manager, Dan, a White man, and told him her version of what transpired. She reported feeling threatened by Simone and said she no longer felt safe. Dan called Simone into his office and said, *"You made Kim feel uncomfortable. Saying 'do you want to take it outside' made her feel threatened."* Simone attempted to explain what happened from her perspective. Dan's final words were, *"It's important you understand your response to Kim can be perceived as threatening."*

Two weeks later, when Simone sat down with Dan for her employee evaluation, she noticed hers was prewritten. He informed her she needed to work on improving her, "*communication*" with coworkers stating, *"We need to make sure we don't have threatening behavior in our office again. We want everyone to feel safe here."* He then asked Simone, *"Is there anything you want to add?"* Simone replied, *"No, you've already formed your opinion, I don't have anything to say"* and left his office. A few weeks later, Dan went to Simone's cubicle, *"Your productivity is down, your work used to be above average, now you are operating at standard. I've notice you are not going above and beyond like you used to and seem disengaged from your colleagues."*

I've met far too many PoC who describe a similar experience in their workplace. For PoC to feel valued and believe they matter, your organization's actions must match its DEIB messaging. Take what occurs in cross-cultural interactions seriously, address it immediately, explore it from multiple perspectives, mitigate your own bias in the process—all before making a final decision. Below are questions to practice exploring related to the above vignette so when this happens in your workplace you are more prepared to arrive at a socially just outcome.

Questions to Explore

- Explore thoughts and feelings that might be occurring for Kim. Why might Simone believe Kim's behavior to be threatening?
- Explore thoughts and feelings that might be occurring for Simone.
- Explore any cultural differences between Kim and Simone.
- Imagine the only thing that has occurred so far is the incident between Kim and Simone. Kim has come to Dan's office. Using the diagram in Figure 5 below and your own best thinking, generate questions Dan could ask Kim when she arrives to his office that could lead to a different outcome than the one described above.
- Generate questions Dan could ask Simone when he goes to meet with her that could lead to a different outcome.

Supervisor/Manager/Leadership: Stop and Reflect So You Respond Versus React

Though the points below mostly apply to cross-cultural interactions when the person in a position of authority is White, they can also be useful for Leaders of Color.

- What was I taught growing up about Black, Indigenous, Asian, and Latine people? About White people? (Examine your stereotypes, assumptions, beliefs about all groups).

Leaders Leading When Cultures Clash

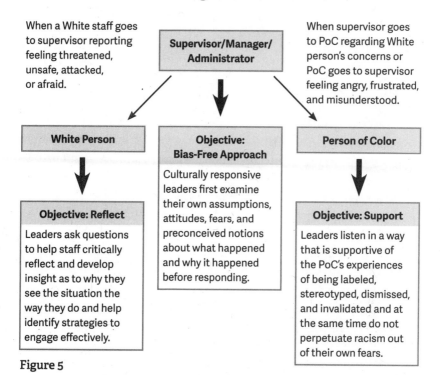

When a White staff goes to supervisor reporting feeling threatened, unsafe, attacked, or afraid.

Supervisor/Manager/Administrator

When supervisor goes to PoC regarding White person's concerns or PoC goes to supervisor feeling angry, frustrated, and misunderstood.

White Person

Objective: Bias-Free Approach

Person of Color

Objective: Reflect

Leaders ask questions to help staff critically reflect and develop insight as to why they see the situation the way they do and help identify strategies to engage effectively.

Culturally responsive leaders first examine their own assumptions, attitudes, fears, and preconceived notions about what happened and why it happened before responding.

Objective: Support

Leaders listen in a way that is supportive of the PoC's experiences of being labeled, stereotyped, dismissed, and invalidated and at the same time do not perpetuate racism out of their own fears.

Figure 5

- How was conflict handled in my home growing up? Did we attack one another, avoid the conversation, or did we openly and honestly engage in conversations that helped us move through the conflict?
- Do I tend to handle conflict in my professional life in the same way I engage conflict in my personal life? Does it hinder or help facilitate positive change? Does it lead to a fair outcome?
- How were crying, anger, and mistakes dealt with in my family growing up?
- How do I want to leave the White person feeling and thinking once this issue has been addressed?
- How do I want to leave the PoC feeling and thinking once this issue has been addressed?
- What do I know about the White person (What is my relationship like with them)?
- What do I know about the Person of Color (What is my relationship like with them)?

When you find yourself managing cross-cultural conflict, consider the following:

- *Do I really care about this person?* If you find yourself disliking the person you are talking with as the conversation unravels, chances are no new insight is happening for either of you. Try to find the good in that person.
- *What are our common beliefs?* Starting with where you agree, your understanding of their intent, or what you see good in that person can be a way to connect. For example, *"I know you're here because you care about the families we serve and are committed to their well-being."*
- *Was there a point in my life when I saw the world like this person does?* Refrain from holding the enemy image of the other. This is a good opportunity to practice humility by remembering a time you behaved, acted, or thought in a similar way. Asking questions will assist you in examining their perspective and deepen your insight on what is going on for them. This approach works better than general ideas that feel empty, e.g., *"We care about all our staff."*
- *What is the foundation of this person's world view?* When viewpoints do not consider racism, privilege, and oppression, they are often built on a foundation of an individual's experience outside of race, e.g., *"I was poor growing up, and I made it."* Asking questions that encourage the person to examine how they came to their conclusion can lead to uncovering their lack of understanding.
- *What work have I done to understand racism, power, and privilege?* When management has not done the work to understand how racism operates in subtle and not so subtle ways, they can easily dismiss a PoC's experiences. Ask questions to deepen your insight into their perspective.
- *Whose interests are being served?* Whose interests are served by the questions you ask and the statements you make? Ask questions that seek to understand and help inform you of your next steps that lead to a fair and just outcome.
- *Is it difficult to retain PoC in our organization?* Have there been situations like this before where PoC are viewed as the problem? Have I been working as a leader to address institutional racism within our organization?

The following Learning Conversation Stems are used to help you think about questions you might ask to deepen your understanding in the conversation with both White staff and the PoC. Asking questions and active listening involve truly trying to see another point of view rather than planning your next argument or making your point without all the facts. It is much more difficult to dismiss someone else's perspective when you care about them and when they know you have taken the time to really understand where they are coming from.

They are not in any order, nor should you limit yourself to these questions. The more questions you ask, the deeper the conversation will go, the easier questioning will become. While at first it may feel awkward, it will likely feel more natural as the conversation evolves.

White Person	Person of Color (PoC)
• You said _____ can you expand on that more?	• What happened?
• Clarify what you mean by _____?	• How are you feeling about all of this?
• I'm not sure what you mean by you were feeling _____ say more.	• I'm wondering if _____ would make sense?
• What are your hopes for the both of you?	• Tell me more…
• What would it mean to you if you did say/do something that was (e.g., racist)?	• I think I heard you say _____. Did I understand that correctly?
• Tell me more specifically, what made you feel unsafe?	• Have you had other experiences like this before?
• What do you mean by "she was aggressive"?	• What concerns you most about what happened?
• Say more about why this is important to you?	• What are your thoughts about how this can best be resolved?
• Help me better understand why you feel that way.	• What are your hopes for the both of you?
• Can you be more specific about how you came to believe _____?	
• Would you be open to hearing how Simone experienced how you engaged?	

In situations like the one above, when a White coworker harms a PoC, it is important that the two do not engage with one another until the White person understands their impact. Initially when you are talking with Kim, she is likely to make herself the victim or focus on her intent. You will need to work with her in developing insight. Until she becomes aware of the impact of her actions, do not allow the two to meet to discuss what occurred. It will only make things worse if Kim tries to defend herself or further makes Simone the problem. If Kim can recognize her impact, check in with Simone to find out if she is ready to engage. Have them meet with one another when Simone is ready and include a third person in the room who can help guide the conversation if necessary.

White leadership can perpetuate racism when they make decisions out of a fear of being called a racist. This fear often causes them to lower their expectations of Staff of Color and will impede their professional growth. For example, I've seen leaders who allow PoC to exhibit behaviors that are not tied to their culture and are legitimately unacceptable in the workplace, but they won't hold them accountable due to their fear. In these situations, PoC don't receive the same mentoring and guidance for professional growth and advancement as their White coworkers. Instead, everyone walks on eggshells around the PoC, have private conversations about them, and avoid interacting. Expressions of anger and other emotions should be accepted in the workplace. However, no one should be permitted to threaten, hurt, harm, or dehumanize another person because they feel anger. When leadership do their personal work to grow in Awareness of self and develop Knowledge of other cultures, they are better able to discern when to take appropriate action, and where workplace culture needs to change to be more inclusive. As I've heard said before, all criticism is not racism.

GAINING COMMITMENT AND INSTITUTIONALIZING CHANGE

You are not obligated to complete the work,
but neither are you free to abandon it.

—Unknown author

18

Bring Decision-Makers
on Board

Y OU MAY BE TAKING ON this work because you are a Person of Color who is tired of the experiences you and other PoC are facing in your workplace, because you hold an administrative position in your company and see the need for change, or were hired or assigned the role. Whatever the case may be for how you came into your position, it is critical to your organization's success that you do not do the work in isolation. Find support and commitment from your colleagues and those higher in your organization—administrators, management, board, superintendent, and others who have power and influence. Things will become more difficult and disruptive before they get easy, and you will need support and allies by your side.

Anticipate your organization experiencing a disequilibrium as people begin to feel their workplace shifting. Prepare for resistance from inside and out. Know that the more impact your organization makes as it engages in DEIB work, the more some will attempt to hinder progress. They will do their very best to ensure that anything you do to bring about equity and create a welcoming and inclusive workplace for those who have been marginalized is stopped. Public records requests of your DEIB trainings, having cameras off while secretly videotaping, sharing the information with conservative media sites, miseducating the public on purpose, sending hate mail, and opposing Critical Race Theory being taught in our schools are just a few examples of what we are up against in the United States.

When "you know what" hits the fan, and it will, you do not want all fingers pointing at you, making you a scapegoat or "cause of the problem." When Seattle Public Schools hired a new superintendent, I was told that if anything I did got in the papers again, I would no longer have a job. Given that I had no control over what people decided was newsworthy, and the fact that I was doing what they hired me to do, I had not realized that another Woman of Color would be the one to end four years of work. DEIB requires shared ideas, thinking, and responsibility. Change that emerges because of growing conversations and understanding will require taking huge risks so ensure what you do is sanctioned by the powers that be—and that you are not doing the work alone. Not only will your job be on the line when (not if) things don't turn out the way you or others intended, your own emotional and mental health will be at stake. Following are ideas for gaining commitment.

Getting Administrators on Board

- Identify at least one to five people (or more), whom you can approach and who will likely support DEIB efforts. These people could be your colleagues, board members, managers, supervisors, or other administrators, depending on your position within the organization.
- Once you have identified people who could potentially support this work, bring them together to outline changes that need to occur to address DEIB and why. Based on everyone's understanding, experiences, past conversations, and knowledge, what case can you make for diversity, equity, inclusion, and belonging?
- Identify people who may become barriers to the work. What might they say or do that could impede progress? Prepare qualitative and quantitative evidence supporting the need for this work.
- Request a meeting with leadership. Invite those same people who support the work to meet and discuss benefits, barriers, needs, and concerns to the meeting. It doesn't have to be everyone, but it should not be you alone.
- If DEIB is already a part of your organization's written mission or vision, use that language to help make the case for what needs to be accomplished. Reminding people of their commitment helps to hold leadership accountable to walk their talk.
- If you have little experience in DEIB work, you may want to reach out to a DEIB consultant for guidance. FYI: Do not ask a PoC to do this work for free. If leadership is committed to DEIB, they need to allocate their resources in ways that demonstrate they are invested in all ways.

- When seeking to fulfill leadership positions, embed DEIB questions in the interview process to gain a sense of candidates' commitment.

Making the Case for DEIB

You may work for an organization that will not take on a DEIB initiative unless the data shows there is a need. Following are some of the ways you can make the case for DEIB.

- Survey all staff on their workplace satisfaction and understanding of DEIB. For example, questions that reveal most of your staff are operating under color-blind thinking or believe they do not have bias can help prove the need for culturally relevant professional development.
- If you have a high number of Staff of Color, focus groups are a great way to uncover what their workplace experiences are like. You should do this with White staff as well.
- Consider who your organization is there to serve and uncover any data that shows the need to improve services.
- Assess what has been done in the past to address DEIB. It is good to acknowledge what is already being done so the conversation is not approached solely from a deficit model. Assessments don't always need to be formal. You can invite a group of people to brainstorm together. If nothing is being done, spend time thinking about how you will make the case for this work. How will your organization benefit from DEIB? Do not wait for a lawsuit.
- Look up research on the value of diversity, how organizations benefit, etc. There is a great deal of research available to you. Have conversations identifying the values of a diverse, inclusive workplace?
- Hire a DEIB consultant to do a formal organizational assessment.

Remember your role is to lead the way. You will not need one hundred percent buy-in to create a cultural shift. Remember the 10/80/10 makeup of your organization. While literature varies in what percentage constitutes a critical mass (30–40% for change to occur), there is wide agreement that you don't need everyone on board to affect change. Getting those within your organization to see the benefits of this work requires others working alongside you. It's far more effective to convey "we" have a concern versus "I" have a concern.

Of course, if you were hired or assigned to lead equity work, the "I" versus "we" won't present as much of a challenge. However, you will still likely face the challenge of getting some leadership and staff involved in the work. The point is, don't go alone on the journey. You need others to help move the needle. It is too easy for your voice to be marginalized when you advocate or work alone. Without true commitment from leadership, meaningful change will not happen.

I recall working with a midsize nonprofit organization years ago. The staff were committed to the work. On their own, they began caucusing, holding meetings, engaging in race conversations, and identifying racist practices. They had one Administrator of Color supporting them, but supervisors, managers, and other leaders, including the board, were not a part of these early conversations. Over time, a significant divide developed between leadership and staff. Staff were pointing fingers at leadership, and leadership disengaged for fear of making mistakes. I was hired to train, coach, and consult with leadership and staff with the hope I could help to bridge the divide.

As staff worked together on issues of DEIB, their understanding of how racism permeated throughout their organization grew. As their knowledge increased so did their feelings of anger as well as their demand for immediate change. Staff were insisting leadership participate in the work with them and support changes to their organization. But getting leadership to be a part of the process wasn't so simple. The bus had already left, and the almost all-White leadership had been left behind. They felt a great deal of anxiety engaging in race conversations midway in the journey. But that's not how the racially diverse staff saw it. Leadership's apprehension and avoidance was proof their leadership was not only resistant to change but also racist.

Unbeknownst to staff, leadership felt inadequate, fearful of making mistakes, and worried about being seen as racist. Leadership's fear caused them to be labeled in the very way they tried to avoid being seen. By the time I was brought in, there was already a culture of us against them. Had staff and leadership started together, one that wasn't bottom-up (or top-down in some cases), they likely would have encountered fewer bumps and potholes in the road.

I have also come across leaders who will *say* they value DEIB and even agree to workshops and other initiatives that support the work but who do not take on an active role in the process. These leaders don't attend workshops or actively participate when they do. They don't ask for updates on progress or provide needed resources. There is no mention of DEIB during staff meetings, and no one is held accountable to adjust their practices. These leaders are willing to use DEIB like a trophy to display in the window, only they don't do anything to earn it.

This will cause you a great deal of frustration. However, if you can initially get their commitment, albeit superficial, see it as a small win. Though it won't be enough, it is a start. In these situations, you may need to begin with what you have and address barriers along the way. As an example, you might share with leadership the impact it is having on staff when they are not actively engaging in the professional development.

One of my first roles as Director of Equity and Race Relations for Seattle Public Schools was to co-facilitate three committees established to address institutional racism: Community Engagement, Policy, and Professional Development. Once the work began, the first fifteen minutes of every meeting was spent convincing committee members the work we were tasked to do would eventually move beyond committee work. They had seen so little progress in the past that it was hard for them to believe that the time and energy they invested in these meetings would lead to change. My response over and over was, *"They hired me and formed this committee to address racism; let's do the work and deal with the pushback if or when it comes."*

While this work can be slow, find ways to make it take root so when you are no longer working there, the work continues. And if leadership begins to back out the moment things become challenging, point to things in place, e.g., your job description, the strategic plan, the mission and vision statements, or a policy, to hold them accountable for maintaining their commitment. As the Director of Equity and Race Relations, I regularly reported to the Superintendent and the School Board, so fortunately these committees were able to accomplish a great deal. Get the commitment upfront, keep leadership informed along the way, and hold them accountable to stay the course.

19

Establish an Equity Team
to Maintain the Work

STAFF'S DEVELOPMENT OF their Awareness of self, Knowledge of others, and Skills in engaging across cultures are critical in their being able to contribute to dismantling institutional racism through Action and Advocacy work. Because staff make up your organization, they play a key role in advancing change from within. Rather than being reliant on one or two people or telling individuals what to do and how to do it, those within must learn to look at their work through an equity lens and become agents of change. This will be their journey, and your role is to guide them on it. As those within become better equipped at identifying racist policies and practices, they can work together in their collective understanding to dismantle racism and replace them with equitable practices.

Glenn Singleton, in his book *Courageous Conversations About Race: A Field Guide for Achieving Equity in Schools and Beyond*, came up with the idea of developing Equity Teams as an approach in dismantling institutional racism in schools. I recommend every organization establish an Equity Team. When done right, they are an effective way of bringing in multiple voices and perspectives to address racism. I have found that when organizations do not have an Equity Team, the work is usually led by one or two people, typically by someone higher up in the organization who ends up making all the decisions. This decreases buy-in, increases resistance, and maintains White cultural norms and racist practices by taking an individualist approach to a collective problem.

When organizations do have an Equity Team, members often flounder around unsure of the team's purpose or direction. When this happens, members stop showing up to the meetings, believing they are just a waste of time. Some individuals wrongly perceive themselves as the Equity Police, seeing it as their job to patrol and point out any wrongdoings from their colleagues. This brings about further division amongst staff and feeds into the tension and resistance against racial equity work, rather than the growth and support Equity Teams are meant to provide.

When done effectively, Equity Teams can be one of the most effective ways of generating institutional change. Below are guidelines for establishing an effective Equity Team. If you already have one in place, the ideas below can help you identify ways to strengthen your Equity Team's efficacy.

Goal of the Equity Team's Work Together (What Will They Do?)

Your first step as will be to identify one to three people who can assist you in laying the groundwork for your organization's Equity Team (ET). These people may or may not end up being on the Equity Team. Their role will be to help you establish important and logistical aspects of the Equity Team such as goal, purpose, and roles. By providing key information in advance, potential ET members will be able to gain a sense of what they are being asked to commit to, so they can make an informed decision as to whether they want to apply to join. You will need to develop a statement that informs potential ET members of the work.

> Example: *The Equity Team will work collaboratively to identify institutional practices, policies, decision-making processes, allocation and use of resources, and other areas necessary for dismantling and mitigating racism in our workplace.*

Purpose Statement (Why Will They Do It?)

An Equity Team consists of a group of people who have different roles within an organization who become the eyes, ears, and voices for the whole organization or department. They assess the needs of staff and the communities they serve by, for example, collecting and analyzing data and other information to determine where change needs to occur. Equity Teams not only assess the need for change, but they also develop a plan of action. Develop a purpose statement that messages why your organization values DEIB.

Example: *We believe everyone should have access to health care regardless of their income, race, class, gender, sexual orientation, ability, religion, or immigration status and feel welcomed and included when utilizing _____ (organization's name) services.*

Determine Roles and Responsibilities of the Equity Team

The roles and responsibilities of the ET may change over time as team members dig into the work and uncover new responsibilities; they might also realize roles they've originally identified are no longer needed. Regardless, you will want to generate a list of roles and responsibilities so they have an idea of what they are being invited to do. Clarifying role and responsibility of the ET will help to minimize confusion and assist potential members in determining if they want to join. Following are some ideas to help you determine what your Equity Teams Roles and Responsibilities might include:

- Provide leadership in creating a culturally responsive work environment.
- Assess the needs of our _____ (program, department, organization) as it relates to past, present, and future race and equity work. Note: This does not need to be a formal assessment.
- Research and develop plans for ongoing culturally relevant professional development for staff.
- Aid in creating a supportive learning environment whereby staff can engage in ongoing courageous conversations. For example, determining norms and Foundational Beliefs.
- Lead staff in dismantling institutional racism in policy and practices.
- Utilize the strengths and resources of staff to support racial equity.
- Practice and model engaging effectively across cultures.
- Continuously critically examine self, take risks, and practice skill building.
- Keep issues of racial equity at the center of the organization's work.
- Participate in ongoing culturally relevant professional development to continue to learn and grow your understanding and leadership abilities.
- Meet monthly for two hours.

- Work on a subcommittee to accomplish ET goals.
- Develop a strategic plan identifying one to three things to work on throughout the year.

Identify Your Area of Focus

It is important you know what you mean by diversity. If you are unclear, your organization will be unclear. Lack of clarity will cause the DEIB work to lose its power and impact. Those who are intent on derailing the conversation will make it about anything and everything, "*What about the Irish?*", "*What about the skateboard community?*" or "*Why don't we have a White history month?*" Your role as an Equity Leader is to address those groups who historically have been marginalized through past and present policy and practices, resulting in an unlevel playing field, e.g., race, gender, class, sexual orientation, ability, age, immigration status, and religion. If your organization is early in its DEIB journey, limit your focus to one area so you can grow and learn along the way. If you pick multiple areas to focus on, you are likely to go wide, with minimal impact, rather than deep in your organization's growth and understanding.

If you choose race, staff from other marginalized groups will likely initiate pushback. Any type of ism in your organization should not be tolerated and therefore should be taken seriously and addressed immediately. With that said, rather than have the Equity Team taking on all marginalized groups at once (essentially watering down the impact of the work), choose one area of focus. I recommend Equity Teams focus on race first. Race is the most difficult conversation for White staff to have and the one PoC are most frustrated aren't being had. If you choose race, you will need to be prepared for the "*What about...*" comments. Rather than playing the oppression Olympics, honor legitimate concerns and help people in the organization understand why it is important to focus on just one area first and why you are starting with race.

> Example: "*You are bringing up a great point. We want everyone to feel welcomed and included, and LGBTQ+ employees should not feel they do not belong. This is why we are venturing into equity work. We are planning to address not only race but also LGBTQ+ and other groups that are marginalized. Given that we*

are new to the work, we decided to focus on one area until we have a better understanding of how to effectively create change. We chose race because... In the process we hope to learn what works and what doesn't, with the goal of dismantling all forms of institutional isms."

Do not let every issue become the Equity Teams' focus. Get clear about what you do and do not mean by diversity, equity, inclusion, and belonging. Bear in mind all identity groups are important, but not all groups are impacted by discrimination in the same way or to the same degree. It helps if you have data to support your decision. As the team gains momentum and makes progress, you can and eventually should expand your focus to include other groups.

Developing the Application Process

Do not select people to serve on the ET. Instead, develop an application process inviting everyone in your organization or department to apply. Selecting individuals will reinforce the biased and privileged practices you are trying to change. No one should be able to say they did not hear about the opportunity or wonder why they were not asked to join. The process should represent the very change you seek within your organization rather than the familiar "good old boy" network. News that you are developing an ET should be discussed at leadership and staff meetings. And all leaders should be expected to support the process by granting anyone who wants to participate permission to apply.

Following are examples of what you might include in the application process.

Examples of Application Questions

When creating the application, specify a maximum number of words so you are not reading pages and pages of information.

- How would our organization benefit from having you on our Equity Team?
- Describe your motivation and interest for being on the ET.
- What personal or professional experiences do you have that help you understand issues of diversity, equity, inclusion, and belonging?

- Why should we select you for the ET? What would we miss out on if we did not choose you?
- Describe your personality and how you work with others?
- Are you willing and able to commit to attending all monthly meetings and make this work a priority? What if any barriers may prevent you from attending meetings regularly?
- Describe your vision for the impact the ET could have on our organization.
- Given that we are starting with race, is there an area of need that you see as a priority that would strengthen the impact of the ET effectiveness? If so, please explain.
- Please share any ideas you have for increasing the success of the ET.

Demographic Information

If your organization is large, consider including demographic information to aid you in selecting people who will represent diverse voice, experience, and perspective. People may feel it is inappropriate to share personal information about themselves so explain why you are asking. Demographic information might be specific information asked directly about applicant's race, age, role, and years at the organization, or it could be asked more generally. Following is an example of the latter:

> Our goal is to create an Equity Team with as much diverse representation as possible. We would like team members to consist of diverse staff so we are best able to generate new ideas, foster creativity, and aid us in considering all aspects of our organization. Please share with us, to the extent you are willing and comfortable, the following information: Your current and past roles within this organization, how long you've worked here, your age, race, ethnicity, gender, sexual orientation, religion, immigrant status, or any other identities that might speak to the diverse perspective you would bring to the committee. If you have any concerns about this question, do not hesitate to reach out to me. Please keep in mind that responding to these demographic questions is not mandatory but simply our attempt at making the ET as heterogeneous as possible.

Logistical Information to Consider Including

In addition to including the Equity Team's goal, purpose, roles and responsibilities, and focus, you will also need to figure out logistics they will need to know before they can determine if they are interested in applying.

When the Equity Team Will Meet

It is a challenge to come up with a day and time that will work for everyone. Determine this in advance so those applying are aware of when the meetings will occur to determine whether they are available and can make the commitment. This also gives them an opportunity to gain support from their supervisors. You will also want to consider including the first meeting date of the ET. Make sure it is far enough in advance that people can put it on their calendars.

Meeting Frequency

Most ETs meet at least once a month, the same day every month for a minimum of two hours. Include an initial half- or full-day retreat to accomplish some of the groundwork and spend time getting to know one another and begin building community.

Compensation

Few nonprofit or government organizations can provide its members with a stipend. However, if this is a possibility or if they are required to meet after work hours, make a concerted effort to find funding (even a small stipend) to honor the participants' time and efforts. This will also convey the organization's commitment to DEIB.

Number of ET Members

A minimum of three staff members and a maximum of 8–12 is a good group size, though the number will depend on the size of your organization. Exceptionally large organizations may need to have an Equity Team in every department. If this is the case, you will want to create a central office ET representing one member from each of the departmental Equity Teams. Keep in mind the smaller the Equity Team, the less diverse perspectives. The larger the committee, the more difficult it can be to get things moving.

Duration of Member Commitment

ET members should be prepared to serve a minimum of two years on the team. Some will need to commit longer, so everyone doesn't leave the committee at the same time, resulting in new members floundering and trying to find to their way. If your organization is small, these same people may serve on the ET for years.

Date the Decision Will Be Made

Let staff know how long you believe the application process will take and when they can expect to hear from you. Think about how you will inform those who were not selected. Explain why you cannot select everyone who applies if you receive more applications than you have seats for. Also, let those who were not selected know that there will be other opportunities for them to support DEIB efforts.

Identify Your Equity Team Members

This is probably the most difficult part of the application process. You will either have more applications than you need or not enough. You and those you have selected to help with the process will need to sit down together and review the applications. Think of it like trying to put together pieces of a puzzle. If, for example, you have three African Americans but no Asian representation, you may have to turn down one or two of the African American applicants and identify who in your organization can bring voice and input from an Asian perspective.

This means one of you will need to approach someone in your organization who is Asian and explain why you are inviting them to be on the ET. It's critical you do not tokenize them.

> *"Heather, I noticed you didn't submit an apllication to be on the Equity Team. I was hoping you would. You have demonstrated over the past year a willingness to share your story and talk openly about racism. You also have great relationships with your colleagues. They listen to you. I know how busy you are, but in all honesty, right now we only have Whites and Blacks applying. I'm worried there won't be any Asian voices represented and was hoping you'd apply."*

Being Asian is one of the reasons you are asking this person, but it is not the only reason. If it was, you should not be asking them.

When you were generating ideas about who to personally invite because their voice was not represented, why did you think they would be a good fit? Tell them that. If they are the only Asian person in your organization, name the elephant by speaking that truth and the need for their voice. Also, keep in mind, because someone is a Person of Color, it does not mean they would bring in diverse voice and perspective. Particularly if they have assimilated into White cultural norms.

The First Year

The committee will have a lot of work to do to get grounded before trying to affect change within the organization. It takes at least a year for an ET to build community, practice engaging in courageous conversations, and ground themselves in how they will work together, before making any progress visible to the organization. Allow the team time for forming, storming, and norming as they settle into their roles to perform. The team should start, at minimum, with a half- or full-day retreat to build relationships as ET members and work through logistics described below. If the ET meets for two hours once a month in a year, it totals 24 hours. One day is not nearly enough time to begin making an impact on your organization. At that rate it will take them years to figure out what they are doing.

You or someone else from your organization can facilitate the retreat, but it should not be a member of the Equity Team. They should be able to fully participant in the process. If need be, hire an outside consultant. Following are suggested areas for the committee to brainstorm, discuss, and determine as a committee. All of this may not get accomplished during the retreat and may have to continue into the first couple of meetings.

Introductions

Each person shares something about themselves, their why for joining, and what they hope to offer the ET. Remember, you read their applications, but they did not read each other's.

What We Already Know

Review the goal and purpose of the ET, share leadership's commitment to their work, go over their roles and responsibilities, how often everyone will meet, and give members the opportunity to ask clarifying questions. Any questions you cannot answer should be taken to leadership and then brought back to the ET at the next meeting. Ask the ET what is missing that they would like to know that would help them better serve in their role.

What Needs to Be Determined

You will not be doing all the work. Ask others to volunteer to take on various roles to ensure leadership is shared and they function as a team. Below are suggested roles to consider. ET members will be hesitant to take on the role of cochair. Inform them of what the role involves and encourage them that they can do it with the support of one another and your guidance. The expectation is not to be perfect in it but rather to develop their leadership skills and share responsibility.

- One person to volunteer to cochair with you. It's important you share leadership and cultivate new skills in others, whenever possible. The cochairs are responsible for managing the meetings. This may include, but is not limited to, developing the agenda, facilitating the meetings, redirecting members when they get off track, soliciting ideas for the next meeting.
- Someone to volunteer to be the secretary. This person is responsible for taking minutes, e-mailing them to everyone, and sending out upcoming meeting reminders.
- Someone to volunteer opening or closing each ET meeting with a DEIB-related inspirational poem, quote, video, or song to keep the team centered and enthusiastic about the work. Committee members can send their suggestions to this person.
- One or two people volunteer to oversee the Equity Team's professional development. The ET will need to continue to learn and grow together so they develop the lens to lead. This role involves finding articles, books, videos, conferences, and other means of learning. Those leading professional development may teach a short lesson or facilitate the learning process. For example, books can be purchased for all team members to read and discuss chapters. Each member is assigned a chapter and comes up with questions and facilitates the discussion. Committee members can contribute by sharing their ideas, preferences, and resources. Professional development should happen regularly throughout the year. It may be a ten- to fifteen-minute learning opportunity, or it may take an entire meeting..

- Determine the name for your Equity Team. Equity Team is a general term used to describe a group of people working together on DEIB efforts. However, the ET can call themselves whatever they choose. Many Equity Teams refer to themselves as JEDI— something you will want to avoid. In *Scientific American*, Sara E. Brownell, Nita A. Kedharnath, Susan J. Cheng, and W. Carson Byrd wrote *"Why the Term 'JEDI' is Problematic for Describing Programs that Promote Justice, Equity, Diversity and Inclusion."* They make many valid points that I would not have considered had I not read their article: "They are a religious order of intergalactic police-monks, prone to (white) saviorism and toxically masculine approaches to conflict resolution (violent duels with phallic lightsabers, gaslighting by means of "Jedi mind tricks," etc.)."[1]

Norms and Foundational Beliefs

As mentioned earlier, it is essential your team operates under norms that guide them in engaging in courageous conversations. It will eventually be important for leadership and staff to also become aligned and grounded in these norms.

- Identify norms for having courageous conversations. Once these are agreed upon, put them on table tents or poster paper and bring to every meeting. As mentioned in Chapter 13, consider giving the ET norms rather than having them decide. Consider assigning members a norm to read and teach to one another. ET Members should be expected to practice using these during meetings and in their work and personal lives. This is a part of their leadership, and practicing will help them model what they desire from staff.
- Brainstorm together Foundational Beliefs the ET believes are necessary to move the work forward as they engage one another and the rest of the organization. What approaches do they agree are helpful or harmful in the process? Will the approach become a bridge or a barrier to success? See Chapter 4.

Identify DEIB Goals

The first year is meant to provide the ET with an opportunity to build relationships, have questions answered, accomplish some groundwork, and learn together. While it is important to spend time building relationships and processing issues occurring within your organization, at some point they will need to begin working on impacting change. If they spend too much time getting grounded, members will begin to complain the meetings are a waste of time. They each have a *why* for joining, and if they do not soon feel like they're making a difference, they may start to miss meetings or drop out altogether. Following are ideas for determining where to start and how to approach their work.

Assess

Work together on the Multicultural Organizational Identity Development (SMOID) in Chapter 20 to determine what stage your organization is currently operating in. Next do an organizational scan by brainstorming what your organization has done in the past and is currently doing to address DEIB. Depending on the size of your organization, everyone on the ET may not be aware of small or even big wins. The purpose of this process is to put everyone on the same page before identifying what more needs to be done.

Narrow Your Focus

The ET will not be able to do all that needs to be done. It's important to narrow your focus and agree on a few areas to work on in the upcoming year. Below is one process to help the team come away with two or three priorities.

- Now that you are all aware of past and present work, divide members into small groups. Have them brainstorm two or three things they believe the ET should focus on first. These should be ideas that are within the team's locus of control. Each idea should be written on a separate sheet of chart paper and include bullet points on why they believe it should be a priority.
- Each group will report out suggested areas of focus and share why they believe they should be the priority.
- Other groups will then ask clarifying questions before moving on to the next group's suggestions. After each group presents, they put their poster on the wall, and then the next group reports out. This process continues until every group has shared.
- With all the posters on the wall, team members look at what they've come up with. Similarities are identified, crossed out, and added to one poster so there are no duplicates.
- If one idea is too big, you may need to break it down further into

bite-size chunks. For example, hiring and retention is a huge area. You may need to narrow the focus to one aspect of the hiring process, e.g., developing culturally relevant interview questions. If you determine you want to revamp the entire hiring and retention process, several subcommittees may need to be formed.

- Once everyone's ideas are up on the walls, give members sticky dots and have them vote by placing their dots next to their top three or four choices. The ideas with the highest number of votes become your areas of focus and a part of your strategic plan. Keep the other ideas for future discussion.

Developing a Strategic Plan

- Have Equity Team members form subcommittees to work on areas they identified. This may mean that there are people who need to be invited to work on the subcommittees who are not a part of the Equity Team. For example, if one of the focus areas is hiring and retention, someone from HR must be on that subcommittee even if they are not a member of the ET. This could also be a good time to invite those who applied to be on the ET, but were not chosen, to get involved.
- Plan for a one-year strategic plan versus two-, three-, four-, or five-year plans. As the ET begins mapping out and implementing the work, they will gain a better sense of barriers that exist. It is likely that the work will unravel more that needs to be done than was initially anticipated. Planning too far ahead when you do not know where the work will lead can cause your plan to end up on a shelf forgotten.
- Do not take on more than the ET can handle. Make sure the areas of focus are within their locus of control and that they have the capacity to see it through. Making gains will provide momentum as they achieve small wins. For example, having leadership provide funding for staff professional development is a win.
- Find a strategic plan template that everyone uses to record the process and progress.
- The subcommittees will need to meet outside of the monthly ET meetings. There simply is not enough time to work on your goals during the meetings. Your monthly ET meetings are a great time for subcommittees to give updates and for the team to provide

input, generate additional ideas, suggest ways to remove barriers, review their work, etc.

- Reach out to supervisors and managers of ET members to ensure they provide them with the time needed to meet in their subcommittees. Their meeting time should be hassle-free.
- Inform higher-ups of the ET's plan. Keep them regularly updated so leadership supports their efforts. I've seen Equity Teams get far along in their work, excited about their progress, only to be told by leadership their work cannot be supported due to, e.g., union restrictions, budget, funders, etc. Nothing will deflate a committee's momentum quicker than being informed all their hard work and time invested in meeting and planning was for naught.

Leadership's Roles and Responsibilities

In this section, leadership is defined as those who have an administrative role and/or decision-making power. It's important that someone in a leadership position serves on the ET, but it should not be the person who holds the top position within your organization, i.e., the CEO, principal, or president unless your organization consists of a small group of close-knit staff. It is not a good use of their time to be involved in the detailed planning, and this is an opportunity for others to practice leading. However, leadership should be regularly updated on progress being made.

The ET could generate a list of roles and responsibilities they would like leadership to take on in support of their work. Or, you might have leadership generate ideas. In some cases, leadership won't know what they can do to support DEIB work. Whatever ideas are generated for leadership's role and responsibility, it should be shared and agreed on by both leadership and the ET. Following are ideas to help you think about what leadership's support might include:

- If you are the Equity Leader in your organization, you need to serve on the Equity Team.
- If your organization does not have a Director of DEIB, someone from leadership (e.g., assistant principal, assistant VP, manager) needs to be designated to serve on the Equity Team. This should not be the person at the highest level of the organization, and they should have some decision-making authority. This person does not need to lead the Equity Team though they can initially until other

ET members are willing to take on that role. They can also cochair with an ET member.

- Supervisors and managers provide time for their staff to serve on the ET and remove barriers that may hinder their participation. This might include lessening staff's workload.
- An ET representative should have time on board, cabinet/leadership, and staff meeting agendas to report progress.
- Leadership utilizes the ET best thinking on issues that arise, since they make decisions for the entire organization.
- Leadership actively participates in DEIB professional development with staff. Not only do they attend, but they model the work by taking risks and being vulnerable.
- Leadership participates in professional development together to specifically address their unique needs.
- Leaders encourage courageous conversations amongst staff during meetings, one-on-one, and other opportunities, e.g., admit when they don't have the answers, seek support from staff to find solutions, apologize when making mistakes, are uncertain of next steps, etc.
- Leaders support a learning environment where people learn from their mistakes versus punitive.
- When conflict occurs, repair and support (versus call out culture) are leaders' first objectives.
- Leadership is intentional about including diverse voices and perspectives in decision-making.
- Leadership is open to feedback and suggestions about DEIB from the ET and other staff.
- Leadership regularly speaks to staff about the value and importance of DEIB work.
- Department leadership regularly provides time during meetings for DEIB discussions, e.g., after workshops have occurred.
- The annual budget includes funds for staff's professional development.
- Budgets are provided for the purchase of learning materials and other types of professional development opportunities ET members require for their ongoing learning.
- Dates are identified throughout the year for culturally relevant professional development.

- Leaders hold staff accountable for attending DEIB workshops. If a staff member is unable to attend a session, there are alternative options for learning the content.
- Leadership provides space on the website to keep community and staff informed of its DEIB efforts.

The Appendix is an Antiracist Leadership Practices tool to assist leaders in supporting DEIB work not specific to the Equity Team.

Board's Roles and Responsibilities

If your organization has a board, it is imperative that they are involved in DEIB efforts. They play an essential role in shaping the culture of your organization and need to support the work.

- Create a budget for a department of equity and race so they have the resources to do their job. This should include administrative staff, and at minimum, one other equity lead, depending on the size of your organization.
- Participate in the hiring of a DEIB director. This position should not be at a managerial level, nor should it be an add-on to an already existing role, e.g., the HR person's job. This position should report directly to the executive director or the board of directors.
- Have the DEIB director report progress and challenges directly to the board at minimum quarterly so the Board is kept aware of DEIB efforts.
- Engage in their own professional development individually and collectively as a board so they develop an equity lens, can ask essential questions, and support equity and inclusion efforts.
- Increase the racial diversity of the board.
- Support the creation of a DEIB policy.
- Participate in including DEIB language into the mission and vision statements.
- Review existing policy through a DEIB lens or assign that task to a group.
- Hold the person who reports directly to them, e.g., the executive director, accountable for institutional change.
- Ensure that decisions are being made through an equity lens that has the best interests of those historically marginalized.

- Ensure that resources are being allocated equitably.
- Listen to Staff of Color and make changes based on what the board learns.
- Meet with Communities of Color and listen to their concerns. Use this information to make changes within the organization.
- Call one another in when things are said and done that further marginalize underrepresented groups.
- Develop their own strategic plan to ensure that changes amongst the board are occurring.
- Make decisions based on DEIB, not on the philanthropists who provide the institution funding.
- Seek funders who support DEIB efforts.
- Designate a board representative to serve on the Equity Team.

You may want to consider waiting until your organization has made some progress before inviting students, parents, or community members to join the Equity Team. In most situations, it is more effective to start from the inside and work your way out. For example, if you decide culturally relevant professional development for staff is an area of focus, you may not want students and parents hearing what educators are doing and saying in their learning journey. At the same time, if your goal is family and community engagement, you will need representatives from the community involved in the planning. You will need to decide what will be needed to progress.

Listed in the Resources section are books, articles, and videos to help your ET grow in their understanding of racism, power, and privilege. It is important that your ET continue their learning and that some of the learning happens together. Also, consider developing a library of resources for staff within your organization to support ongoing learning beyond any professional development that you might provide them. If you purchase books, create a system for staff to check out the resources. The library of resources can also be utilized for new hires as a part of their onboarding so they can familiarize themselves with the work that your organization began before they joined.

Finally, keep track of the work your organization is doing. Try and be as transparent as possible by updating everyone of the progress being made.

Establish an Equity Team:
Commitment to Change and Be Changed

- If you do not already have an Equity Team, talk with administrators and/or your colleagues in your organization about the idea of establishing one. Get a sense of their thoughts, ideas, and barriers you may encounter.
- Identify two or three people in your organization who can begin helping you with the process of establishing an Equity Team. If you already have one, have the ET read this chapter and identify ways they can improve how they function as a team.

20

Determine Your
Organization's Stage of
Multicultural Development

THE FIRST RACIAL IDENTITY DEVELOPMENT model was developed by William Cross in 1971. In his model, Cross described five stages of identity development Black people go through as they become more aware of racism and its impact on their lives. His model was, at onetime, the most cited in counseling literature. Additional models were later developed to acknowledge the process of identity development for other groups, i.e., Asians, multiracial, Latine, gay and lesbian, and Whites. Racial Identity Development later became known as Racial/Ethnic Identity Development (R/EID) and considers an individual's comfort level with racial issues. The models are not meant to function in a linear fashion but rather recognizes people can move in and out of stages at different times in their life and be in more than one stage at the same time.

Noticing similarities between individual R/EID models and stages organizations were going through, Dr. Jennifer Wiley, a friend and colleague, and I used the same concept to develop this Multicultural Organizational Identity Development tool. Cultures Connecting adapted the model based on our work with hundreds of organizations. Stages of Multicultural Organizational Identity Development is a useful tool to guide a group of people in identifying where their organization most closely fits. From there they will be able to ascertain steps needed to move them further along in their organization's development.

Stages of Multicultural Organizational Identity Development (SMOID)

Following are stages organizations go through as they address (or fail to address) racism, power, and White privilege. The earlier stages typically operate more heavily under White norms[1] designed to maintain institutional power. Organizations may exhibit indicators from several stages simultaneously, but the organization will likely function predominantly in one stage. Organizations are more circular in nature rather than operating in a linear progression from one stage to the next. They can move up, down, or even skip stages as they work toward building a diverse, equitable, inclusive, and belonging environment. They do not need to meet all indicators to fit in a stage. Given that this work is adaptive, there is no natural progression or "evolution" from one stage to the next. Each organization will look different. Get ready because the working environment will become more challenging before it gets better. It will require a sustained effort over time for your organization to become a multicultural organization.

Stage 1: Pre-Encounter

Pre-Encounter is like Unconscious Incompetence—your people in your organization don't know what they don't know. Organizations in this stage do not recognize institutional racist practices and the impact it is having on their Employees and Clients of Color. Bias in decision-making, hiring, policies, practices, and procedures go undetected. Institutions in the Pre-Encounter stage often foster a Eurocentric monoculture that is run by White leadership operating under White norms, values, and beliefs benefitting White staff and White clients. Whiteness is unquestionably centered. There are usually few People of Color working in the organization, and those who do have either assimilated into White culture or experience fatigue in the workplace culture.

Pre-Encounter Indicators
- Employees do what they are told and uphold the system's institutionally racist practices without questioning the status quo. When changes are suggested, it's common to hear *"They're never going to let you do that"* or *"Things are fine the way they are"* and *"This is the way it's always been done."*
- PoC who have assimilated to White culture do not see a need for change. Their attitude is *"Don't rock the boat or make waves."*

- PoC who have not assimilated commonly experience microaggressions which go ignored. When brought to the attention of their supervisor, their experiences are invalidated, and they are made to feel they are being too sensitive or are the problem. *"I've worked with Bob for a long time, he's never treated me that way"* or *"I'm sure he didn't mean it that way."* This type of gaslighting causes fatigue, and they may search for other employment.
- Leaders function as managers, rarely if ever think outside the box in ways that grow the organization to become more multicultural. They continue to do things the way they have always been done, never questioning who is benefitting or being harmed from their practices. *"I'm just doing what I was told to do"* is a common refrain.
- Overt and covert institutional messages support the dominant culture. When PoC ask questions or raise concerns that bring inequity and social justice issues to the forefront, others respond by minimizing the issue (*"That's not needed."*). If the complainant persists, they are often deemed the problem: *"I've worked here for 25 years, and no one has complained about that before."*
- Individual racist, sexist, and homophobic acts go unchallenged. Inappropriate jokes, statements, and e-mails are disregarded. *"It was just a joke."* When someone persists in voicing their concerns, they are told it is being handled though nothing changes.
- Systems and practices are focused on equality rather than equity. There is a belief that everyone should receive the same thing rather than recognizing the impact of racism and the importance of providing resources based on need. *"We don't need to single out Students of Color; if we work with all students, those who have earned it will rise to the top."*
- The myth of meritocracy (believing that people are where they are solely due to their hard work) is popular rhetoric. There is no recognition of the unearned privileges that come with being White: *"I've worked hard. No one ever gave me a handout."*
- When PoC and women bring up ideas, they are ignored. However, when a White male suggests the same thing, it is well received as if it was the first time it was mentioned, and he is praised for *his* ideas.
- Leadership is tightly controlled versus widely shared. There is limited diversity of voice in decision-making settings, and usually the diversity is gender versus race. Opportunities to "sit at the

table" are restricted. There are a few people who control information. There is little interaction between leadership and staff.

- Environmental microaggressions dominate the space. The physical environment reflects dominant culture, i.e., pictures, artwork, celebrations, protocols, language, and positions of power. When PoC are included, they are tokenized in brochures and other materials but not sought out for their talents and abilities. Looking from the outside in, it may appear as if the organization is racially diverse, but the few PoC are only used to convey a sense of inclusion.
- The ethos of the organization is based on dominant culture's norms, values, beliefs, attitudes, discourse, and rituals. This is commonly communicated with statements like "*Assume positive intent.*" Religious accommodations are viewed as unnecessary. When requesting a place to pray, a Muslim may be told, "*Did you come here to work, or did you come here to pray?*"
- White employees are often hired because of who they know in the organization. "*Good fit*" is often a deciding factor in who gets hired or promoted.
- When PoC apply for a promotion, they are instructed to develop more skills, and reasons for not being promoted into leadership are vague. If the lack of PoC in leadership and other key roles is challenged, a common defense is "*We hire the most qualified people for the job.*"

Stage 2: Encounter

The term "Encounter" is used in various REI/D models to describe what is commonly referred today as an awakening. An Encounter can happen in two ways. An individual or subgroup within the organization does ongoing DEIB work to understand power, privilege, and oppression. As they gradually increase their understanding of racism, their perspectives begin to shift. They have a desire to "do something," but like Conscious Incompetence, they don't know enough to know what to do.

A PoC may have always known racism exists, but their ongoing education expands their comprehension and provides them with new language to better articulate their experiences and identify racist practices. Cross refers to this process as a "series of eye-opening experiences" in that it happens over time. In this stage individuals and subgroups become less tolerant of institutional racism, and "doing something" can mean focusing on individuals as the problem, rather than the institution.

An Encounter can also occur when something obviously racist (to most) happens external to the organization. The murder of George Floyd is an example of an Encounter moment that caused many organizations to seek out DEIB consultants for the first time. It can also occur internally in the organization, e.g., a lawsuit, finding themselves center of media attention, data revealing significant racial disparities, someone does something racist that is difficult to ignore. Whatever the reason, disregarding the issue is no longer an option. It is not uncommon during the encounter for people within to take sides, make excuses for why the work isn't needed, or justify the racist act. In this stage there is usually division.

In the Encounter stage, very little change occurs. Leaders are too afraid of "doing it wrong." White staff are fearful of making mistakes. And PoC don't feel it's safe to disclose their experiences and are not trusting anything will change.

Encounter Indicators

- Individuals in the organization begin to quietly, and sometimes publicly, question and resist the way things are and have always been. They begin to deepen their understanding of inequity within their organization. These individuals want things to change but may not know how to go about it.
- Many people within the organization remain in the Pre-encounter stage, denying that things need to change despite contrary evidence. Cognitive dissonance is often operating, where people say one thing but do another. PoC receive contradictory messages, overtly being told they are appreciated and valued, but nonverbal signals convey otherwise through policies, practices, everyday microaggressions, and denied promotion.
- Leaders may hope it will all blow over so they can go back to "business as usual."
- Some will blame individuals or groups who are pointing out the problems rather than become curious about institutionally racist practices: *"If they tried harder, they might get promoted to management"* and *"It's their attitude that's the problem."*
- When a racist incident has occurred, the individual is blamed for their actions. It is seen as an isolated incident that can be

rectified by sending the individual to training, coaching, or even firing them.

- There is a continuum of perspectives throughout the organization from "*It's about time we started talking about racism*" to "*I don't notice differences. I treat everyone the same.*" Many White people are in a state of disbelief that racism is an issue in their organization. Pain, anger, surprise, and confusion are common emotions that surface.
- During unstructured time, relationships are formed based on similarity. People begin taking sides, and their thinking is reinforced by surrounding themselves with those who share their same attitudes and beliefs.
- PoC within the organization are tokenized. They are held up as proof the organization values diversity and to show racism does not exist within their institution. I was once told by the principal of my children's elementary school, "*We have diversity. The cafeteria lady is Black.*"
- White people continue to be hired at a disproportionate rate. When this is brought to the attention of Human Resources the common responses are, "*People of Color didn't apply*" and "*We can't find qualified PoC.*"
- When a PoC struggles, he or she is blamed for having cultural deficits ("*Your English needs to improve*"), individual shortcomings, ("*We've had a number of complaints from your colleagues*"), or performance issues rather than examining institutional racism.
- The more conversations about race are happening, the more intense emotions become. As racism is examined and White people grow in their discomfort, the conversation is viewed as divisive rather than a necessary part of the process.
- DEIB work may get started but quickly comes to an end when White people complain about its "divisiveness." If a PoC disagrees with the need for race conversations, their voice affirms the need to discontinue the discourse.

Stage 3: Pre-Transformation

In Pre-Transformation, the organization is in a state of disequilibrium. Leadership recognizes something needs to be done, though they do not know what to do, and resistance is gaining momentum. Many consider the conversations a waste of time and make money-making statements like *"We have work to do"* or *"I can't believe that we are spending time on this; this is the workplace, not a place to be having touchy feeling conversations."* Statements like *"This just divides us"* and *"That was just one incident"* are a common form of resistance. Typically, the responsibility is put on the shoulders of one person, who is assigned the role of addressing DEIB, regardless of whether they have the qualifications or experience. This is frequently a person in Human Resources or a PoC because of their race. It is added on to their current job and usually comes with no added pay, resources, authority, support, or training.

Pre-Tranformation Indicators
- Little is done to make meaningful change. Leaders are not fully convinced DEIB is necessary and worth investing time and money in.
- Rather than a true commitment to change, leaders are most concerned about how much time it will take and how much it will interrupt their daily work.
- Leadership is cautious about looking incompetent, afraid of making mistakes, and uncertain in how to lead DEIB efforts.
- Leadership believes one person can "fix" the problem and assign that one person "do the work" rather than seeing an institutional problem that requires everyone's involvement including theirs.
- If an Equity Committee is formed, it is window dressing, rather than for any real substantial change.
- PoC in the Pre-Transformation stage are angry and deeply hurt. They are less likely to have the bandwidth to tolerate their White colleagues' lack of awareness. They don't believe White people are as naïve as they appear and don't have the emotional capacity to "meet them where they are at."
- PoC are more likely to call White people out by labeling, shaming, and blaming than calling them in by asking questions and being curious. There is little if any self-reflection as to why their approach isn't working. Anyone who doesn't agree with them is the problem. Their behaviors exhaust and intimidate White people, leaving them walking on eggshells.
- White allies who are new in their allyship are fearful their Colleagues of Color will see them as racist. Like PoC they too are reactionary, quick to point fingers, and fail to see opportunities for their own personal growth.

- Terms like racist, White fragility, gaslighting, and microaggressions are often overused and incorrectly applied. They become a weapon to put White people in check.
- PoC and White allies are seen as the problem. How they engage their colleagues becomes the issue. This lends credence to the belief that the issue isn't racism, it's "them."
- When PoC and Whites allies raise concerns, their voices are marginalized.
- Evidence of racist practices continues to surface through language, attitudes, beliefs, bias, who gets hired, promoted, etc., and little is done to address it. This fuels the hurt, anger, and feelings of hopelessness of PoC.
- Private versus public conversations become the norm. What is being discussed at the watercooler and in private Zoom chats are not occurring during staff meetings. Us versus them is typical in this stage.
- There is chaos in the organization. Staff and leadership do not have the skills to lean into the tension and are all over the map in what they believe needs to be done, so nothing gets done.
- No one is listening except to those who reinforce their own beliefs. There is more breaking than there is bridging. When conversations become intense, they are quickly shut down. Shaming and blaming are occurring from all sides both publicly and privately. New hires are at a loss as to what is happening and why. They may be pulled in to take sides.
- Race conversations focus on Black and White issues, leaving out the experiences of Indigenous, Latine, and Asians.
- There is considerable anxiety, nervousness, fear, anger, confusion, depression, frustration, and withdrawal. Few look forward to the workday.
- White women's tears can quickly shift the direction of the conversation away from race issues toward minimizing White staff's discomfort.
- Leadership is still defined by those who hold positions of power.
- Those wholly committed to equity work continue to move forward and seek support outside the organization. They know they need help.

Stage 4: Transformation

Transformation is similar to Conscious Competence in that the organization is growing in its ability to identify racial issues and are actively attempting to make changes. Though they are not confident in what they are doing—or if it is working, and how best to transform their organization—they maintain their commitment to DEIB. Different strategies are tried but are not well thought out or organized. Committed people have difficulty collectively agreeing on objectives and desired outcomes. Their newfound enthusiasm unleashes a fervor that causes them to take on anything and everything and much too quickly. It's as if they are trying to make up for lost time. Regardless of the reason, little progress is being made, and what has been done is not likely to stick.

Movement toward organizational alignment is slow going, but as they engage in culturally relevant professional development, common language and collective understanding is transpiring. There are still those who are resistant, but more people are shifting their thinking. Color-blind ideology is gradually being replaced with cultural and racial literacy. Those leading the work are beginning to tire with no clear direction or way to get wherever it is they are trying to go. In their zeal for change, PoC and White allies sometimes still struggle to bridge the divide with those who are not where they "should" be in this work. Tension, conflict, and lack of direction is still apparent.

Transformation Indicators

- An Equity Team is formed or reformed with renewed vigor and commitment though the Committee still struggles to find their focus. Too much time is spent processing and/or complaining about the problems rather than identifying actionable steps.
- Instead of assigning one person to do all the work (as in the Pre-Transformation stage), leadership places the responsibility on the shoulders of the ET with little involvement, believing it's best to leave it up to them.
- Leadership and the Equity Team are not working collaboratively and are frequently at odds with one another.
- Diversity statements versus policies are being written, and not everyone is aware of what exists.

- Quantitative measures are overvalued, and qualitative measures are minimized. If it can't be measured, it's not likely to be funded or supported.
- Pressure from leadership to "to do something" intensifies. This is more out of a need to showcase, rather than a commitment.
- Efforts to change are top-down or bottom-up and usually fail to include diverse voices and perspectives.
- Attempts are made to identify aspects of the organization that perpetuate institutional racism, but leadership is not aligned in how to go about this or what their role is. There is a fear of failure. Some leaders are doing more than others.
- Those leading equity are providing professional development for staff with little knowledge of how to effectively facilitate. When outside trainers are brought in, it is to address an immediate issue, e.g., microaggressions, rather than being strategic in their approach.
- Comments like *"We've already done that"* and *"Just tell me what to do"* begin to surface during workshops. Staff are struggling to understand how awareness of self, knowledge of others, and practicing skills *is* doing something. They grapple with the idea that it will lead to their knowing where to take action and how to advocate for change. In other words, they seek a technical solution to an adaptive problem.
- Some staff and leaders are not taking the professional development seriously. Those who remain resistant cite examples of ways in which their needs have not been met with statements like *"...but you don't see me forming a committee."*
- White staff are taking an individual approach to the conversation, citing personal examples of how they differ from other White people, hindering progress by making it about them rather than the collective.
- People of Color may mentally and emotionally check out of workshops on race or refuse to attend altogether, stating, *"I just want White people to do their work."* White people may look to PoC to teach them about racism as their second, unpaid job.
- Affinity groups and/or caucusing are put in place, but there is a need for structure and common understanding of its purpose. Some White people may feel it is divisive.
- The structure of the organization is in a state of flux as the work

is gaining momentum; displeased employees are leaving, and new staff are being hired.

- What has been achieved is not an integral part of the organization. If leadership or board members who are supporting DEIB were to leave, the work could potentially stop.
- There is still energy around DEIB efforts, but people who are leading the efforts are being stretched too thin and beginning to feel some burnout. They are not being compensated for the extra work.
- The organization realizes there are both internal and external issues but are overwhelmed by how much needs to be done and where to begin.
- The culture is learning to become more inquiry based, asking strategic, exploratory, and critical questions.
- Discussions are happening about bias in hiring and the need to be intentional in hiring and retaining PoC. However, recruiters fail to recognize PoC won't stay if the organization is not internally prepared to receive them.
- Different feelings have surfaced. Some are frustrated more isn't being done and not fast enough. Others are angry and feeling loss with how much things are changing too quickly. Leadership is anxious that things are getting worse not better.
- Small wins are occurring, but they are not celebrated. Other than those leading the equity efforts, few in the organization are aware of what has been accomplished.
- Attention and focus are on eliminating disparities for one group (e.g., race vs. ableism, sexism, ageism, heterosexism, classism, homophobia, etc.) without an understanding of intersectionality. This is a source of angst for other marginalized groups.
- Norms for difficult conversations are brainstormed and agreed upon. However, they are unaware of how norms like "assume positive intent" and "safety" maintain racist practices and run contrary to the work.
- Tone policing is transpiring. PoC who are more assertive, direct, and unapologetic about speaking up are encouraged to act and talk differently. The PoC whose communication style are aligned with dominant cultural norms are sought out and invited to the table. The organization struggles to recognize that diversity is not about fitting people into an existing system.

- The eagerness of allies can be overwhelming, tiresome, and some-times come across as disingenuous to PoC.
- Leadership is unsure of their role and feel incompetent in their ability to guide their staff. They seek a coach to guide and support them.
- Outside consultants who can provide an assessment, professional development, and help guide the organization are sought after.

Stage 5: New Identity

With support from a consultant, and through trial and error, there is more clarity in the direction they are heading. People within are consciously competent in some areas and unconsciously competent in others. The organization begins to feel a cultural shift as all levels of the organization are becoming involved in the transformation. Leadership and staff begin to feel comfortable with the discomfort and are taking more risks, recognizing this is a necessary part of the process. As their New Identity is taking form, momentum is building throughout the organization. There is new understanding that this work is a way of *being* versus *doing*, and leaders begin to model what the work looks like. The organization is more accepting of the time it will take to transform the organization and demonstrate a willing-ness to stay the course.

The organization is seeing the positive effects of their hard work through improved relationships, courageous conversations, and applied learning. Equity is at the center of most conversations, and there is talk of improving services the organization provides for mar-ginalized communities. When conflict erupts, as it inevitably will, people are better at working through the tension. Staff who do not support the direction of the organization are quieting their voices, and more are leaving, whether by choice or force.

New Identity Indicators

- The culture is becoming much more inquiry based, asking strate-gic, exploratory, and critical questions.
- "Us against them" mentality is being replaced by collective respon-sibility for institutional change.
- The Equity Team has identified Foundational Beliefs and norms to operate under as they engage the work.

- The Equity Team and leadership are working together collaboratively. They have gained clarity about what they are trying to accomplish and have a better understanding of how to approach the work.
- Leadership values the role of the Equity Team and relies on them for ideas and input on important matters.
- A strategic plan is underway to address DEIB and includes hiring a DEIB Director if one is not already in place.
- The focus becomes on changing systems and providing resources and support when needed, geared toward individuals success.
- Hiring and retention is examined through a DEIB lens so more diverse staff are hired and promoted.
- People recognize they can't do everything but begin to believe that they can make a difference. Their focus is on what's in their locus of control.
- The organization's mission, vision, policies, and practices are being revised to ensure they include DEIB language and support continued transformation.
- Staff and leadership are becoming clearer of their own *why* for the work.
- Leadership regularly discusses the importance of fulfilling the organization's DEIB mission and vision with staff.
- When decisions are made, they include diverse voices and reflect the interests of the diverse cultural and social groups they serve.
- Leadership and staff are committed to eradicate all forms of oppression within the organization.
- Race conversations move beyond a Black and White dichotomy to include other marginalized groups.
- Efforts are being made to cultivate PoC leadership skills.
- Leadership sees themselves as learners, and they meet with outside consultants for coaching. They are in relationship with leaders from other organizations engaged in DEIB efforts, recognizing the need for support and critical friends.
- Leadership and staff are seeking other means outside the organization to grow in their understanding of DEIB, e.g., books, podcasts, conferences, and so on.
- Leadership model transparency and vulnerability as they learn alongside their staff.

- Privilege, oppression, racism, antiracism, and other language that felt threatening in the past are common in meetings and used to critically examine the organization's policies and practices.
- Affinity groups are running more effectively. Staff recognize the need for a safe space where people are free to explore DEIB without fear of offending or harming nongroup members.
- In race discourse, conversations focus on racial groups rather than on individuals within a racial group. PoC are no longer having to take care of White people and their internal need to be an exception to any rule.
- When people are called in for harmful words or actions, they are more likely to be open and appreciative of the feedback.
- The organization recognizes that this work is ongoing with no end.
- Board participates in professional development, asks critical questions, and supports the transformation process.
- Small and big wins are celebrated.
- DEIB is a part of the onboarding process for new hires.
- Courageous conversations are viewed as an opportunity for individual and collective growth.
- Staff and leadership have appreciation for the personal and professional growth that comes with taking risks. They begin to realize perceived and actual costs are different for PoC who take more risks than their White colleagues.
- White allies are doing their personal work. They are visible in the organization and are advocating and supporting change in ways that bridge and help move the work forward.
- Undoing all isms is the focus of the organization, and when isms do occur, they are immediately addressed.
- Quantitative and qualitative measures are both valued. Listening Sessions are occurring to gain a better understanding of the needs, fears, and concerns of PoC.
- Leadership is defined more broadly to include those who are taking a lead in the diversity, equity, inclusion, and belonging efforts.

Stage 6: Social Justice in Action

The organization has transformed itself considerably. Leadership, staff, and board members are all becoming increasingly unconsciously competent in the way they talk about DEIB and center equity in their work. They are living into this work in their personal and professional spheres of influence to stand against all forms of oppression.

Leadership and staff are developing relationships across cultures within and outside the organization. Engaging in courageous conversations has become a norm. People are more authentic in how they show up in the work and feel a sense of belonging. They are skilled and effective in developing policies and strategies that work toward liberating diverse staff and clients at all levels of the organization. The culture is one that values its diversity. Partnerships are formed with other organizations to support not just racial justice but other social justice initiatives. People understand advocating for diversity, equity, inclusion, and belonging is for our collective humanity, not solely for the benefit of one group.

Social Justice in Action Indicators

- The organization is less reliant on outside consultants. Funding is allocated to train trainers within the organization. They are more inclined to look inward for support, ideas, and resolution.
- There is less need for caucusing/affinity groups unless people need space to process the impact with same group membership. Staff can have courageous conversations with one another as issues arise inside and outside the organization.
- Ongoing learning is a regular part of workplace. Some are mandatory while others are optional. Leaders participate in facilitating some of the workshops.
- Problems are addressed with a restorative justice approach. Solutions are sought to remedy the impact on those harmed and the person who authored the harm in a way that leads to growth rather than immediate dismissal or other punitive measures.
- Healing circles are a part of the culture to address harm done due to institutional isms and to work through issues as they arise.
- Multicultural versus monocultural skills are valued, encouraged, and cultivated by the organization. They recognize the value of diverse voices, perspectives, and identities and are intentional about who is represented at all levels of the organization.
- Clients and staff can bring their different identities into the organization without feeling they will be judged negatively, excluded, or passed over for promotion.

- Different holidays and cultures are recognized and honored. Staff are given flexibility to take time off to acknowledge and celebrate religious holidays and cultural practices, e.g., Yom Kippur, Ramadan.
- Everyone knows the importance of DEIB, their role in it, and accepts responsibility for infusing it into their everyday workplace practice.
- Accountability measures are in place to ensure the work continues through the efforts of leadership and staff.
- People become agents of change, not just in their professional lives but also in their personal lives.
- The organization is a place where staff and leadership feel they belong and enjoy working there.
- The Director of Equity has one title versus multiple functions, e.g., HR Director.
- The Director of Equity has the budget needed to support DEIB efforts and enough staff to help carry out the work.
- The Director of Equity reports to the head of the organization or the Board so they are not hindered in their ability to give programmatic or individual feedback to members.
- The Equity Team is running smoothly and effectively with fewer challenges. They are valued in the organization as a source of support in moving the work forward. People know who they are and are clear about their purpose.
- There is a standardized hiring process that is intentional in seeking diverse candidates for all levels of the organization, including interview questions pursuing candidates who have experience and are committed to being a part of a multicultural organization.
- Anyone serving on the interview committee is required to attend implicit bias training, so they become skilled at recognizing their own bias and bias in other panelists.
- Individuals are given the support and resources needed to succeed and advance in the organization.
- The onboarding process of new hires includes DEIB workshops, resources, and a contact person to help them successfully navigate their workplace environment.
- Exit interviews include examining how the organization was

successful or failed to support staff's multicultural experiences. Changes are made based on themes that are occurring.

- The organization regularly accesses their progress, the climate, and well-being of staff.
- The board is clear about their role and responsibilities in DEIB.
- The makeup of the Board is diverse.
- The board and leadership receive regular updates on progress and play an important function in ongoing DEIB efforts.
- When the board is in the position to hire an executive leader, they seek out someone who is committed and grounded in DEIB.
- The organization shares its resources with other agencies, e.g., partnering in learning opportunities.
- The organization addresses systemic racism that is hindering their progress.
- As they continue to evolve internally, external services have become a central focus.
- The organization is actively working on a regional, national, and global level to eliminate all forms of oppression.
- Communities most impacted by decisions made by the organization are involved in the decision-making process whenever possible.

Specialized Resources

Jackson, B. W. "Theory and Practice of Multicultural Organization Development." In *The NTL Handbook of Organization Development and Change*, edited by B. B. Jones & M. Brazzel, 139–154. San Francisco, CA: Pfeiffer, 2006.

Jackson, B. W., & Hardiman, R. "Multicultural Organization Development." In *The Promise of Diversity: Over 40 Voices Discuss Strategies for Eliminating Discrimination in Organizations*, edited by E. Y. Cross, J. H. Katz, F. A. Miller, & E. W. Seashore, 231–239. Arlington, VA: NTL Institute, 1994.

Jackson, B. W., and Holvino, E. V. "Developing Multicultural Organizations." *Journal of Religion and Applied Behavioral Science (Association for Creative Change)* (Fall 1988): 14–19.

Okun, Tema. *White Supremacy Culture.* dRworks. Dismantlingracism .org.

The Social Justice Training Institute (2008). "Creating Social Justice on Campus: Sharing Best Practices and Lessons Learned." Presentation at the White Privilege Conference by Jamie Washington, Kathy Obear, and Vernon Wall.

Your Organization's Stage of Multicultural Organizational Identity Development (SMOID): Commitment to Change and Be Changed

- Identify which stage your organization most closely fits by checking all areas that best describe what is taking place within. Consider engaging in this process with your Equity Team, staff, and/or leadership.
- Generate ideas on steps needed to move to the next stage.

SUSTAINING YOURSELF WHILE MAINTAINING YOUR COMMITMENT

You cannot save the world by sitting
in the upholstered arm chair. It takes the effort,
the action, the work, the endurance that exposes
the body to fatigue and hurt and exhaustion and pain.

—John Hiram Jackson

21

Radical Self-Care

ONE DAY WHILE WAITING for a light to turn green, I witnessed a man getting hit by a car while walking across the street. He went flying over the hood and landed flat on the pavement with an apparent thud. He instantly jumped up and with both hands immediately started patting himself as if to confirm he was still alive. Leading equity work is emotionally, physically, and mentally exhausting to the point where there will be days you will feel as though you have been struck by a moving vehicle. You will wonder if you will be able to get back up again. Becoming grounded in this work paired with self-care will be critical in your ability to stay the course. Because when you do get knocked down, you will need to jump back up.

The more you move racial equity work forward, the more challenges you will face. Some days you will take one step forward, and the next find yourself two steps back. You will experience immense judgment and pressure from inside and out. At times, community, coworkers, and even leadership will cause you to doubt your abilities and commitment. Some will say you are not doing enough; others will argue you are doing too much. The more you move DEIB efforts forward in your organization, the more resistance you are likely to experience from White communities and individuals who don't want to see change.

Your organization may find itself in the news because of its DEIB efforts, and it won't be to praise your progress. I know. I've been there before. During my role as Director of Diversity for Seattle Public Schools, I received two "Schrammie" awards. When local Seattle broadcaster Ken Schram was alive, he would award people who he believed made "bonehead decisions and/or the most appalling of asinine behavior." Apparently, I was boneheaded twice. Because I had sent students to the White Privilege Conference, a federal investigation was done on my department falsely accusing me of misusing government funds.

If you are PoC, you may have the added burden of experiencing microaggressions as you lead your organization on its journey toward racial justice. The list of challenges is endless, so get ready. Consider small steps you will take to embed self-care into your daily routine; it will strengthen your mind, body, and spirit so you are prepared to withstand the heat.

From early childhood through much of my young adult life, I would put the needs of others before myself. I rarely said "no" when someone needed something and had what I've heard referred to as "*the disease to please*." Though this tendency wasn't the root cause, I eventually came to understand I was being driven by an unconscious need for others to like me. It took a lot of therapy, self-help books, and mindfulness before I could believe that self-care itself wasn't an act of selfishness. I was eventually able to change my mindset and behaviors.

When I recently read civil rights activist Audre Lorde's quote, "*Caring for myself is not self-indulgence, it is self-preservation, and that is an act of political warfare,*" I spent significant time wondering what she meant by "an act of political warfare."[1] I contemplated if she meant without self-care, we won't have the bandwidth to change institutional isms. Or maybe when she made the statement, she knew racism was literally killing Black, Brown, and Indigenous people and saw self-care as fighting back. I also considered if she was referring to the corporations who value the dollar more than the lives of PoC. She made that statement while battling cancer, which eventually took her life. Though I'll probably never know what she truly meant by it, I do know those five words have caused me to feel a deeper conviction for my own self-care and yours.

Leading your organization through deconstructing its policies and practices and reconstructing a new way of being is tough and demanding work. If you are not careful, you will quickly burn out or, worse yet, become sick. But even self-care can be hard work, and I know if you don't take care of yourself, your commitment to social justice will consume you and you will end up giving yourself away until there is nothing left. Below are ways I practice improving my psychological (how I think), physical (my body), social (relationships), emotional (feelings), and spiritual (connection to a higher power) well-being. They are in no specific order. I hope you find them helpful in your journey for justice.

Self-Care Practices

- Identify other people leading this work who you can call on when things become challenging. People who are not doing this work won't truly know what you mean by a "bad day" even when they try their best to understand. Seek out a critical friend who will keep you from going down a self-deprecating path when others in your workplace place blame on your shoulders.
- Attend social justice conferences to engage like-minded colleagues and to meet other people leading equity work whom you can learn from and connect with.
- Resign from any boards you serve on and other professional volunteering you may be doing. This work in and of itself is a more than any one person can manage to lead. You will need to free up your schedule as much as possible so you can rejuvenate.
- Refrain from working on the weekends if your work does not require it. Meaning if your organization is not operating during the weekends, then neither should you. Checking e-mails and bringing work home is not going to get you caught up for long. Do what you can during the week, and then let it go.
- Be intentional about spending time with family and friends. These should be people that bring you joy—not drama—into your life.
- If you have children in your home, take time to just be present with them. When driving together in the car, do not talk on the phone. Someone once told me, "*Social justice starts at home.*" Whose interests are being served when you put all your time and attention into your work while your family falls apart? If you have fur babies, know that they need your love and attention too.
- Set aside guilt-free time to do things you love doing. Indulge in your favorite shows, work in your garden, read a book (not work related), or go for long walks or drives. Even scheduling little mini getaways, sometimes by yourself if that's what you enjoy doing.
- Go to bed at a reasonable hour. I don't need to tell you how important your sleep is. If you have a problem falling asleep or frequently wake up in the middle of the night because work is on

---

your mind, put a pad of paper next to your bed so you can quickly write down your thoughts to clear your mind. I try to go to bed by 7:30 p.m. each night so I have time to unwind by reading. I prefer fantasy books about kick butt women with swords. It's a great way to escape reality if you like that kind of thing.

- Wake up 10–15 minutes earlier in the morning for quiet time to meditate, journal, read scripture (if that's you), or just reflect. Don't rush to work every morning, arriving stressed before the day has even begun.
- If you have the financial means, have someone clean your home at least once a month so you are not spending most of your weekends cleaning. I remember the first time realizing a friend had a cleaning lady. I always associated it with being lazy. Now I associate it with self-care and class privilege.
- Let people do things for you. When they offer their help, don't push it away. You do not need to prove to anyone that you are capable. And if you are a PoC, recognize that exceptionalism is a part of our racist culture.
- Be in touch with your body. Find time to get in a little exercise by walking during your breaks or even doing 5- to 10-minute work-outs in the morning. (DON'T SKIP WORK BREAKS!)
- Walking with friends and family during weeknights or weekends is a great way to exercise and maintain relationships.
- Set your alarm to do yoga or stretch at your desk.
- Bring healthy snacks to work so you can replenish your body. If you find yourself in your car a lot, put them in your glove com-partment. This can help you to avoid fast food. And stay hydrated!
- Receive compliments others give you. People will be quick to tell you what you did wrong and slow to tell you what you did right. Really take in the accolades. Don't make it a habit of always giving the credit to others or minimize the hard work you've put in. Practice just simply saying thank you. Make a folder for compliments on your computer. When people send you e-mails thanking you, telling you how awesome you are, save those mes-sages. When you have a bad day, read a few of the compliments to remind yourself you are making a difference.
- Practice complimenting yourself by speaking positively about who you are as a person and things you've done or are doing

well. Write down 3 or 4 character traits about yourself. Come up with affirmations to repeat to yourself when you need to hear them. Affirmations really work. You are likely your biggest critic. Why not learn to be your biggest fan too?

- Do not skip *any* medical or dental appointments. Schedule physicals, mammograms, and prostate exams. You are no good to anyone if you are sick.

- Take vitamin supplements regularly if you are getting up in age or are not consuming nutrients your body needs. Find out from your health practitioners which ones you should be taking.

- If you enjoy massages, schedule them periodically to help work out the stress that builds up in your body. And do not cancel your appointments! If you don't like massages, soak in a hot tub every now and again.

- Use the time you spend alone in your car as a time for reflection. Listen to music that lifts your spirit, podcasts that inspire you, and audible books that help you grow or clear your mind.

- Do not let "selfish" become a bad word. It is only bad when people in your life use it as a tool to get from you what they want. Practice saying the words "No" or "I can't." When someone asks you what you are doing on Saturday ask, "Why?" before telling them, "Nothing." It is OK if you don't have anything planned and want to keep it that way. Don't stretch yourself thin.

- Inform people in your life when you are working on something that is increasing your stress level. Let them know you may be a little crankier or a little less present. Tell them what you need from them, and then thank them for supporting you when the stressful time has passed.

- When you hurt someone, apologize. Don't find ways to justify your actions. This simple action will help you release the internal guilt that comes with being human. Ignoring it when you've wronged someone will slowly eat away at you.

- When you attend family functions, give yourself permission to bring a store-bought item. It's OK if you don't have the capacity to cook or bake that homemade dish you are famous for.

- Seek out a mental health therapist if you need a professional to talk to. Do inner healing work to face past hurt and harm done to you. There's no shame in therapy.

- Uplift a PoC. We are constantly bombarded with spoken and unspoken messages conveying we are not beautiful, smart, talented, brilliant, gifted, etc. It may not sound like self-care, but it will lift your spirit to speak light into another person.

While leading equity work has its challenges, you will also find it immensely rewarding as you take steps to improve the lives of those who have existed on the margins for far too long. You will be changed in many wonderful and surprising ways, and you will be left feeling your sacrifices were worth it.

Assess what you are doing well in different areas of your life and where you need to improve, then commit to improving that aspect of your life in small ways. Indigenous peoples have what they refer to as a Balance Wheel, also known as a Medicine Wheel, to describe this. Continually strive for balance in your psychological, physical, mental, social, and spiritual life, and when one area becomes off-kilter, address it so it does not have a big impact on other facets of your life. While you will never achieve complete and total balance, working on self-improvement in these and other ways feels good and can bring about a sense of joy and inner peace. I feel so much better when I'm taking care of myself, I know you will too.

Make Self-Care a Habit:
Commitment to Change and Be Changed

- One way to consider areas that you need to nurture is to take an inventory of the psychological, physical, mental, social, and spiritual aspects of your life. Go through the above ideas for self-care and determine which ones will benefit you personally and add your own ideas.
- Choose one beneficial thing and commit to making it a habit. Identify small steps that will lead to big change. When one area becomes a habit, gradually take on other self-care practices.

All the best to you as you lead your organization through diversity, equity, inclusion, and belonging. And remember, social justice starts at home.

APPENDIX

Antiracist Leadership Practices

On a scale of 0–4, rate your leadership practices as it pertains to Diversity, Equity, Inclusions, and Belonging (DEIB) for your clients, communities, staff, and your personal continued growth. Place a ✓ in the box that most closely reflects your practices. This survey will take a minimum of 15–20 minutes to complete. The Institutional portion can be completed by a group of leaders.

Rating			Description of Rating
0	Never	I'm stuck	I'm not sure what to do. I could use some help getting started.
1	Rarely	I'm avoiding	I know what I could be doing, I just need to do it more.
2	Sometimes	I'm developing	I do an adequate job with this, but I could commit to doing more.
3	Often	I'm applying	It's a regular part of my leadership practices, but I've missed opportunities.
4	Always	I'm incorporating	Whenever possible, I'm doing this.

Antiracist Practices Each question pertains to PoC even when not explicitly stated.	Never 0	Rarely 1	Sometimes 2	Often 3	Always 4	Wherever you scored a 0–2, what steps can you take to improve your practice? What more do you need to know? What questions do you have? What are your fears or concerns? What support do you need?

All Staff

		Never 0	Rarely 1	Sometimes 2	Often 3	Always 4	
1	We regularly discuss DEIB, e.g., during staff meeting.						
2	We are engaging in learning together as it relates to DEIB.						
3	We practice naming how race and privilege play out in our group dynamics, e.g., during meetings.						
4	We celebrate small wins as they relate to DEIB.						
5	When our words and behaviors negatively impact others, we call one another in.						
6	We are inquiry based, asking strategic, exploratory, and critical questions as they relate to DEIB.						
7	When I provide staff feedback, I ask questions, so they are thinking about their work through a DEIB lens.						

Antiracist Practices Each question pertains to PoC even when not explicitly stated.	Never 0	Rarely 1	Sometimes 2	Often 3	Always 4	Wherever you scored a 0–2, what steps can you take to improve your practice? What more do you need to know? What questions do you have? What are your fears or concerns? What support do you need?

Staff of Color

		Never 0	Rarely 1	Sometimes 2	Often 3	Always 4	
8	We regularly practice the seven norms for courageous conversations. If not these, we have our own.						
9	Staff of Color know they can talk with me about experience of racism and that I will address it.						
10	When Staff of Color experience racism, I address it immediately and/or advocate on their behalf.						
11	I take steps to ensure Staff of Color know that I see them, care about them, and that they matter.						
12	I listen to concerns of Staff of Color and make changes based on what I have learned.						
13	I take the initiative to engage in conversations with Staff of Color about race, racism, and race relations.						
14	I work to ensure the burden of DEIB work does not fall on the shoulders of Staff of Color.						

	Antiracist Practices Each question pertains to PoC even when not explicitly stated.	Never 0	Rarely 1	Sometimes 2	Often 3	Always 4	Wherever you scored a 0–2, what steps can you take to improve your practice? What more do you need to know? What questions do you have? What are your fears or concerns? What support do you need?

Self

15	I continually assess and challenge my stereotypes, so they do not impact my expectations or engagement with others.						
16	When I offend or make mistakes, I lean into the impact of my words and actions, not my intent.						
17	When I offend or make mistakes, I give myself grace; I use what I've learned to practice engaging differently.						
18	I continually engage in self-reflection exploring how my privileged identities impact how I see and experience PoC.						
19	I do not consider myself color-blind and seek to understand experiences through a racial lens.						
20	I take time to learn about diverse groups' experiences and culture beyond what I provide to my staff.						

	Antiracist Practices Each question pertains to PoC even when not explicitly stated.	Never 0	Rarely 1	Sometimes 2	Often 3	Always 4	Wherever you scored a 0–2, what steps can you take to improve your practice? What more do you need to know? What questions do you have? What are your fears or concerns? What support do you need?
21	I know when to take an adaptive vs. technical approach when engaging Staff and/or Communities of Color.						
22	I recognize my power and privileges and use them to build a culture of DEIB.						
23	I know my racial/ethnic identity and power influences the way staff and Communities of Color see me. We talk about this.						
24	I learn to pronounce every staff and client's name correctly rather than shorten or change their names.						
25	I share with staff my learning and insights, so they feel they can engage others in their learning journey.						
26	I practice regular self-care and create balance in my professional and personal life, so I have the capacity for DEIB.						
27	I talk with staff about DEIB often enough they know it is a priority to me.						

	Antiracist Practices Each question pertains to PoC even when not explicitly stated.	Never 0	Rarely 1	Sometimes 2	Often 3	Always 4	Wherever you scored a 0–2, what steps can you take to improve your practice? What more do you need to know? What questions do you have? What are your fears or concerns? What support do you need?
28	I embrace discomfort and take risks to try new DEIB practices.						
29	I model, for my staff, courageous conversations, culturally responsive practices, and humility.						
30	I approach DEIB with a historical understanding, not a blank slate mentality.						
31	When I need help, I ask colleagues or seek support from a DEIB consultant.						

Institutionally

Note: If the below are not within your scope of work, respond based on whether you are advocating for these changes.

32	Our evaluations include culturally responsive and relevant practices.						
33	Our Staff of Color are provided opportunities to gain experience and advance.						
34	We use data, e.g., from our climate survey, to inform us on opportunities for growth and success.						

	Antiracist Practices Each question pertains to PoC even when not explicitly stated.	Never 0	Rarely 1	Sometimes 2	Often 3	Always 4	Wherever you scored a 0–2, what steps can you take to improve your practice? What more do you need to know? What questions do you have? What are your fears or concerns? What support do you need?
35	Our newsletters, website, social media, and marketing materials include multicultural content throughout.						
36	We include community voices to better understand their needs and concerns and make changes accordingly.						
37	When planning events, we are mindful of holidays and do not schedule events on those days, e.g., Yom Kippur						
38	We have flex holidays so staff can take days off for important celebrations and do not have to use personal leave.						
39	Our mission and vision statement has a DEIB focus.						
40	We implement equitable policies and practices based on DEIB principles.						
41	We have a strategic plan in place to address DEIB.						
42	We are mindful of how institutional racism impacts PoC, and we allocate our resources equitably.						

	Antiracist Practices Each question pertains to PoC even when not explicitly stated.	Never 0	Rarely 1	Sometimes 2	Often 3	Always 4	Wherever you scored a 0–2, what steps can you take to improve your practice? What more do you need to know? What questions do you have? What are your fears or concerns? What support do you need?
43	Our hiring practices are through a DEIB lens, e.g., interview questions, advertising, job descriptions, etc.						
44	Anyone participating on a hiring panel is required to participate in implicit bias training.						
45	When possible, we support minority-owned businesses, e.g., ordering food, copies, books, and other materials.						
46	Our materials are translated in other languages, and when needed we use interpreters.						
47	We encourage staff to take regular breaks, go on vacation, and take sick leave when needed.						
48	Our Staff of Color receive the same pay as their White counterparts.						
49	We have PoC in leadership positions.						

Questions to Discuss

What do you notice about your Antiracist Leadership Practices?

_____

_____

_____

_____

Choose one practice you scored yourself a 4 on and discuss specifically successes, challenges, insights, lessons learned, etc.

_____

_____

_____

_____

Choose one of your 0–2 scores and share with your group challenges you are facing in making this a part of your Antiracist Leadership Practices. Ask your group a question that will help you improve in this area? What will you have the courage to commit to changing?

_____

_____

_____

_____

What other Antiracist Leadership Practices are you engaging in?

_____

_____

_____

_____

Do not be daunted by the enormity of the world's grief. Do justly now. Love mercy now. Walk humbly now. You are not obligated to complete the work, but neither are you free to abandon it.

--Pirkei Avot

Acknowledgments

Ubuntu.
I am because we are.
—South African proverb

I am grateful to my God for the guidance and grace that has brought me this far. I never would have imagined my life to be what it is today. Being shy as a child, struggling through K-12 and early college, I never dreamed I would some-day have a doctorate degree, own my own business, write a first book, let alone this second one, and then use what I've accomplished as tools to fight for social justice. There is no doubt in my mind that my success is due to God.

Given that I have some insecurities about my writing, I was ecstatic when I received the e-mail from Caylie Graham, Assistant Editor and Rob West, Acqui-sition Editor. When I met them both personally, I knew I wanted New Society Publishers to publish my manuscript. They seemed as excited about publishing my book, as I was. It eased my insecurities and lifted my spirits to be told they've been waiting for a book like this one for a long time, and in Rob's words, it "fills an immense gap." I am so grateful to all of the people at New Society Publishers. I was surrounded by a team of people who were truly invested in the success of my book. Thank you, Caylie Graham, for everything you did to put the publication of *Inside Out* into action and for your constant encouragement. Sue Custance and Diane McIntosh for your creativity with the book cover. Greg Green for rede-signing my graphics so they fit into this book. The Marketing Team, Sara Reeves and EJ Hurst, for meeting with and coming up with great ideas for how to get this out there to readers. Betsy Nuse, thank you so much for all the hours you invested in polishing it so my words came together more smoothly.

A huge thank you to my business partner Ilsa M. Govan. She's kind of a big deal to me. I know much of this book would not be possible without her. Many of the concepts have been shaped through our work together. So much so, I'm not always able to discern her ideas from mine. Ubuntu. I am because we are.

I thank the organizations, leaders, and staff I've had the opportunity and privilege to work with over the past twenty plus years. Your trust in me to lead

245

you in courageous conversations has furthered my growth as a consultant. Many things written in this book have come from the questions you've asked, the times you've challenged my thinking, and those moments you've offered up praise reinforcing my commitment by reminding me that I am making a difference.

To my husband, Gary, who is one of my biggest fans. I sometimes overhear you praising me to your friends. It makes me smile and brings me joy to have you by my side every step of the way.

To my sister Suki who is always so supportive and will do anything to help in my success.

Special thanks to Leticia Nieto for everything you poured into this book. I'm still in awe that you agreed to write my foreword. I've always been a big fan of your work! To Emilie Hard, friend and colleague, for all the time you time spent editing. Your suggestions, praise, and encouragement were much needed. To Jill Nathanson, Librarian at Rutgers University, for your willingness to edit my manuscript even though we have never met. The laser-like focus you provided in pointing out small things I would not have seen myself were invaluable. To Debra Robinson Baker for proofing my hardest chapter and offering helpful suggestions. Thank you.

Thank you, Erin Jones, author of *Bridges to Heal Us: Stories and Strategies for Racial Healing*, and Dr. Jennifer Wiley for playing a big role in coming up with the title of this book. Erin, when you said, "The title will live with you forever," I knew I couldn't just settle. I almost did. I appreciate Ilsa Govan, Richard Kim, Jerod Grant, Kenzie Gandy, Jovan Hollins, Karena Hooks for generating ideas.

There is nothing like having girlfriends who want the best for you. I must thank my Sista girl, Karena Hooks with Hooks Global. Thank you, Karena for your words of encouragement, late-night phone calls when I should have been asleep, and for being there for me as I processed my writing insecurities. Thank you for being the first person to offer to read my manuscript and for suggesting the chapter on self-care. It's so like you to make self-care a priority. To my Sisters Andrea Gleason and Linda DeCuire who, after a great meal and lots of laughter, got serious with me about getting my manuscript to a publisher. Thank you for not letting me off the hook until I gave you a date and for holding me accountable. I should probably be thanking you both after God because this book would probably still be gathering dust if you hadn't pushed back on all my excuses.

Finally, I want to acknowledge everyone out there who is bringing about change. Keep shouting, marching, fighting, and writing for social justice. You are generating a critical mass that is reminiscent of the Civil Rights Movement. Never underestimate the power of collective will and its ability to keep hope alive. We are making history together as each of us finds a way to do our part in making the United States great for all her people.

References, Readings, and Resources

Books and Articles Cited in the Text

Banaji, Mahzarin and Anthony Greenwald. *Blindspot: Hidden Biases of Good People.* New York: Delacorte Press, 2013.

Broadwell, Martin. "Teaching for Learning (XVI)." *The Gospel Guardian* 20, no. 41 (1969): 1–3.

Calderón, JLove. *Occupying Privilege: Conversations on Love, Race, & Liberation.* Love-N-Liberation Press, 2012.

Crenshaw, Kimberlé. "Demarginalizing the Intersection of Race and Sex: A Black Feminist Critique of Antidiscrimination Doctrine, Feminist Theory and Anti-racist Politics." *University of Chicago Legal Forum* Vol. 1989: Iss. 1, Article 8.

Cross, Jr., William. *The Negro-to-Black Conversion Experience. Black World* 20, no. 9 (1971): 13–27.

DiAngelo, Robin. "White America's Racial Illiteracy: Why Our National Conversation Is Poisoned from the Start." *Salon* (April 10, 2015).

DiAngelo, Robin. *White Fragility: Why It's so Hard for White People to Talk about Racism.* Boston: Beacon Press, 2018.

Dillard, Annie. Quotation. In Palmer, Parker J. *Let Your Life Speak: Listening for the Voice of Vocation.* San Francisco: Jossey Bass, 2020.

Govan, Ilsa and Tilman Smith. *What's Up with White Women: Unpacking Sexism and White Privilege in Pursuit of Racial Justice.* Gabriola: New Society, 2021.

Heifetz, Ronald, Alexander Grashow, and Marty Linsky. *The Theory Behind the Practice: A Brief Introduction to the Adaptive Leadership Framework.* Boston: Harvard Business Press, 2009.

Hollins, Caprice and Ilsa Govan. *Diversity, Equity, and Inclusion: Strategies for Facilitating Conversations on Race.* Lanham: Rowman & Littlefield, 2015.

Katz, Judith. *White Awareness Handbook for Anti-Racism Training.* Tulsa: University of Oklahoma Press, 1978.

Kendall, Frances E. *Understanding White Privilege: Creating Pathways to Authentic Relationships across Race*, 2nd ed. New York: Routledge Publishing. 2013.

Lorde, Audre. *A Burst of Light and Other Essays.* Garden City NY: Ixia Press, 2017.

McIntosh, Peggy. "White Privilege and Male Privilege: A Personal Account of Coming to See Correspondences through Work in Women's Studies." Working Paper 189, Wellesley Centers for Women, Wellesley, Mass (1988).

Mukhopadhyay, Carol C. "Getting Rid of the Word 'Caucasian,'" in *Everyday Antiracism: Getting Real About Race in School*, edited by Mica Pollock, 12–16. New York: New Press, 2008.

Nieto, Leticia, Margot F. Boyer, Liz Goodwin, Garth R. Johnson, and Laurel Collier Smith. *Beyond Inclusion, Beyond Empowerment: A Developmental Strategy to Liberate Everyone*. 2nd ed. Olympia: Cuetzpalin Publishing, 2014.

Oluo, Ijeoma. *So You Want to Talk about Race*. New York: Seal Press, 2018.

Singleton, Glenn E. *Courageous Conversations about Race: A Field Guide for Achieving Equity in Schools and Beyond*. 3rd ed. Thousand Oaks: Corwin, 2021.

Steele, Claude. *Whistling Vivaldi and Other Clues to How Stereotypes Affect Us*. New York: W.W. Norton, 2010.

Sue, Derald and David Sue. *Counseling the Culturally Diverse: Theory and Practice*. 4th ed. New York: Wiley & Sons, 2003.

Sue, Derald, Christina Capodilupo, Gina Torino, Jennifer Bucceri, Aisha Holder, Kevin Nadal, and Marta Esquilin. "Racial Microaggressions in Everyday Life: Implications for Clinical Practice." *American Psychologist* 62, no. 4 (2007): 271–86.

Takaki, Ronald. *A Different Mirror: A History of Multicultural America*, rev. ed. Boston: Back Bay Books, 2008.

Wile, Daniel B. *Collaborative Couples Therapy: Turning Fights into Intimate Conversations*. Workshop attended in Renton, Washington, July 2011.

Zinn, Howard. *A People's History of the United States*. New York: Harper, 2005.

Readings

Brown, Brené. *Dare to Lead: Brave Work. Tough Conversations. Whole Hearts*. New York: Penguin Random House, 2018.

DiAngelo, Robin. *White America's Racial Illiteracy: Why our National Conversation Is Poisoned from the Start*. The Good Men Project, 2015.

Ibram, Kendi X. *How to Be an Antiracist*. New York: One World, 2019.

Irving, D. *Waking up White and Finding Myself in the Story of Race*. Cambridge: Elephant Room Press, 2014.

Kivel, Paul. *Uprooting Racism: How White People Can Work for Racial Justice*. 4th ed. Gabriola: New Society, 2018.

Resources for Equity Leaders
Land Acknowledgment
Maps:
Locate the Indigenous Peoples land you are on. native-land.ca/.
First Peoples' Map of B.C. fpcc.ca/stories/first-peoples-map.

Video:
Honor Native Land: A Guide and Call to Acknowledgment. usdac.us/nativeland.

Websites

Asian Nation: Asian American History, Demographics, & Issues.
asian-nation.org/assimilation.shtml.

National Education Association: nea.org.

Project Implicit: a researched based test you can take online that measures your
unconscious attitudes and bias: implicit.harvard.edu/implicit/demo/take
atest.html.

Racial Equity Tools offers tips and resources for organizational change work:
racialequitytools.org/home.

Reducing Stereotype Threat: reducingstereotypethreat.org.

Rethinking Schools provides articles and resources for teachers looking to infuse
social justice in their practice: rethinkingschools.org/index.shtml.

Teaching Tolerance has free resources including DVDs, CDs and publications for
educators, parents, and kids: tolerance.org/index.jsp.

Videos

Cultures Connecting YouTube Channel: DEIB related videos
youtube.com/playlist?list=PLyt2WdCXfeTcQOMPkt1jRs7VtPUFUosuv.

Race: The Power of an Illusion: This three-part series is an eye-opening tale of
how what we assume to be normal, commonsense, even scientific, is actually
shaped by our history, social institutions, and cultural beliefs.
newsreel.org/video/race-the-power-of-an-illusion.

Unnatural Causes: Consists of 7 short videos addressing how racism affects
health. (4 hours) California Newsreel. unnaturalcauses.org/

Notes

Introduction

1. Latine (pronounced Lateenae) is a relatively new term replacing the binary masculine and feminine "Latino/a" and "Latinx." Latine is a gender-neutral term adopted by those of Latin descent and is a way to speak gender inclusively. It calls us to shift our paradigm from seeing gender solely in terms of she/her/hers or he/him/his, girl or boy, to a broader understanding that acknowledges gender fluidity and appreciates the complexity of our genders. Note: Latine is controversial in the Latino/a community. Not everyone agrees with the term.

Chapter 2: See Yourself as a Part of the Work

1. Gender diverse acknowledges the fluidity of gender and is all-encompassing versus the restricting traditionally held notions of gender identity. It is like saying Latine.
2. A. G. Johnson, *Privilege, Power, and Difference*. (New York: McGraw-Hill, 2001), 23–24.
3. Annie Dillard Quotation. In Parker J. Palmer, *Let Your Life Speak: Listening for the Voice of Vocation*. (San Francisco: Jossey Bass, 2020), 80.
4. Cisgender describes a person who identifies with the gender they were assigned at birth. If, for example, you were assigned the gender of male at birth and throughout your life always identified with that assignment, you would be considered cisgender male. Not everyone identifies with the gender they were assigned at birth, and there are those who do not identify as male or female. They use they/them pronouns rather than he/him or she/her.

Chapter 3: Why We Don't Know How to Talk About Race

1. This overview comes from an accumulation of my readings over the years, but I would say the main source is Ronald Takaki's book *A Different Mirror: A History of Multicultural America*.

Chapter 4: Establish Your Foundational Beliefs

1. Ilse Govan quoting Jamie Washington to the author, December 2013.
2. Frances E. Kendall, *Understanding White Privilege: Creating Pathways to*

Authentic Relationships across Race, 2nd ed. (New York: Routledge Publishing, 2013), 39.

Section II: Finding a Framework to Guide You

1. This fourth component was influenced by Judith Katz in her book *White Awareness: Handbook for Anti-Racism Training.*

Chapter 5: Be Aware of Yourself as a Racialized Being

1. Mahzarin Banaji and Anthony Greenwald, *Blind Spot: Hidden Biases of Good People.* (New York: Delacorte Press, 2013), xiv.
2. Claude Steele, *Whistling Vivaldi and Other Clues to How Stereotypes Affect Us.* (New York: W.W. Norton, 2010), 59.

Chapter 7: Gain Skills to Effectively Engage across Cultures

1. JLove Calderón, *Occupying Privilege: Conversations on Love, Race, & Liberation.* (Love-N-Liberation Press, 2012), 43.
2. Simon Moya-Smith, "Native American Teens Pulled off College Tour Are Latest Victims of the Push to Police White Spaces," *NBC News* (May 7, 2018). nbcnews.com/think/opinion/native-american-teens-pulled-college-tour -are-latest-victims-push-ncna871981.
3. Ilse Govan quoting Jamie Washington to the author, December 2013.

Chapter 9: Plan for the Journey, Not an Event

1. Martin Broadwell, "Teaching for Learning (XVI)," *The Gospel Guardian* 20, no. 41 (1969): 1–3.

Chapter 10: Be Mindful of the Language You Use

1. Kimberlé Crenshaw, a scholar and activist, coined the term "intersectionality" in 1989 in a paper she wrote for the University of Chicago Legal Forum. This new language provided a tool for Equity Leaders to consider how various combinations of identities can create different outcomes.
2. See Chapter 2: See Yourself as a Part of the Work.

Chapter 11: PoC Fatigue—When to Walk Away and When to Engage

1. Derald Sue et al., "Racial Microaggressions in Everyday Life: Implications for Clinical Practice," *American Psychologist* 62, no. 4 (2007): 271–86.
2. Robert Jones Jr. (@SonofBaldwin). See John A. Powell's blog post "Resistance and the Rebirth of Inclusion." Accessed June 14, 2022. blogs.berkeley.edu/2016/11/28/resistance-and-the-rebirth-of-inclusion/.

Chapter 13: Adopt Norms for Engaging in Courageous Conversations

1. Anita Garcia Morales shared this quote from Parker Palmer's Courage and Renewal program with the author, August 2012.

Chapter 15: Strategies for Engaging when Someone Offends You

1. The language "Building a Platform" comes from Daniel Wile's workshop *Collaborative Couples Therapy: Turning Fights into Intimate Conversations*.

Chapter 16: Strategies for Engaging when You Witness an Offense

1. This statement comes from a puppet named Keisha Jones created by Trey Moe for a series of YouTube videos.

Chapter 19: Establish an Equity Team to Maintain the Work

1. J. W. Hammond, Sara E. Brownell, Nita A. Kedharnath, Susan J. Cheng, W. Carson Byrd, "Why the Term 'JEDI' Is Problematic for Describing Programs That Promote Justice, Equity, Diversity, and Inclusion," *Scientific American*, September 23, 2021. scientificamerican.com/article/why-the-term-jedi-is-problematic-for-describing-programs-that-promote-justice-equity-diversity-and-inclusion/.

Chapter 20: Determine Your Organization's Stage of Multicultural Development

1. White norms designed to maintain institutional power include

"Either/Or" Thinking	Power Hoarding
Worshiping the Written Word	Progress Means "Bigger, More"
Defensiveness	Sense of Urgency
Paternalism/Saviorism	Secrecy
"Objectivity"	Only One Right Way
Competitive Individualism	Fear of Open Conflict
Scarcity Mentality	Right to Comfort
Quantity over Quality	

Chapter 21: Radical Self-Care

1. Audre Lorde, *A Burst of Light and Other Essays*. (Garden City NY: Ixia Press, 2017), 130.

Index

About the Author

CAPRICE D. HOLLINS was born and raised in Seattle, Washington, where she currently lives with her husband Gary, and their two children (who are no longer kids) Matae and Makena. She has three adult stepchildren, Jovan, Akilah, and Marques, and three grandchildren Gia, Amaya, and MJ. She received her Associate of Arts and Sciences from Shoreline Community College and Bachelor of Arts from Seattle University. She attended California School of Professional Psychology–Los Angeles campus where she  received her Master's in Arts and a Doctorate in Clinical Psychology with an emphasis in Multicultural and Community Psychology.

In her free time, Caprice loves to watch old black-and-white movies that bring her back to old memories of lying in bed watching movies with her grandmother. Though she now realizes just how sexist and racist they are, she can't help but enjoy them. She loves fantasy novels and can't resist a good read when the protagonist is a kick butt woman with a sword. If she's riding a dragon or fighting alongside elves, even better.

ABOUT NEW SOCIETY PUBLISHERS

New Society Publishers is an activist, solutions-oriented publisher focused on publishing books to build a more just and sustainable future. Our books offer tips, tools, and insights from leading experts in a wide range of areas.

We're proud to hold to the highest environmental and social standards of any publisher in North America. When you buy New Society books, you are part of the solution!

At New Society Publishers, we care deeply about *what* we publish—but also about *how* we do business.

- Our books are printed on 100% **post-consumer recycled paper**, processed chlorine-free, with low-VOC vegetable-based inks (since 2002).
- Our corporate structure is an innovative employee shareholder agreement, so we're one-third employee-owned (since 2015)
- We've created a Statement of Ethics (2021). The intent of this Statement is to act as a framework to guide our actions and facilitate feedback for continuous improvement of our work
- We're carbon-neutral (since 2006)
- We're certified as a B Corporation (since 2016)
- We're Signatories to the UN's Sustainable Development Goals (SDG) Publishers Compact (2020–2030, the Decade of Action)

To download our full catalog, sign up for our quarterly newsletter, and to learn more about New Society Publishers, please visit newsociety.com

ENVIRONMENTAL BENEFITS STATEMENT

New Society Publishers saved the following resources by printing the pages of this book on chlorine free paper made with 100% post-consumer waste.

TREES	WATER	ENERGY	SOLID WASTE	GREENHOUSE GASES
47	3,700	20	160	20,300
FULLY GROWN	GALLONS	MILLION BTUs	POUNDS	POUNDS

Environmental impact estimates were made using the Environmental Paper Network Paper Calculator 4.0. For more information visit www.papercalculator.org